A Celebration Of The Thought Of John Paul II

On The Occasion Of The Papal Visit To St. Louis

A Celebration Of The Thought Of John Paul II

On The Occasion Of The Papal Visit To St. Louis

Edited by

Gregory R. Beabout

St. Louis: Saint Louis University Press

Distribution
Saint Louis University Press
3663 Lindell Blvd.
St. Louis, MO 63108

PRINTED IN THE UNITED STATES OF AMERICA

Table of Contents

Permission

Three of the chapters in this book have appeared previously in earlier, slightly revised, forms. They are reprinted here with permission. Chapter One appeared in *Communio* 24 (Winter 1997) 713–727. Chapter Three appeared in the February 1998 issue of *First Things,* 19–25. Chapter Eight has been excerpted from *His Holiness: John Paul II and the Hidden History of Our Time* (New York: Doubleday, 1996), with the permission of Mr. Bernstein.

Preface

The visit of Pope John Paul II to St. Louis on January 26–27, 1999 is clearly cause for great celebration. He has been called the most recognized person in the world. While his face is widely recognized, the vitality of his thought and writings may need a fuller introduction.

The essays in this volume come from a Saint Louis University conference, "A Celebration of the Thought of Pope John Paul II," on January 22–23, 1999. The essays were prepared and published in anticipation of the conference.

The conference and this book share three main goals: celebration, preparation and education.

First, we want to celebrate the thought of the pope. Before his election to the papacy, Karol Wojtyla was a bishop who actively participated in the Second Vatican Council and wrote a book on its application. Before that, he was a philosophy professor who had published widely in ethics and action theory and who had gained an international reputation with his blend of Thomism and phenomenology. Before his two dissertations, he studied languages and literature as an undergraduate and made a contribution to the arts as a poet, dramatist and actor. During his papacy (as is well known) he has written and spoken on a wide range of topics including moral, cultural, social, economic and political issues. In addition to the several books he has written during his papacy, he has produced encyclicals and other documents on a wide range of topics and at an almost unbelievable rate. In the spirit of celebration, we chose commentators who recognize that the ideas of John Paul II are and have been important in shaping the church and the world. The topics covered in this volume, while representative of the pope's thought, are by no means exhaustive.

Second, we planned the conference to help people in the St. Louis community prepare for the pope's visit. There is a special timeliness here that might be noted. The first day of the conference falls on January 22, 1999. This day marks the 26th anniversary of the announcement of the Supreme Court's decision in the case of *Roe v. Wade*. Since John Paul II has become perhaps the world's most articulate defender of the dignity of every human life from conception to natural death, it seemed very fitting to mark the *Roe* anniversary with lectures on the thought of John Paul II. But since this emphasis on the dignity of human life is part of a deeper and broader view of a range of topics, the conference and the book might serve as a way to gain a fuller understanding of the thought of John Paul II in preparation for his visit to St. Louis.

Finally, we planned for this book to provide information about the thought of John Paul II. While there is a growing literature of books and scholarly essays about John Paul II, the popular press and the electronic media have done relatively little to explore the thought behind the man who is Pope John Paul II. It is our hope that this volume will contribute to that worthwhile educational goal.

G.R.B.
St. Louis, MO
Respect Life Month
October, 1998

Foreword

𝕴f I had ten minutes with the pope, my first reaction might be to do what many American Catholics would do.[1] I'd want to tell him what's wrong with the Church and what he should do about it, or I'd want to tell him what's wrong with the world and how he should fix it.

But after all the work that has gone into preparing for the conference that this book is based on, I think I would reconsider. It takes so many people to pull off a conference like this, including preparing a book like this and having it ready by the time of the conference, that I have had to rely on the help of scores of people. A lot of these people have volunteered their help, in big ways and small. For many of the people that I turned to for help with this project, especially when I was asking for volunteer help, the person would ask "Will I get to meet the pope when he comes to St. Louis?"

So if I had ten minutes with the pope, I would probably divide up my time into five-second segments. That would give me 120 slots. This might not be enough for all the many people who helped in this undertaking, but it would be a start.[2] Five seconds isn't much, but I had plenty of people help me who would be happy just to have the opportunity to see the Holy Father face to face, to touch him, or to receive his apostolic blessing.

Of course, being a philosopher, when it came to my five seconds, I'd want to say something. There's not much that you can say in five seconds, but I would try. I would probably lean over and whisper in the Holy Father's ear: "Go easy on the Jesuits."

On second thought, I wouldn't mind being given another ten minutes. And if I were, I'd ask the Holy Father to hear my confession. I don't really have in mind the sacrament of reconciliation. I'm thinking of Augustine's *Confessions*, of the way that he tells the story of his soul, of his life. I would tell him something like this.

"As an American Catholic, I have two confessions: one as an

American, and one as a Catholic. First, I don't remember where I was on November 22, 1963. I say this because, for my entire life, almost everyone that I have listened to and respected has been able to describe in vivid detail where they were when they heard that President Kennedy was shot. But I don't remember it. Of course, I was only three and a half years old, but that hardly seems like an excuse. My wife, who is a year older than me, remembers the event. My older brother was in kindergarten, and he remembers it. I have secretly wondered if I may be the first citizen in our nation's history who does not remember the day when Kennedy was shot.

"Second, I don't have any recollections of the pre-Vatican II church. For example, I don't remember going to Latin mass. I was baptized in Latin, and my parents tell me that I went to mass in Latin for the first several years of my life, but I have no memory of it at all. My whole life, I have heard countless accounts of what the Church was like before Vatican II (some have told me it was wonderful; many have painted it as terrible), but I have no memory of it at all.

"In contrast, I remember exactly where I was on October 16, 1978 when I heard the news that 'an archbishop from Poland' had been elected pope. I was a freshman in college at Loyola University Chicago at the time. When I heard the news, I was walking north nearing the 6700 block of Sheridan Road. I remember the way the sunlight cast a warm glow on the brick buildings when I first heard the surprising news. My mother's side of the family is Polish, and I was astonished and delighted at the report.

"A year later, on October 5, 1979 when I was a nineteen year old sophomore, classes were cancelled on the day you celebrated mass in Grant Park in Chicago. My friends and I left campus early to get a good spot. After reserving our place with a blanket, someone had a football, so we organized a pick-up game of touch football in the park as we waited for you. We joked about how you might join us and that we could teach you American football; we had heard you were a sportsman and that you enjoyed soccer. And then the moment came when you drove by in your popemobile. You were moving slowly and waving to the crowd as you made your way down the street and into the park where you celebrated mass. I was one of the million people with you in Grant Park at that mass.

"During my junior year (1980), I studied in Rome. My diary that I kept from that time records the casualness of regular bus rides from the campus down the hill to the Vatican. On All Saint's Day, some friends and I went to Campo Verano, a cemetery in Rome, where you celebrated mass. Over our Thanksgiving break in late November, the students organized a ski trip to the Italian Alps. When we got there, we heard that you were skiing on the same mountain. As we sped down the mountain, we looked all over in the hopes that we would see you. (Many of the students joked about wanting to see if you ski with your robes on!) On December 3, 1980, the students from our campus got tickets for a 'private audience' with you. It wasn't really very 'private'; there was a gathering of perhaps two thousand people. I remember the excitement of the crowd as you walked down the aisle, and the vitality in your eyes which I could see as you got close to my row. I am usually not a camera buff, but I wanted to take pictures to show my family. When you came to my row, I had to decide whether to take your picture or reach out to touch you. At the last second, I decided to take your picture. There were dozens of cameras flashing, and mine must have flashed right in your face. I was perhaps three feet from you when you reached your hand toward me and shook the hand of the person next to me. I still have the picture.

"The twenty years of your pontificate have been my entire adult life. During that time, I have gone to college, gotten married, gone to graduate school, had five children and taught as a professor for ten years. My interests in theology and philosophy have developed over those twenty years, and increasingly I have been drawn to a study of your writing. In our parish, my wife and I participated with a group of families who had young children that met in one another's homes to study *Familiaris Consortio* and your 1994 Letter to Families. In my capacity as a philosophy professor, I have been given the opportunity to pursue the study of your thought and writing both in my research and in my teaching. In the classes I teach, I have had the opportunity to introduce your writing to many students, especially your social encyclicals, *Redemptor Hominis*, *Laborum Exercens*, *Sollicitudo Rei Socialis*, and perhaps my favorite, *Centesimus Annus*. Since the publication of *Evangelium Vitae*, I have been called upon to explain your teaching in that encyclical to various groups. And for almost a year now, in preparation for this conference and your visit to St. Louis, I have been deeply involved in the study of your thought.

"I would like you to know how this conference, which is a celebration of your thought, came to be. But to tell that story, let me back up a bit. In 1993, two of my colleagues, Dr. William Monahan and Dr. Charles Ford, invited me to join with them in an effort to form a faculty group dedicated to the promotion of the dignity of human life. We met with a group of about a dozen faculty for several meetings. While the faculty involved included male and female members of religious orders, most of the participants were lay faculty.

"In November of 1993, after a series of preliminary meetings, Saint Louis University Faculty and Staff for Life was formed. Our central vision was to make more visible the commitment of faculty and staff of Saint Louis University to the pro-life teachings of the Church. Our charter includes the following goals: 1) to provide a forum to foster multi-disciplinary dialogue and collaboration among Saint Louis University faculty, staff and students concerned about human life; 2) to educate the community about life issues and the reasons behind pro-life positions; and 3) to foster further faculty involvement in the non-partisan, non-denominational academic study of pro-life activities. To carry out those goals, we began with several modest events. We sponsored a panel discussion for faculty on "How We Discuss Abortion in our Teaching" and another on "How Abortion Affects Women." We hosted various pro-life intellectuals who have spoken to our group and to other interested faculty and staff; these have included Dr. Wanda Franz, Dr. Edmund Pellegrino, Fr. Richard John Neuhaus, David Reardon, and others. We also sponsored presentations by our own faculty, including William Brennan and Kevin O'Rourke.

"Most of these activities were designed to be rather small. But to mark the historic 25th anniversary of the *Roe v. Wade* decision, we decided to organize two larger activities. First, we published a letter in the *University News*, the school newspaper, on the sacredness of all human life. This letter was signed by 100 Saint Louis University faculty and staff. We also sponsored a major event, an address by Professor Peter Kreeft titled "Why We Work for Life." Professor Kreeft's lecture drew a capacity crowd to the largest room on the campus. In fact, we had to bring in extra chairs.

"After that event, I secretly hoped that our association would not have another major event for several years. It is hard work to organize such an event. Also, one might hope that the *Roe* decision be overturned as we seek to build a culture that affirms life. It was true that many people came from the community to our university to hear an academically informed defense of the pro-life position, and many students do not hear often enough an articulate and intellectually informed defense of the pro-life position. We knew that we had a duty to continue in such efforts. Nonetheless, the steering committee of our group agreed that we didn't necessarily want the work and responsibility of holding a major speaker every year on January 22nd, the anniversary of the *Roe* decision. 'Perhaps in five years we will do it again,' I said to my colleagues. 'In the meantime, we can go back to doing smaller events.'

"And then came the news that you were coming to St. Louis. When it was announced that you would be here on January 26, 1999, I checked a calendar and realized that the Friday before your arrival would be January 22nd, the anniversary of the *Roe* decision. It seemed clear that our association should sponsor another lecture on January 22nd, but that this time we should have a speaker on the theme "John Paul II and the Gospel of Life." As I started to think about this, it seemed that we really needed to do more than just have a single lecture. Since the Jesuits have always had a reputation for excellence in education, and since their charism has traditionally included the task of explaining and defending the teachings of the Church, it seemed fitting to put together a conference at Saint Louis University (the second oldest Jesuit university in the United States) of great speakers to provide a multi-disciplinary forum that celebrates and articulates the intellectual legacy of your thought. Following the teaching of the Second Vatican Council, we knew that lay people have an increased responsibility to shape a culture that promotes the dignity of the human person. So our group, under the guidance of a steering committee of lay faculty, decided to plan a conference to celebrate your thought.

"In light of all of this, we set five goals for ourselves in planning the conference: 1) to mark the occasion of your visit to St. Louis with an academic conference celebrating the intellectual legacy of your ideas, 2) to mark the occasion of the 26th anniversary of the Supreme Court's decision in the case of *Roe v. Wade* with a major lecture that presents an informed account of the abortion issue and a reasoned presentation of the pro-life position from an academic perspective; 3) to provide a forum for academic discussion of some of the central issues of our day, (abortion, economics, culture, families, etc.,) and show how those themes have been addressed by your thought; 4) to bring some of the leading thinkers who have written on your ideas to our campus and to our University community; 5) to provide an opportunity for the people of the St. Louis community and beyond to prepare for your visit by participating in a conference on your thought.

"With these goals in place, we went to the Jesuit Marchetti Endowment Fund with a request for a grant to offer this conference. We were strongly encouraged to proceed, and it was suggested that we go to the Chancellor's Office for additional support. Fr. McGannon has been tremendously supportive. Additionally, we went to the Student Government Association, which offered assistance for the conference as well. Many offices of the University have been quite helpful in planning this project, including the Dean of the Graduate School and especially the office of University Public Relations which also helped with many of the details of event planning. We are deeply grateful for all this support.

"Since we got the go ahead to proceed with the conference, we have been working on all the tasks that it takes to prepare for such an event. Each of the speakers graciously agreed to provide a written version ahead of time. The first eight chapters of this book constitute the lectures presented at the conference.

"Looking back, I vividly recall the crisp fall air on the lake shore in Grant Park during the outdoor mass with a million people in Chicago. I assume that many people in St. Louis will have similar memories formed during your visit here. Our hope is that this conference will help people prepare for your visit by deepening the understanding of your thought, and that this book will serve as an aid for those seeking to continue in the study of your thought.

"I suppose that makes ten minutes and five seconds. We've been working for almost a year to prepare for your visit. Welcome to St. Louis, Holy Father."

G.R.B.
St. Louis, MO
October 16, 1998
The 20th Anniversary of the Election John Paul II to the Papacy

NOTES

[1] When John Paul II visited New Orleans in 1987, Walker Percy wrote an essay in which he gave the pope five minutes of his mind. See "If I Had Five Minutes with the Pope," in *Signposts in a Strange Land.* Edited by Patrick Samway. (New York:

Farrar, Straus and Giroux, 1991). Since I'm not really giving advice, I figured that I could follow Walker Percy's lead, but take ten minutes, or more.

[2] The list of people who have helped, in various ways, would include Don Brennan, William Brennan, Fr. James Blumeyer, Wade Bradshaw, Stanley Bray, Katie Burke, Angela Chierek, Chris Collins, Nathan Cooper, Fr. Denis Daly, Laura Di Franco, Alison Dunehoo, Kevin Dyer, Jason Eberl, Mary Beth Erickson, Mary Flick, Charles Ford, Laura Geiser, Meg Gleason, Gregory Gronbacher, Maurico Gutierrez, Kelli Hauser, Pat Henning, Joe Hodes, Jim Hitchcock, John Kerr, Cheryl Lampert, Kate Larsen, Fr. Michael Mahes, Mary Catherine Martin, Fr. Barry McGannon, Clair McGlynn, Mike McGlynn, Patty Mecadon, Ron Modras, William Monahan, Jean Monahan, Carol Murphy, David Murphy, Pat Norris, Kathleen Parvis, Randy Rosenberg, Fr. Richard Rousseau, Bonnie Sabin, Ed Sabin, Pete Salsich, Tom Shaw, Machele Spencer, Ken Trupke, Dan Van Slyke, Daryl Wennemann and Todd Wiseman. Since I have drawn on the help and support of so many people in so many different capacities during this project, I am certain that this list of people who deserve thanks is quite incomplete. Be assured that I would like to thank all of the people who helped with the conference and this book. A special word of thanks belongs to my children for their understanding and patience, and for my wife. Without her support, this probably would not have been possible.

CHAPTER ONE

John Paul II and Theology

Avery Dulles, S.J.

I. John Paul II's Theological Development

It is not necessary to review the biography of John Paul II, which has often been recounted.[1] I shall not be concerned with Karol Wojtyla the actor, poet, sportsman, linguist, musician, though all of these interests have probably affected his theology in one way or another. Nor shall I attempt to assess his political influence, vast though it has been, or even his pastoral ministry as bishop and pope, although his theology is not wholly separable from his concerns as a pastor. But to place his theology in context I shall give a brief sketch of his intellectual and spiritual development.

As a Pole living through the horrors of the Nazi occupation, the devastation of World War II, and the harsh domination of the Russian Communists, the young Wojtyla learned to cope with adversity. His faith was strengthened by the guidance of Jan Tyranowski, a remarkable layman who was a tailor in Kraków. As a young man Tyranowski had been a leader in Catholic Action and in the Marian Sodality. During the Nazi occupation he ran a kind of informal academy of fellow parishioners, with Wojtyla as a prominent member. Tyranowski trained the group in ascetical and mystical theology, and introduced them to the works of St. John of the Cross and St. Teresa of Avila. He also organized a "living rosary" of young men who turned in prayer to the Blessed Virgin to save Poland from its perils. Tyranowski seems to have been

1

an authentic mystic, and he gave Wojtyla a lasting respect for Carmelite spirituality. Wojtyla at one point considered becoming a Carmelite.

After his first year at the Jagiellonian University (1938–1939), Karol Wojtyla's course of study was interrupted by the war. He labored for two years in a stone quarry connected with a chemical plant and in 1942 secretly entered an underground seminary organized by the future Cardinal Adam Sapieha. Two weeks after his ordination as a priest in 1946 he was sent to Rome for doctoral studies. At the Angelicum (as the Pontifical University of St. Thomas was then called) he wrote a dissertation on the theology of faith of John of the Cross.[2] He accepted the teaching of the Carmelite saint that faith does not suffice for union with God unless it is vivified by charity, which brings about a personal transformation through participation in the divine life. In pure faith the spirit adheres to God in darkness, without support of any proper representation. In an appendix to the dissertation Wojtyla tried to show that the Spanish Carmelite's teaching on faith agreed with that of Thomas Aquinas, a point that others had questioned.

Before defending his dissertation in July 1948, Father Wojtyla was able to spend his summer holiday of 1947 in France, Belgium, and Holland. In Paris, where he lived at the Polish Seminary, he looked into the worker-priest movement. While he admired the valiant efforts of the French clergy to win the working classes back to the Church, he seems to have been convinced, after a visit to Canon Cardijn in Belgium, that priests should present themselves distinctly as priests instead of taking on lay employments in their effort to reach out to the laboring class.

Upon his return to Poland, Father Wojtyla was assigned to parish duties that included ministry to university students in Kraków. In 1951 he was assigned to further studies in philosophy, and delved into the ethics of a German phenomenologist, Max Scheler. Scheler wanted to build an ethical system on the basis of a personally experienced hierarchy of values. Relying heavily on feeling and emotion, Scheler rejected the role of authority. Wojtyla found some merit in Scheler's personalism, but he believed that this ultimately called for a personal relationship to God and to Jesus as a commanding authority.

After teaching briefly at the seminary faculty at Kraków (1953–54), Father Wojtyla joined the philosophy faculty of the Catholic University of Lublin. In the next few years he became one of the leaders of "Lublin Thomism," a personalist interpretation of Thomas Aquinas, influenced by French philosophers such as Maurice Blondel, Emmanuel Mounier, and Gabriel Marcel.[3]

In 1958, Plus XII named Wojtyla auxiliary bishop of Kraków, thus terminating his full-time academic career. As bishop he continued to work closely with youth groups, and it was partly out of that experience that he developed the ideas for his book, *Love and Responsibility* (Lublin, 1960).[4]

From 1962 to 1965, Bishop Wojtyla was heavily involved in the work of Vatican II. The *Acta Synodalia* of the Council contain some 23 interventions by him, several of them in the name of the whole Polish episcopate, some in writing, and some orally delivered. It may be helpful to refer to several of these interventions.

Regarding the Constitution on the Church, Bishop Wojtyla insisted that the main goal of Church is sanctification and that the teaching and ruling offices are subordinate to this goal. The chapter on the people of God should precede that on the hierarchy, for the hierarchy is only an instrument for promoting the common good of the whole people of God. He welcomed the incorporation of the document on the Blessed Virgin Mary into the Constitution on the Church. But it was a mistake, he believed, to put this chapter at the end of the Constitution, where it appears as a mere appendix. As Mother, Mary built up Christ's physical body, and now she performs the same office toward the Church. Thus this chapter should come immediately after the one describing the Mystery of the Church.

Bishop Wojtyla made five interventions on Religious Freedom. He regretted that the original schema dealt mainly with immunity from coercion, which is a negative and partial conception of freedom. Mere tolerance is too static; it cannot serve as a principle of growth. The Council, he believed, should proclaim the Christian doctrine of freedom on the basis of revelation rather than give a lesson in political philosophy. Christian freedom is grounded in the word of God and in the grace that liberates from sin and its consequences. Finally it should be made clear that religious freedom is limited not only by positive law but by the moral law itself.

Another five of Wojtyla's interventions dealt with the Church in the Modern World. Welcoming the idea of a dialogue with atheism, he suggested that this dialogue should begin with the philosophy of the human person. He encouraged the Council to speak out against utilitarianism, which threatens authentic life by turning persons into means for abstract ends. With reference to the economy, he maintained that the right of private property and of ownership of productive goods should be affirmed against socialist ideologies.

These and other points from Bishop Wojtyla's Council interventions are of interest because they foreshadow ideas that he was to articulate more fully in his writings as pope.

In 1964, Paul VI named Wojtyla Archbishop of Kraków and, three years later, Cardinal. As archbishop and cardinal he was heavily involved in all the synods of bishops from 1967 to 1977. At the synod of 1969, he proposed his views on papal primacy and episcopal collegiality; in 1971, he contributed to the documents on the ministerial priesthood and on world justice; in 1974, he played an important role in the discussion of evangelization; and in 1977, he took an active part in the debates on catechesis.

As a member of the papal "birth control" commission Wojtyla, following the positions taken in *Love and Responsibility*, opposed any liberalization of the doctrine forbidding contraception. Some maintain that he was one of the drafters of the encyclical *Humanae vitae* (1968).[5]

In 1969 he published the first edition of his *The Acting Person*, a work of philosophical anthropology written in dialogue with Marxism.[6] Against Marxist materialism and determinism, this book strongly affirms the priority of the person and the capacity of persons to shape their very identity by the way they act. The English translation, published in 1979, is very hard to read. According to competent scholars the translator considerably modified the text according to her own philosophical thinking.

Cardinal Wojtyla's next work, *Sources of Renewal*[7] (Polish original 1972), is based on conferences he gave to implement Vatican II pastorally in the diocese of Kraków. The fundamental question to be answered by the Council, he says, was the one put by Paul VI: "Ecclesia, quid dicis de teipsa?" ("Church, what do you say of yourself?"). The Church as she travels down the road of history participates in the consciousness of Jesus Christ and shares in his mission. The consciousness of the Church develops historically to keep pace with the cultural shifts in the world in which the Church finds herself and which she is constantly seeking to transform. Vatican II in the estimation of Wojtyla called for a fundamental shift of consciousness in the Church as a whole, leading to a more dialogical posture, as the Church enters into conversation with all groups of people, believers and unbelievers. Her mission is to help all humankind to enter consciously into the communion intended by the triune God. Revelation is an invitation to salvation through communion with God.

In 1976, Cardinal Wojtyla was invited to give the Lenten retreat to the pope and the papal curia. As his theme he chose *Sign of Contradiction*,[8] since he wished to emphasize the need for the Church to stand up in opposition to materialism and secularism in their various forms, whether Marxist or capitalist. The word of God, he holds, encounters an anti-word; the truth of God struggles against the lies of Satan; the obedience of Jesus pays the price for human disobedience. In the course of the retreat he praised Paul VI for having taken a firm stand against contraception in *Humanae vitae*.

Since becoming pope in 1978, John Paul II has been almost incredibly productive. In the midst of all his apostolic journeys and pastoral visitations he has found time to write thirteen encyclicals[9] and seven post-synodal apostolic exhortations. Most of these twenty documents are practically book-length. In addition he has authored two very personal books since becoming pope. The more important of the two, *Crossing the Threshold of Hope*, is a written interview with an Italian journalist, published in 1994.[10] The second book, *Gift and Mystery* (1996), is a brief autobiographical memorandum dealing with his own vocation to the priesthood.[11] Five volumes of his general audience talks have thus far been published in English. To keep abreast of all these publications would be a full-time occupation.

II. Theological Synthesis

The teaching of Karol Wojtyla, before and since he became pope, has been vast and many-faceted. He writes as a philosopher, a theologian, and a pastor. As bishop and pope he has sought to carry out faithfully the agenda set forth by Vatican II. As a scholar he has roots deep in the tradition, and remains in many respects the faithful disciple of Thomas Aquinas and John of the Cross, both of whom he studied in depth. But he is also at home with new currents in personalist phenomenology. A man of deep faith and prayer, he has broad interests in literature, science, politics, and social studies. It is scarcely possible to bring this great variety of interests and concerns into any kind of schematic unity.

Formidable though it be, the challenge can to some degree be met.

John Paul II does have a central vision and message that students of his thought should be able to articulate. One of his salient convictions is that faith in Christ can bring mutual understanding and reconciliation to peoples of various cultures. As a Slav who has lived in Western Europe and traveled widely on other continents, Karol Wojtyla sees himself as charged with interpreting different cultures to each other. More particularly, he aspires to mediate between the traditions and mentalities of Eastern and Western Europe.

The present pope also has a chronological understanding of his mission. He situates his pontificate historically between Vatican II and the end of the millennium. The advent of the third millennium, he says, may be seen as a hermeneutical key for his entire conduct of the papacy. Vatican II, in his view, providentially prepared the Church for the challenges of this period. It marks a vital stage in the growth of the Church's self-awareness and hence in its maturation. John Paul II is no restorationist, hankering for the simplicity of an earlier age. Just as human beings come of age by understanding what and who they are and by freely living out their own identity, so too the Church comes of age by discovering, freely embracing, and living out its own vocation in Christ.

Within these parameters we may undertake a rapid overview of the pope's dynamic apostolic vision.[12]

1. *Anthropology*. Permeating all the pope's work is his anthropology. He understands human existence in personalist and dynamic terms. By a responsible use of our own freedom we make ourselves the kind of persons that we are. Human beings come to themselves by relating to others in loving service and dialogue. They are created in the image of the triune God, and for that reason they are essentially social beings, called to communion and solidarity with others. To be human is to be a bodily creature, weak and sinful, but at the same time filled with boundless desires and summoned to a higher life.

2. *Christology*. The supreme model for human existence is Jesus Christ, who totally gave himself for the redemption of every man and woman. The intense personalism of John Paul II therefore leads to a boundless universalism. Christ in his concrete uniqueness is the center of the universe, the goal of human history, and the focus of each individual's personal quest for salvation. The appearance of Jesus Christ on this planet is not a mere accident. "Through the Incarnation," writes

John Paul II, "God gave human life the dimension that he intended man to have from his first beginning" (*Redemptor Hominis*, 1).

As Son of God, Jesus reveals the Father's character as merciful love; as perfect man, he also reveals humanity to itself. He is the norm by which the Christian life, and indeed all human life, is to be judged. God does not come into the world in order to crush or diminish human freedom but to guide and direct freedom to its proper goal. The purpose of freedom is that we may responsibly choose the true and the good. Jesus offers himself to all as the way, the truth, and the life. He is the truth that sets us free.

In relation to redeemed humanity, Jesus has a threefold office as prophet, priest, and king. He is the teacher, sanctifier, and ruler of those who follow him, and in this way he becomes the unique savior of all who are saved. Every human being is called to pass through the Paschal mystery in order to achieve the goal of redemption. It is a universal law of human nature that by generously giving ourselves, we fulfill ourselves at the deepest level. Suffering itself, accepted as a participation in the sufferings of the God-man, can be redemptive. This pope does not simply theorize about suffering; he lives it out by offering an example of illness and affliction patiently endured.

3. *Trinity*. In his Christology John Paul II is Christocentric, but he avoids Christomonism. He views Jesus Christ in relation to the other two divine persons. As the eternal Logos, Christ owes his entire being to the Father, from whom he proceeds, and as man he seeks to carry out his mission from the Father who sent him into the world. He was conceived by the Holy Spirit, who thereafter empowered him for mission. Faithfully carrying out his charge under the guidance of the Spirit, Jesus gave his life away, and by this sacrifice made his life fruitful for others. Having totally surrendered himself into the hands of the Father, Jesus is able to join the Father in sending the Holy Spirit to carry on his own mission. The Holy Spirit universalizes the work of Jesus Christ, so that Jesus may come into union with every individual. The theology of John Paul II, while remaining Christocentric, is pneumatological and Trinitarian.

4. *Mariology*. John Paul II is keenly conscious of the unique role of the Blessed Virgin Mary in the history of redemption. Just as Jesus was totally receptive in relation to his Father, so she is the model of receptivity and obedience, as is indicated by her words, "Behold the handmaid of the Lord." In her total self-giving to God, she embraces

virginity, but that sacrifice renders her not sterile but fruitful; it qualifies her to be the mother of the Incarnate Word. John Paul II calls her the most perfect disciple, inasmuch as she, more than anyone else, may be said to have heard the word of God and faithfully obeyed it. In his words from the Cross, Jesus indicated that she was to have a maternal relationship to the disciples, represented by John. As the mother of Christ's physical body, she was appropriately chosen to be the mother of the Church, his Mystical Body.

5. *Ecclesiology*. John Paul II understands the Church in personalist terms. It is not a mere thing, a mere institution, but a living reality constituted by persons who achieve their selfhood by consciously affirming their own identity. The Church is a mystery that lives by the grace of Christ and the Holy Spirit. Its mission is none other than that of Christ its Lord.

The mystery of fruitful obedience, first accomplished in Jesus and in Mary, is subsequently realized in the Church, which becomes fruitful by its bridal relationship to Christ, who loved the Church and gave himself up to make her holy. The obedience of the Church in faithful discipleship does not constrict the personal growth of the members but opens up a path whereby they can be led to the fullness of life that is to be found only in Christ. The Church, marked by receptivity and obedience, has a Marian character leading to life and holiness. Like Mary, the Church is virgin, bride, and mother.

The Church is a communion of persons, a community of disciples. The community itself, as stated above, is not a merely human fellowship. It is humanity brought into a higher and more consciously experienced union with Christ through the Holy Spirit, or rather through the inhabitation of all three divine persons. Thus the pope is favorable to what might be called a *communio* model of the Church. The Church for him is a mystical or mysterious communion of human beings joined together by the Holy Spirit, the Spirit of Christ. Vatican II, with its interpersonal understanding of the Church as People of God, marks a vital stage in the maturation of the Church.

The interior grace of the Holy Spirit is not reserved to those who are formally members of the Church. God in his providence makes it possible for every human being to be associated in a salvific way with Christ and the Paschal mystery. This orientation to Christ opens up a multiplicity of potential relationships to the Church as the body of Christ, which serves as his instrument for the redemption of all.

Christians of other communions, adherents of other religions, and nonreligious persons of good will, provided that they are open to the leading of the Spirit, can be related in salvific ways to Christ and the Church.

The Church has a visible aspect insofar as it becomes historically tangible in the creedal, societal, and sacramental structures with which it has been endowed. As a sacrament of Christ in the world, the Church participates in his threefold office as prophet, priest, and king. As prophet it teaches and bears witness; as priest, it sanctifies, and as king it orders human life in accordance with the will of Christ. As the "social subject of responsibility for divine truth," the Church has been endowed by its founder with the gift of infallibility (*Redemptor Hominis*, 19). The institutional aspects of the Church, for the present pope, are subordinate to its character as interpersonal community.

6. *Sacraments*. John Paul II has written extensively about several of the sacraments, including the Eucharist, penance, marriage, and ordination. The Eucharist for him is the sacrament that most perfectly expresses and accomplishes the union that exists among the members of the Church, binding them together in Christ, who continually builds up the Church through the Eucharist. In that sacrament the Church relives the Paschal mystery. The sacrament of penance, for this pope, constitutes a personal encounter with the crucified Christ, who utters through the priest the words of forgiveness and reconciliation—words directed to the individual penitent.

Matrimony, as treated by John Paul II, manifests the nuptial union between Christ and the Church. The permanent, loving, monogamous union between the Church and her Lord provides the model for Christian marriage. The sexual union of husband and wife expresses their total mutual self-giving within the commitment of marriage. Men and women who are called to celibacy can show forth in other ways the bridal relationship between Christ and the Church.

7. *Priesthood*. Priesthood in the Church is conferred in a general way upon all the members, including the laity, through baptism and confirmation, and in a special way upon certain ministers through ordination. All Christians are called to participate in Christ's threefold office as prophet, priest, and king, because they must bear witness to Christ, share in his consecration, and order their lives according to his example and precepts.

Participation in the threefold office takes on a special quality in the case of those ordained as bishops or presbyters, since they are called to maintain the Church in the unity and truth that come from Christ. Their tasks are to proclaim the word of God with authority, to administer the sacraments, to bring about the Eucharistic sacrifice, and to govern the People of God with pastoral authority. Acting in the name of the Church, priests offer prayers and sacrifices on her behalf. Sharing in Christ's role as head and bridegroom, they act in his name with regard to the faithful. There should be no blurring of the distinction between them and the laity. The general priesthood of the faithful and the ministerial priesthood of the ordained are distinct in kind.

8. *Primacy and Collegiality.* The ministerial priesthood is exercised on the highest level by the bishops, who are gathered about the successor of Peter as the center of their unity. For John Paul II, the unity among the bishops is brought about by means of primacy and collegiality, neither of which can be properly exercised except in combination with the other. Through councils, synodical assemblies, and meetings of episcopal conferences the bishops build up their solidarity with one another and with Rome as the center of unity. By their collegial activity they assist the pope in exercising his primatial office.

To prevent an unwholesome clericalism it must always be kept in mind that the hierarchical leadership has an essentially servant character. The hierarchy exists not for its own sake, but for the sake of the whole Church; not to lord it over the laity but to perform a necessary service on their behalf. The purpose of all ministry is to contribute to holiness, the ultimate purpose of the Church.

9. *Mission.* Endowed as it is with a universal import, the Church must avoid being narcissistically turned in upon itself. Like Jesus himself, the Church is sent into the world to accomplish God's saving work. It is always in a state of mission. Every Christian has a share in the missionary responsibility of the whole Church, in accordance with the state of life and vocation of each individual.

The outward mission of the Church may be studied under two headings, evangelization and humanization. In the thinking of John Paul II, these two are in the last analysis inseparable. They are two sides of the same coin. The world cannot achieve unity and peace except in the truth, which is most fully disclosed in the person of Jesus Christ. Humanity cannot achieve its God-given goal except by personal transformation in Christ, by sharing in his holiness. Conscious of this, the pope dares to challenge the world not to be afraid, but instead to open up its doors to Jesus Christ.

10. *Evangelization.* By evangelization John Paul II, like Paul VI, means the whole process of bringing the world into a conscious and explicit adherence to Christ as redeemer, in whom alone creation can achieve its fulfillment. The responsibility for the proclamation of the gospel and the ministry of the sacraments rests especially on the ordained, who must stimulate and direct the evangelizing efforts of the whole Church. The laity are called to evangelize by bearing witness to Christ and by transforming the temporal order according to the norms and ideals of the gospel. Large portions of humanity are still in need of primary evangelization; they have not as yet heard the call of Christ and the gospel. Many parts of the world are today in need for reevangelization, since the faith of earlier generations has not been effectively passed on.

11. *Humanization.* Multitudes of persons, although endowed with human nature from their conception, are caught in situations in which they are unable to develop their basic human powers. The world is full of starving, uncared-for children and of adults who live in political fear and economic misery. Sharing in the compassion of Jesus, the Church is called to collaborate in building what Paul VI called "a civilization of love." This involves work for peace, for solidarity among peoples and nations, for justice and human rights. In our time, more than ever before, the Church must make itself a champion of the poor, the weak, the elderly, the unborn, and the newly born. The grace of Christ, mediated by the Church, gives hope for a human fulfillment beyond all that this world can offer.

In a broader sense of the word, biblical revelation calls for the humanization of the world itself, as the environment for human activity. The vocation to "subdue the earth" (*Genesis* 1:28) does not authorize us to exploit and pollute the earth, the seas, and the atmosphere in irresponsible ways but gives us the mandate to make the world what Vatican II calls "a dwelling worthy of the whole human family" (*Gaudium et Spes*, 57).

12. *Social and Natural Sciences.* The Church as such does not have specific programs for the ordering of human society, but it does have a body of social teaching that articulates the basic principles. For John Paul II the first essential would seem to be the rights of the individual person, which are sacred and inviolable. The state is under a strict

obligation to protect the God-given rights of the citizens, including the freedom of conscience and religion. Individuals perfect themselves by seeking truth and moral integrity in community, serving one another. Authentic community is threatened today by currents of utilitarianism and collectivism that would treat persons as mere means. The pope warns against institutions and programs that would subordinate the good of human subjects to political power, economic development, or technological progress, pursued for their own sakes.

To translate these general principles into concrete proposals is properly the task of the laity, who are called to involve themselves in the spheres of politics, business, and the secular professions. Ever on guard against clericalism, John Paul II wants to give scope to the Catholic laity to be creative in their initiatives and to enter into mutually acceptable collaborative arrangements with other persons of good will. The laity are called to see to it that the gospel has its leavening impact on the spheres of culture, law, and politics. The leadership of the Church must remind the laity of their responsibility to bring the gospel to bear on the new worlds of science and communication that are in such rapid flux today. These spheres are what John Paul II (with an implied reference to Paul's preaching in the Areopagus in the seventeenth chapter of *Acts of the Apostles*) calls the "Areopagi," or cultural centers, of the modern world.

The pope recognizes the important contributions of science to the development of human understanding. In his addresses to the Pontifical Academy of Sciences and to university professors he has repeatedly insisted on the need for a lively dialogue between science and theology. He holds up Albert the Great as an example of a theologian who embraced and mastered the scientific knowledge of his day. In the Counter Reformation, he believes, the proper distinction between the orders of knowledge was blurred, with the result that Galileo was erroneously condemned. Anxious to prevent any repetition of such errors, he has expressed openness to the theory of evolution and to various cosmological hypotheses, provided that these are not linked with some kind of materialist and reductionist philosophy. As a former professor the pope envisages the Catholic university as a place where the various disciplines interact, to the enrichment of all, including theology.

13. *Critique of Cultures*. In the pope's vision, the gospel cannot take hold of individual persons and societies except by being incarnated, so to speak, in cultures. Western European culture, in spite of its past

greatness, no longer suffices for a world Church. Every cultural sector, including those of Asia and Africa, has a proper contribution to make in showing forth the full riches of Christ the redeemer. By implanting itself in various cultures, the gospel preserves, elevates, and purifies those cultures, supplementing whatever may be lacking in them.

In some of his recent writings the pope draws a broad contrast between two cultures—the one a culture of life, the other a culture of death. Since Jesus came into the world in order that men and women might have life, and have it more abundantly, Christianity is committed to a culture of life. But in many countries, not excluding prosperous societies such as our own, the pope sees alarming symptoms of degeneration and decay. He finds a falling away from truth and a disregard of God's creative plan. Forgetful of permanent and transcendent truth, people are turning more and more to the quest for utility, convenience, and personal pleasure. In a consumerist culture, primacy is given to entertainment, gadgets, and luxury items. People seek freedom without responsibility, even to the extent of falling into hedonism.

In this context the Church hears a call to evangelize not only individuals but cultures themselves. In so doing, the Church and its representatives must not fear to become signs of contradiction. The faithful following of Christ is not intended to be a path of ease and popularity. Inspired by the example of Christ and that of the martyrs, Christians must be prepared for rejection, even to the point of the cross.

14. *Grounds for Hope.* John Paul II, however, gives no scope for discouragement. With his eyes fixed on Christ and the Holy Spirit, he is convinced that the divine Lord of history is in control. Even in the midst of poverty and oppression, many are reaching out—he says—for the meaning of life; increasing numbers are disposed to hear the message of the gospel, provided that it be authentically proclaimed to them. Even before being explicitly accepted, the gospel exerts a beneficial influence on the ideas and values that are shaping the world of our day. Movements for peace, justice, human rights, and protection of the environment are basically sound. A large patrimony of truth and holiness survives in Protestant and Orthodox Christianity. In secular humanism and in the non-Christian religions the pope finds rays of divine truth and seeds of the word of God. These seeds, he believes, must be cultivated so that they can come to flower and fruition.

In the hope of achieving greater unity in the truth, the pope holds out a constant invitation to respectful and friendly dialogue. Vatican II and Paul VI summoned the Catholic Church to dialogue with other churches, with world religions, and with those who have no religious belief. Such dialogue, John Paul II insists, must not be aimed at weak pragmatic compromises but at unity in the fullness of truth. In this dialogue proclamation will have its place.

15. *The Coming Millennium.* The teaching of John Paul II manifests a lively consciousness of the situation in which Christianity stands today. He defines his pontificate in relation to the coming of the third millennium, which is now scarcely a year away. We stand therefore in an Advent season, awaiting the celebration of a great jubilee of the birth of Christ. Like every Advent, this should be a time for prayerful examination of conscience and repentance for our past errors. Conscious of their failures, past and present, Catholics should beg forgiveness of those whom they have injured. Looking forward in hope, they must renew their confidence in the Holy Spirit, through whom Jesus was conceived in the womb of the Blessed Virgin. The millennium jubilee, properly celebrated, may usher in a renewal of the Church, a new outburst of apostolic energy, and a more universal adherence to Christ as the way, the truth, and the life.

Conclusion

This brief panorama is not intended to take the place of a detailed study of the pope's teaching on particular points. It may nevertheless be useful because John Paul II has written so voluminously on so many topics that it is easy to lose sight of the unity and coherence of his program. Thanks to an excellent philosophical and theological formation he has been able to present a fresh combination of classical Thomism and modern personalist phenomenology. From this standpoint he has made himself a faithful guardian of the deposit of faith while showing an astonishing openness to dialogue with other churches, other religions, and the secular worlds of science and technology. Deeply influenced by his experience of the Second Vatican Council, he has forged a Christocentric humanism capable of encountering and respectfully challenging the dominant ideologies and spiritual movements of our day. The Catholic Church and, I believe, the world have been greatly blessed by the intellectual leadership of this brilliant pope.

NOTES

[1] The most complete biographies to date are Tad Szulc, *Pope John Paul II: The Biography* (New York: Scribner, 1995) and Jonathan Kwitny, *Man of the Century: The Life and Times of John Paul II* (New York: Henry Holt, 1997). For the intellectual development of the pope see especially George Huntston Williams, *The Mind of John Paul II* (New York: Seabury, 1981) and Rocco Buttiglione, *Karol Wojtyla: The Thought of the Man Who Became John Paul II* (Grand Rapids, Mich.: W.B. Eerdmans, 1997).

[2] Karol Wojtyla, *Faith according to Saint John of the Cross* (San Francisco: Ignatius, 1981).

[3] For a collection of philosophical pieces mostly stemming from this period see Karol Wojtyla, *Person and Community: Selected Essays* (New York: Peter Lang, 1993). As commentary one may recommend Kenneth L. Schmitz, *At the Center of the Human Drama: The Philosophical Anthropology of Karol Wojtyla/Pope John Paul II* (New York: The Catholic University of America Press, 1993).

[4] English translation: Karol Wojtyla, *Love and Responsibility* (New York: Farrar, Straus, and Giroux, 1981).

[5] Tad Szulc, *Pope John Paul II*, 253–55.

[6] Cardinal Karol Wojtyla, *The Acting Person* (Dordrecht, Holland: D. Reidel, 1979), "translated and revised from the 1969 Polish edition, *Osoba i czyn*. This definitive text of the work established in collaboration with the author by Anna-Teresa Tymieniecka" (quoted from the title page).

[7] Karol Wojtyla, *Sources of Renewal: The Implementation of Vatican II* (San Francisco: Harper & Row, 1980).

[8] Karol Wojtyla, *Sign of Contradiction* (New York: Seabury/Crossroad, 1979), translated from the Italian original of 1977.

[9] *The Encyclicals of John Paul II*, ed. I. Michael Miller (Huntington, Ind.: Our Sunday Visitor, 1996). This volume, 1008 pages in length, contains splendid introductions by the editor and a thorough index to the first twelve encyclicals.

[10] *Crossing the Threshold of Hope* (New York: Knopf, 1994).

[11] *Gift and Mystery: On the Fiftieth Anniversary of My Priestly Ordination* (New York: Doubleday, 1996).

[12] I shall not attempt to give specific references for the points in my doctrinal survey, since nearly every sentence would call for a footnote. My principal sources have already been mentioned.

CHAPTER TWO

John Paul II and Philosophy

John Kavanaugh, S.J.

The writings of Karol Wojtyla, John Paul II, may strike many readers as being at first sight diffuse and multipolar. His poetry is so conceptual, his philosophy so lyrical at times, his dramas so theoretical, his encyclicals so dense with economics, family life, political tactic, and philosophical observation, that the judgment of complexity is understandable. And yet, his work is an expression of his life—a convergence of forces which, precisely by their gravitational relationship to each other, yield an integrated totality, no part of which can be grasped without pulling along the others.

The same phenomenon occurs when we probe into the philosophical career of the man. He is Thomist, but that is mediated by his Polishness. He is personalist, but that is mediated by his communitarianism. He is socialist,[1] but only in contradistinction to collectivists. He is a phenomenologist, but this is mediated by theological commitments.[2] He is philosopher, but that is mediated by his poetry which is, again, a fragment that is mediated by his experience as actor, priest, member of the resistance and person of faith.

Wojtyla's life and work, consequently, is a "dialectical" totality. Any approach which is one-sided, dualistic or reductionistic will lead one astray. Each aspect of his life and thought cuts through and across the other aspects. The meaning of each part rests upon its relation to the other parts and the living totality itself. His phenomenology is Thomist, socialist, poetic, evangelical, dramatic, political and traditionalist. His Thomism is radical, phenomenological, contemporary, personalist and transcendental.

In the book, *At the Center of the Human Drama*, Kenneth Schmitz portrays the complex interconnection of Wojtyla's work as dramatically centered in philosophical anthropology. He portrays the central concern of the pontiff's career to be an affirmation and defense of the human person as embodied, dramatic and self-revelatory. The "Acting Person," which served as the title for Wojtyla's major philosophical work, is truly an "actor," an agent in history who unfolds a unique drama of life which is both natural and personal.[3] It is this human drama which, I think, might be most serviceable as a starting point in understanding Wojtyla's philosophical outlook, since it connects with every area of his life and teachings. An understanding of the human as both a natural being and a personal reality is a key not only to his philosophy but also to his ethical stature as quite possibly the most persistent and consistent defender of human dignity. The theme of personal dignity resonates through most of his projects as a teacher in homilies and encyclicals. And it is intimately related to his central faith commitment to God Incarnate in Jesus Christ.

In this examination of the underlying philosophy of human identity and action, I will suggest that the position of Pope John Paul II is a confluence of at least two powerful traditions: Thomism and phenomenological personalism. Each tradition modifies, challenges and strengthens the other. Each of them, moreover, provides a unique quality to Wojtyla's ethical world-view which makes it especially valuable as a contribution to contemporary discourse.

The Thomistic Foundation

Wojtyla's account of human personhood is a rich integration of the Thomistic doctrine of nature revealed in capacities actualized by performance with a phenomenological rendition of personal consciousness. A human is a particular instance of a natural kind favored with endowments of self-understanding and self-possession. Each person embodies the objectively constituted structure of human nature and the potentialities for experienced, expressed personhood.

Much of modern and contemporary philosophy is marked by an absence of any philosophical anthropology and the ethical implications derived therefrom. Marxists and other modern and post-modern thinkers, haunted by a fear of some ossified and static doctrine of human nature, exhibit a marked avoidance of things ontological. This has led them to shun any project of objectively grounding the demand for justice and right order in some "foundational" anthropology.

As opposed to the experience of most contemporaries, Wojtyla's philosophical training in Thomism contributed a metaphysical ballast to his thought which would not only support prophetic calls for human equality and political-religious freedom, but also provide a philosophical anthropology to ground ethics.[4]

Thomas Aquinas' account of "nature" includes, as one of its prominent meanings, an identification with essence—*what* a being actually is—but from the viewpoint of the proper powers and activities unique to that class of beings which share such endowments or dispositional properties. What a being is, is revealed in the actions which both specify and realize that being. "Nature" expresses the whatness of a being from the point of view of action and actualization. The end or purpose of human nature is to realize and fulfill proper human potentialities, the apex of which are rationality and freedom exercised in embodied action. The very expression of human nature—and the fulfillment of it— involves self-reflection and self-ownership, both inherently linked to the power of human rationality.[5]

Thus, for example, when in *Laborem Exercens* Wojtyla brings the Thomistic background to his theory of labor, the notions of "acting for a purpose in mind," "realization of the human," and the alienation of labor are not isolated and ungrounded claims, as they might appear to be in the works of Marx. They are, rather, expressions of the actual objective constitution of human identity expressed in action. Labor, as well as any other human activity, must be evaluated as good or bad in the context of what is proper to man in his rational life. The allusions to Thomas represent the granite-like ethical foundations for Wojtyla's moral discourse. The pope's defense of laborers and their rights is not a matter of rhetoric or a function of majority rule. It is, rather, based on the conviction that if we are to be human, we must be true to our humanity—individually experienced and communally shared—and the constitutive structures of human nature. The issue of labor is one of fidelity to our humanness—not because of class interest or the intensity of oppression felt, but because the human person in "predisposed by his very nature, by virtue of humanity itself" to express and realize human nature concretely embodied in the person who labors.[6]

John Paul's appeal to the doctrine of "nature" is not a mere verbal maneuver. He is quite clearly using the Thomistic-Aristotelian tradition —a tactic which is confirmed and elaborated in *Love and Responsibility*. Although in this work he is dealing primarily with human sexuality, he appeals to the nature of man and even makes preliminary applications to the world of work.

> Man's nature differs fundamentally from that of the animals. It includes the power of self-determination, based on reflection, and manifested in the fact that a man acts from choice. This power is called free will. Because a human being—a person—possesses free will he is his own master.[7]

By nature we are endowed with powers of self-governance. It is precisely the prospect that such powers may be frustrated or repressed that the issues of economics and sexuality are raised. Whether in matters of money or body, a person, who has the proper human power of self-determination, may not be reduced to the status of a passive object to be used as an instrument or means of self-gratification.

> Inherent in the 'employer-employee' relationship there is a serious danger that the employee may be treated as a mere instrument; various defective systems of organizing labor give evidence of this. If, however the employer and the employee so arrange their association that the common good which both serve becomes clearly visible, then the danger of treating a person as someone less than he really is will be reduced. . . How is it possible to insure that one person does not become for the other—the woman for the man or the man for the woman—nothing more than the means to an end—i.e., an object used exclusively for the attainment of a selfish end?[8]

From this section of *Love and Responsibility*, contextualized in the discussion of human nature and its constitutive structure, we can see that ethical questions concerning both human labor and human loving emerge from the disordering of human identity, potentiality and fulfillment—a violation and frustration of human nature. And a special kind of nature it is.

The Phenomenological Personalist

It is not some ahistorical or abstract "nature" which grounds Wojtyla's analysis and critique of our public and personal lives. "Nature" language can seem too remote and rigid for people, and the Thomistic tradition, by itself, is unprepared to articulate the subjective appropriation of nature in history which is the human person.

It is not enough to define a man as an individual of the species *Homo* (or even *Homo sapiens*). The term 'person' has been coined to signify that man cannot be wholly contained within the concept 'individual member of the species', but that there is something more to him, a particular richness and perfection in the manner of his being, which can only be brought out by the use of the word 'person'.

The most obvious and simplest reason for this is that man has the ability to reason, he is a rational being, which cannot be said of any other entity in the visible world, for in none of them do we find any trace of conceptual thinking. Hence Boethius's famous definition of a person as simply an individual being of a rational nature (*individua substantia rationalis naturae*). This differentiates a person from the whole world of objective entities, this determines the distinctive character of a person.[9]

The particular richness of being a human person endowed with rationality infuses work with ethical value because the "one who carries it out is a person, a conscious and free subject, that is to say, a subject who decided about himself."[10] It is based on the fact that labor is ineluctibly an expression of a self-conscious being who is aware of the laboring action and its inherent purpose as personal fulfillment that John Paul is able to insist upon the primacy of labor over capital.

We must emphasize and give prominence to the primacy of man in the production process, the primacy of man over things. Everything contained in the concept of capital in the strict sense is only a collection of things. Man as the subject of work and independent of the work he does—man alone is a person.[11]

Wojtyla's appeal to conscious and free subjectivity, embodied in the expression of human labor, results from his painstaking analysis of *The Acting Person*, which was written nine years after *Love and Responsibility* and nine years before his accession to the papacy in 1978. In this work, he makes it fully clear that he accepts the Thomistic framework of "nature." "Humanness or human nature is equipped with the properties that enable a concrete human being to be a person: to be and act as a person."[12] But it is the living individual being which is the entire career of the natural human. The person is "the existential ontological support and also a living, always expanding synthesis of the dynamism proper to man, the synthesis of action with activations and thus of efficacy with subjectiveness."[13]

Wojtyla contends that it is our reflexivity upon experience as acting persons that enables us to discover and confirm our own self-understanding and comprehend the actualization of our humanness. Thus the phenomenology done in *The Acting Person* is personalist and focused upon the subjectivity of personal life, but only as it is made possible by naturally ontological personal endowments which are expressed and revealed over time.

> Nature does not denote a real and actual subject of existing and acting; it is not to be identified with the ontological foundation of a being. It can only apply to an abstract subject. For instance, in speaking of human nature we refer to something which has the status of real existence as the ontological structure of man only in an actual human being, but which has no real existence apart from him.[14]

Wojtyla holds that human nature is equipped with essential properties that enable a concrete human being to be a person and to act as person. The person is the existential instantiation of humanity concretely expressing humanness in dynamic behavior. It is only because of human potentialities that persons experience themselves as subjective beings. Human rationality and the unique form of consciousness that it exhibits yields the subjective experience of personhood.

> We owe to consciousness and especially to its reflexive function, that man—the subjective autonomous being—has the experience of himself as the subject, which makes his being fully subjective.[15]

The capacity for self-disposition is given in the indubitable human experience of self-consciousness wherein a person is not only immediately aware of the world but aware of his or her very awareness. This awareness is both reflective and reflexive, and insofar as a person is capable of making himself an object of attentiveness he is empowered to make himself an object of disposition. Ultimately, it is the structure of our being human and the structure of our self-conscious engagement with the world that allows us to enter the world as ethical beings and makes us special reposits of moral dignity. "This structure serves as the basis of morality—or of moral value as an existential reality—and it is owing to it that morality as a mode of conduct participates in the innerness of man and achieves a measure of durability in him."[16] *The Acting Person* provides an articulated rendition of the self-conscious dimensions of human rationality, as a foundation for Wojtyla's philosophical anthropology, a complement to the more objectivist Thomistic view of human nature, and a basis for establishing the individual person's uniqueness and incommunicability.

The basis of the pontiff's critique of economic and other activities is the self-determining power of a human being who by nature is *capable* of self-determination. When an economic system represses the human person in his or her subjectivity, that economic system, be it capitalist or collectivist, must be called into question. Herein lies Wojtyla's critique of classical economies as well as dialectical materialism.[17]

Wojtyla sees the major failure of Marxism as a repression of the very humans which Marx himself so passionately defended. It also repressed any idea of species-wide characteristics which could subvert the domination of Party and State. Moreover, dialectical materialism stifles talk about objective moral values and the interior lives of self-conscious, spiritual beings. The human person in the history of most "Marxisms" inevitably became a passive object yielding to the impersonal forces of history, rather than a self-conscious autonomous agent for change.

On a broader level, modern and contemporary philosophy offer false dichotomies as solutions to the question of human identity. On one hand, we are offered an account of the person as pure consciousness or a non-historical ego, dislodged from nature and one's own nature. On the other hand we are offered the image of the human being as a natural object or non-personal animal. Neither account can provide a solid foundation for ethics or for claims of human dignity which underwrite claims for human rights.

Wojtyla proposes an account that is faithful both to our natural animality and our personal capacities for a reflexively conscious engagement of our bodies and our world. This endowment is what makes us ethical animals. This is what marks our moral dignity. The "turn to subjectivity" in modern philosophy resulted in an isolated and encapsulated inwardness cut off from nature and objectivity. Wojtyla's "subject," however, is anchored in a subject (suppositum) of existence. The embodied self is never cut off from the world and nature. Neither consciousness nor nature is absolutized in the union of an embodied-reflexively conscious career, the whole living person.[18]

John Paul II, in all his writing and preaching, affirms the conviction that every arena of human life is to be precisely that: human; for humans, of humans and by humans. Seeing the person as a dynamic integrated totality, moreover, is attractive to John Paul because, as a theologian and believer, he intends to claim these human arenas also for Christ. Economics, politics, social systems, sexuality, and international relations are not only transfused with value as productions of acting persons. They are also intimately related to an integrated faith which impinges upon every arena of human life.

Much of post-modern life, as well as philosophy, has failed in this. We have no shared understanding of human nature or the objective claims that are derived therefrom. We have a profound lack in principles to ground our moral outrage. To this absence, Wojtyla brought his Thomism, a highly developed and tested system, capable of adaptation and contemporary application, invested with a powerful epistemology guaranteeing far more than empiricism, and grounded by a theory of human nature robust enough to support an ethics emergent from the very structures and exigencies of humanness.

Although a rare phenomenologist might accept the ambivalence of his phenomenological method, a rare personalist might welcome what seems to be a "biologistic" emphasis upon nature, and a rare ethician might value his appeal to objective moral standards, Wojtyla's form of phenomenological personalism gives a compelling power to his defense of human dignity. His two philosophical traditions, united to an unshakable Christian faith, converge in a vital unity which offers to contemporary men and women a vision of the human person which is, in this author's opinion, one of the most significant and compelling in contemporary thought.

NOTES

[1] It may seem outrageous to call Wojtyla "socialist," but the response of some commentators to the pope's social encyclicals is an indication of the socialist undertones to his critique of capitalism. *On Social Concern*, for example, was not well received by Catholic commentators sympathetic to Capitalism. One weekly actually gave the final thirty lines of its reportage to a quotation from the *Wall Street Journal*, almost as a corrective to the pontiff's writings. Michael Novak, in the February 24, 1988 issue of the *Los Angeles Times*, found the pope's parallels with the USSR "ungrounded," "uncalled for," as well as "inexplicable" and "outrageous." William Buckley, in the March 18, 1988 issue of *National Review* found the pope's observations a "kind of historical revisionism generally associated with modern nihilists." He prayed that John Paul II might correct his "heart-tearingly misbegotten" encyclical. Secular commentators, such as A. M. Rosenthal and William Safire the *New York Times* and the *International Herald Tribune*, took similar offense at the "boon for the Soviet Union," this "simplistic" and "stultifying" critique of capitalism. Even the Encyclical, *Centesimus Annus*, which, because of its approval of entrepreneurship and freedom, was applauded by the Catholic commentators mentioned above, the more critical of the commentators worried over its challenge to capitalism. Milton Friedman noted that there was "much for the left-liberals" in its concern for unions and justice for workers. John Gray fretted that it perpetuated the "corrupt ideology of the third world." And Shirley Robin Letwin cautioned that it did not repudiate socialism. These comments all appeared in "The Pope, Liberty and Capitalism," a special supplement to the *National Review*.

[2] The great historian of the "Phenomenological Movement," Herbert Speigelburg, noted to me, upon the publication of *The Acting Person*, that the pope was a phenomenologist, yes, but "not quite," since he clearly had ontological and theological commitments which he was not willing to "bracket."

[3] Kenneth L. Schmitz. *At the Center of the Human Drama: The Philosophical Anthropology of Karol Wojtyla/Pope John Paul II* (Washington D.C.:The Catholic University Press of America)1993.

[4] In addition to Schmitz, two fine extended philosophical accounts can be found in *The Mind of John Paul II* by George Huntson Williams (New York: Seabury Press, 1981) and *Karol Wojtyla: The Thought of the Man Who Became Pope John Paul II* (Grand Rapids: Eerdmans, 1997) written by Rocco Buttiglione in 1982 and translated by Paolo Guietti and Francesca Murphy. What is particularly helpful about the latter book is Buttiglione's Introduction to the 1994 third Polish Edition of *The Acting Person* and an excellent "Afterword" bibliographical survey by the translators.

Ronald Modras' "The Thomistic Personalism of Pope John Paul II" (*Modern Schoolman*, January, 1982) and Michael Novak's "John Paul II: Christian Philosopher" (*America*, October 25, 1997) give instructive, but shorter, accounts. See also *A Christian Humanism: Karol Wojtyla's Existential Personalism* by Andrew N. Wozniki (New Britain, Ct.: Mariel Publications) and *The Christian Personalism of John Paul II* by Ronald Lawler (Chicago: Franciscan Herald Press, 1982).

[5] Cf., for example, the exposition of the *Summa Theologica*, Ia.QQ.75–83; 76 on the dynamic unity, 77 on the theory of powers, 79 on intellect and 82–3 on will.

[6] *Laborem Exercens*. Encyclical Letter of Pope John Paul II. There are many editions and some alternative translations of this work. My own pagination refers to the Paulist Press edition which appears in the *Priority of Labor* by Gregory Baum. (New York: 1982). Baum's commentary, while helpful, reads too much Marxism and not enough Thomism into the encyclical; but I believe he is quite right in stressing the socialist and Marxist influences in the context of this letter. Cf. pp. 95, 105.

[7] Karol Wojtyla, *Love and Responsibility*. Tr. By H.T. Willetts (London: Fount Paperbacks, 1982), pp.23–4.

[8] *Ibid.*, pp. 29–30. The economic and sexual parallels are drawn specifically by the author.

[9] *Ibid.*, p.22. This entire passage is reminiscent of Aquinas, not only in its discussion of infra-human cognition and desire, but in its description of the "inwardness" and intimacy, or depth, to human experience, which Wojtyla characterizes as spiritual.

[10] *Laborem Exercens*, p.105.

[11] *Ibid.*, p.119.

[12] Karol Wojtyla, *The Acting Person*, p.84.

[13] *Ibid.*

[14] *Ibid.*, p.77.

[15] *Ibid.*, p.85.

[16] *Ibid.*, pp.22–47, for general discussion. The actual citation is found on page 151.

[17] Cf. *Laborem Exercens*, p.125. Similar to the critique of Marxism, the major failures of Capitalism are found in the repression of personal life through sophisticated forms of slavery. In a homily delivered at Belo Horizonte, Brazil, July, 1980, he spoke, "We cannot be slaves to things we produce, to material objects, to consumerism, to economic systems." (USCC Publication Office) This theme, reiterated in sermons around the world, is powerfully treated in *Redemptor Hominis*, especially sections 15 and 16, as well as in *Sollicitudo Rei Socialis*, (Origins Edition, March 3, 1988), sections 19, 35, 36. Section 27 contains the following passage:

"Superdevelopment, which consists in an excessive availability of every kind of material goods for the benefit of certain social groups, easily makes people slaves of 'possession' and of immediate gratification, with no other horizon than the multi-plication of continual replacement of the things already owned with others still better. This is the so-called civilization of 'consumption' or 'consumerism' . . .

"All of us experience firsthand the sad effects of this blind submission to pure consumerism; in the first place a crass materialism, and at the same time a radical dissatisfaction because one quickly learns—unless one is shielded from the flood of publicity and ceaseless and tempting offers of products—that the more one possesses the more one wants, while deeper aspirations remain unsatisfied and perhaps even stifled."

[18] As Schmitz, *op.cit.*, puts it: "For by this *ascesis* it [the self] prepares—not to find itself a refuge (whether Cartesian, Humean or Kantian, rationalist, empiricist or transcendental)—but to place itself before the transcendent Source of whatever being,

meaning and value the human possesses as a gift received." (p. 137) I have made the observations about this "chastened self" in a review of Schmitz's book in the *Modern Schoolman*, January, 1997, pp. 165–6. Earlier observations in this paper, especially those in the context of human labor, have been offered to the Jesuit Philosophical Association (April 6, 1984) under the title, "The Moral Dialectic of *Laborem Exercens*."

CHAPTER THREE

John Paul II and
The Priority of Culture

George Weigel

I.

℘hat no good deed goes unpunished is nicely illustrated by the terms in which several biographers have recognized Pope John Paul II as a seminal figure in the Revolution of 1989.

Thus Carl Bernstein and Marco Politi, in their 1996 book, *His Holiness: John Paul II and the Hidden History of Our Time*, argue that, yes, the pope played a large role in the collapse of European communism—as co-conspirator with the Reagan Administration in a "holy alliance" that wedded the diplomacy of the Holy See to the anti-communist passions of conservative Republicans and the wiles of the CIA. Jonathan Kwitny agrees with the basic proposition, that "1989" cannot be understood without taking account of the Polish pontiff; but his 1997 biography, *Man of the Century*, inverts the Bernstein/Politi proposition by arguing that the pope, a nonviolent revolutionary on the model of Gandhi and Martin Luther King, Jr., pulled the whole thing off against the machinations of the Reaganites and the CIA.

What these and similar journalistic accounts tend to discount, unfortunately, is the pope's own reading of "the history of our time," whose locus classicus is the 1991 encyclical, *Centesimus Annus*. There, John Paul argued that "1989" could not be understood through the conventional analytic categories of Realpolitik. Rather, "1989" was made possible by a prior moral and cultural revolution, which created the conditions for the possibility of the nonviolent political upheaval that swept Marxism-Leninism into the dustbin of European history. The pope was hardly unaware of the political, military, and economic factors that contributed to the breach of the Berlin Wall on November 10, 1989. But, he suggested, if we want to grasp why "1989" happened when it did and how it did, a deeper reading of the dynamics of history and a more acute analysis of the twentieth century crisis of European civilization are required. Against the Realist school of historiography and international relations theory, in both its left- and right-wing forms, John Paul argued for the priority of culture over politics and economics as the engine of historical change; and at the heart of culture, he proposed, is cult, or religion.

In the years after *Centesimus Annus*, John Paul II has insisted that what was true of the epic changes we call "1989" is also true for the consolidation of free societies in central and eastern Europe, and for the well-being of the established democracies of the West. Democratic polities and free economies, he argues, are not independent variables; absent the habits of the mind and the habits of the heart that make people democrats and that channel their economic energies to good ends, the free society risks becoming a "thinly-disguised totalitarianism" (as he put it in the most controversial section of *Centesimus Annus*). The tendency, even among some celebrants of the pope's role in "1989," has been to dismiss this as so much pontifical rodomontade; and a tone-deaf western media has generally agreed that these are the cranky protestations of an angry old man incapable of understanding the world he helped create (See, for example, Tad Szulc in his 1995 effort, *Pope John Paul II: The Biography*).

But two papal pilgrimages in mid-1997—to Poland in June, and to the 12th World Youth Day in Paris in August—provided ample evidence that John Paul II's reading of contemporary history has not lost its salience, nor has it been blunted in its capacity to generate historical change. Moreover, the pope's re-orientation of Catholic evangelism and social doctrine toward the conversion of culture has given him a distinctive understanding of the requirements of freedom in the third millennium—which he insists, against the backdrop of this fast-closing century of unprecedented wickedness, can be a "springtime of the human spirit."

II.

The pope's June 1997 journey through his Polish homeland took place under two shadows. The first was the memory of his 1991 Polish pilgrimage, the first after the communist crack-up, which was widely (and accurately) regarded as the least successful of his visits to his native country. In retrospect, it is possible to see just how difficult the situation was in those heady days. Poles were still intoxicated with their new freedom and wanted to celebrate it with the man to whom they gave credit for their deliverance; but the prescient pope, who had quickly decoded the new threats to freedom implicit in the value-neutral notion of democracy being exported to east central Europe from the West, wanted to talk about the dangers he saw ahead. The Polish hierarchy had not found an appropriate voice to make its presence felt in the new circumstances of democratic pluralism, particularly on the heated issue of abortion; neither had Catholic politicians who wanted to think with the Church, but who resented being instructed in their duties by bishops who seemed unable to distinguish their episcopal role from that of party bosses. The net result was a tense visit, full of controversies, in which the fervor and the sense of national unity demonstrated in the pope's 1979, 1983, and 1987 pilgrimages was often absent. This unhappy memory hung heavily over anticipations of the pope's June 1997 return home.

The second shadow was Poland's recent political history. In September 1993 a coalition led by ex-communists won the national parliamentary elections and took power in the Sejm. Two years later, on November 19, 1995, Alexander Kwasniewski, the youthful (and, some might say, Clintonesque) founder of the Democratic Left Alliance, defeated Lech Walesa for the presidency of Poland. Walesa's erratic behavior in the years since 1989 made his dismissal by the electorate understandable; but the fact that it was understandable made it no less disconcerting. The icon of the Solidarity revolution had been displaced by a former communist party apparatchik: what had happened to the brave dreams on which "1989" has been built? Is this what happened in a "normal society?"

The combination of these two factors, and concerns about John Paul's health, made for considerable nervousness prior to the pope's arrival. Would a pilgrimage that might turn out to be the pope's farewell fail?

In the event, the pilgrimage was a triumph; as one exuberant Polish Dominican put it, "He's done it again; it's like 1979." But what, precisely, had he done?

The eleven days between John Paul's arrival on May 31 and his departure on June 10 were, to be sure, full of emotion and drama. The pope struck a sympathetic chord and immediately re-connected with his countrymen when he said, at the arrival ceremony in Warsaw, that he had "come among you as a pilgrim . . . filled with profound emotion," because "every return to Poland is like a return to the family home, where the smallest objects remind us of what is closest and dearest to our hearts." Three days later, at Gorzów Wielkopolski, John Paul reminded an immense throng that the late primate, Cardinal Stefan Wyszynski, had told him just after he had been elected pope that "You are to lead the Church into its Third Millennium," and requested that they "ask God on your knees . . . that I am able to meet this challenge." (The crowd chanted back, "We will help you!", a phrase that conjured up memories of strikers in 1970 responding to the pleas of the new communist prime minister, Gierek; the pope answered the chant with a moment of papal whimsy: "I recognize the words but I hope it will be better this time.")

Then there was Mass at Zakopane, the ski resort in the pope's beloved Tatra Mountains. The mayor, in traditional Polish highlander dress, knelt before John Paul on June 6 to thank him for "freeing us from the 'red slavery' and for teaching us how to eradicate from our Polish homeland all that is degrading, humiliating, and all that enslaves us." After Mass, when the tough, craggy Polish mountain people began to sing to John Paul an old folk song about a highlander going into exile ("Mountaineer, who do you leave your beautiful hills and silvery brooks?"), one would have been hard-put to find a dry eye among the half-million present, including the pope.

For eleven days, John Paul (who seemed to get stronger as the visit unfolded) worked the crowds masterfully. When hundreds of thousands of youngsters in Pozna began to chant *Sto lat!* ("May you live a hundred years!"), he was quick to reply, "Don't flatter the pope so much; you'd better think about Paris [the upcoming World Youth Day]." And, more poignantly, when an enormous congregation at the shrine of Czestochowa, home of the Black Madonna, began to chant, "Long live the Pope," John Paul wryly responded, "He does, he does, and he grows older . . ."

But the meaning of the pope's Polish pilgrimage should not be measured simply by the colossal crowds, which topped out at over 1.2 million in Kraków on June 8, when the pope canonized Blessed Queen Jadwiga, co-foundress of the Jagieo dynasty. As in any papal event, what ultimately counts—what historians must finally deal with are the texts. And the twenty-six major texts of this pilgrimage, taken together, spelled out John Paul's distinctive vision of the priority of culture over politics and economics and his Vatican II-driven sense of the "public Church" as, essentially, the shaper of culture. The June pilgrimage was deliberately filled with images of Poland's Christian past: a pan-Central European celebration of the millennium of the martyrdom of St. Adalbert, held in Gniezno; the canonization of Jadwiga; the commemoration in Kraków of the 600th anniversary of the Jagiellonian University's theology department. But this constant evocation of the past was not an exercise in pious nostalgia; rather, it was anamnesis in the service of the present and the future. As the pope put it at the departure ceremony on June 10, "Fidelity to roots does not mean a mechanical copying of the patterns of the past. Fidelity to roots is always creative, ready to descend into the depths, open to new challenges, alert to the 'signs of the times.' . . . Fidelity to roots means above all the ability to create an organic synthesis of perennial values, confirmed so often in history, and the challenge of today's world: faith and culture, the Gospel and life." And that, he said, was why he had wanted to celebrate the canonizations of Jadwiga and John of Dukla, as well as two beatifications, during his pilgrimage: because "the Church's saints are a particular revelation of the loftiest horizons of human freedom."

The canonization of Jadwiga afforded perhaps the greatest temptation to forget present and future in a binge about Poland's glorious past. But the pope stoutly resisted this, and his canonization sermon focused on the fourteenth century queen as a model for Poland today and tomorrow: Jadwiga the queen, for whom power was a question of public service; Jadwiga the diplomat, working to build a community of nations in east central Europe; Jadwiga the patroness of culture, "aware that faith seeks rational understanding," who endowed the university which bears her dynastic name with a gift of her golden scepter; Jadwiga, born to wealth and privilege, whose "sensitivity to social wrongs was often praised by her subjects." The message to Poland's new democracy could not have been clearer: you are the inheritors of a great cultural tradition, and it is that tradition that will enable you to build a genuinely free society worthy of the half-century of sacrifice you made in the name of freedom.

At the commemoration of the 600th anniversary of the Jagiellonian University faculty of theology, held in the collegiate church of St. Anne later that same day, John Paul sent another signal about the Church's relationship to politics. As it happens, Karol Wojtyla was the last student to receive a doctorate from the Jagiellonian University theology faculty before it was shut down by the communist regime in early 1954; and the struggle to sustain serious theological scholarship in Kraków had been one of the hallmarks of his time as cardinal-archbishop of the city. So it might have been expected that the pope would take the occasion of this anniversary celebration to say something about Poland's upcoming parliamentary elections, in which the heirs of the suppressors of the Jagiellonian faculty of theology were contestants. John Paul minced no words about "the dramatic struggle for existence" that that faculty had gone through "at the time of the communist dictatorship." And he reminded the congregation (composed of Poland's leading intellectuals and educators, many of them his old friends) that the Church had "never resigned herself to the fact of a unilateral and unjust suppression" of the theology faculty by the communist regime.

But this was not, he said, a matter of the Church's offended amour propre. Rather, in terms reminiscent of Newman's *Idea of a University*, he insisted that the defense of the theological faculty was a defense of the integrity of the intellectual life, a defense of culture and a defense of the nation. The Church was not protesting the abuse of an ancient ecclesiastical privilege; by fighting for theology's place in the academy, the Church "did everything in her power to ensure that the university environment of Kraków was not deprived of an academic studium of theology" which had made its own "contribution to the development of Polish learning and culture." And a culture cut off from transcendent reference points could not serve the human good, because it could not know the truth about man.

Indeed, the pope's richly-textured address at St. Anne's, in which the politics of the present moment were not mentioned once, seemed to be saying to all concerned (within and without the Church), that while politics were undoubtedly important, the nurturance of culture, especially in the life of the mind, was far more important. You think that parliamentary elections will decide Poland's future? No, the pope suggested, Poland's future really depends on "a lively awareness" that "man does not create truth; rather, truth discloses itself to man when he perseveringly seeks it." That is what universities are supposed to do.

That is why universities are, over time, of far more consequence to a nation than parliaments. And that is why the Church, embodied in her supreme pontiff, is reflecting with you on the meaning of true humanism, that "integral notion of the human person" which is a "condition for the sound development" of the intellectual life, rather than telling you for whom to vote.

Five days before, at Gniezno, John Paul had delivered a similar message about the free society's dependence on a vibrant public moral culture to the presidents of Poland, the Czech Republic, Slovakia, Hungary, Lithuania, Ukraine, and Germany: all new (or newly-reunified) democracies. Politics was not just a matter of winning elections, he reminded them, nor was the success of economic reform to be measured solely by the indices of gross national product. Rather, "the greatness of the role of political leaders is to act always with respect for the dignity of every human being, to create the conditions of a generous solidarity which never marginalizes any citizen, to permit each individual to have access to culture, to recognize and put into practice the loftiest human and spiritual values, to profess and to share one's religious beliefs." The Realpolitik of amoral power had given Europe "this sorely tried century." The birth of a new Europe capable of responding "to its age-old vocation in the world" depended on a European rediscovery of the continent's ancient "cultural and religious roots."

Prior to the pope's arrival, the scent of a valedictory was in the air. Eleven dramatic and intellectually-challenging days later, speculation had already begun about a papal visit in 1999, this time to the Baltic region (where Solidarity was born) and to the Mazurian Lakes where Father Karol Wojtyla loved to kayak. It may not have been "1979 again," as my enthusiastic Polish friend suggested. But John Paul's politics of culture (combined with terminal ex-communist incompetence in the face of catastrophic floods in Poland in July) had their effect: in September, the voters threw out the ex-communists and elected a new parliament led by the old Solidarity coalition, reconfigured.

That parliament is now the steward of Europe's fastest growing economy and east central Europe's most stable polity. And so the great Polish experiment will continue: can democratic pluralism and a free economy be built and sustained on the basis of an intact Catholic culture? That John Paul II gave Poles and Polish culture a living past, rather than a nostalgic past, during his June 1997 pilgrimage bodes well for a positive answer to that historic question.

III.

The evangelical potency of the pope's "culture first" approach to the "Church in the modern world" was also on display in Paris during the 12th World Youth Day in August 1997.

On his first pastoral visit to France in the Spring of 1980, John Paul II, whose affection for the Gallic "Eldest Daughter of the Church" and her culture dates back to his student days, shocked a congregation of 350,000 at Le Bourget Airport by bluntly asking, "France . . . are you faithful to the promises of your baptism? France, Daughter of the Church and educator of peoples, are you faithful, for the good of man, to the covenant with eternal wisdom?" Seven months later, the pope acted on his judgment that the revitalization of French Catholicism was an urgent pastoral need by making what has been, arguably, the boldest episcopal nomination of his pontificate: the appointment of Jean-Marie Lustiger, son of Polish-Jewish parents, as archbishop of Paris.

Lustiger, who had converted to Catholicism as a teenager, had been an innovative student chaplain at the Sorbonne and a Parisian pastor before being named Bishop of Orleans, where he spent a mere thirteen months before his translation to Paris. During his years as chaplain and pastor, Lustiger developed a distinctive analysis of the historical and cultural situation of the French Church. Prior to the French Revolution, the Church in France had been a "Church of power," allied to the political order and in some sense dependent on it. Then came 1789 and the subsequent Terror, during which French Catholicism took the first and (until the twentieth century) hottest blast from secular modernity. Reeling from that massive and bloody assault, the Church divided. A restorationist faction sought the return of the ancien régime: at first tout court; later, when the monarchist option became politically untenable, culturally. This faction produced, over time, the extremism of Action Francaise, Petainism during World War II, and, ultimately, Lefebvrism in the post-Vatican II period. The counter-faction sought an accommodation with secularity and the political left, and eventually gave birth to the bizarre phenomenon of "Christian Marxism." The bitter contestation between these two factions had divided French Catholics for over one hundred fifty years and had drained the Church of its evangelical vigor.

The creativity of Lustiger's analysis lay in its claim that these two factions, far from being the polar opposites they claimed themselves to be, were in fact two variants on the same false option: the determination to be a "Church of power." The two factions divided, of course, on what form of political power was preferable as a partner for the Church. But both agreed (although they could never admit it to each other) that to be the Church in France must mean to be a "Church of power."

Lustiger disagreed. It was the marriage with power, he believed, which had made the Church so vulnerable to the assault of secular modernity. Nor was there any way to mediate between the claims of the accommodationist and restorationist factions: the restorationists regarded *Dignitatis Humanae*, Vatican II's Declaration on Religious Freedom, as heresy (for declaring the state theologically incompetent), while the accommodationists had mistaken the Council's opening to the modern world (in *Gaudium et Spes*) as an invitation to cohabitation with Marxism and, later, post-modernist deconstruction, both of which led in short order to the dissolution of Christian orthodoxy.

In these circumstances, Lustiger proposed, the only option was the evangelical option: to abandon the pretense of power, to eschew alliances with any political force, and to bring France back to her baptismal promises, not through the mediation of politics but through the reconversion of culture. And this, in turn, meant taking the evangelical proposition straight to the molders and shapers of culture: the by-now thoroughly secularized French intelligentsia. After his accession to Paris in 1981, Lustiger began implementing this pastoral strategy of re-evangelization "from the head down" in a dynamic fashion: in a slew of best-selling books, many of them addressing the possibility of faith amidst modernity; by re-founding a seminary (and thus personally encouraging a more evangelically-assertive Parisian presbyterate); and through a direct, personal, weekly outreach to students and the professoriate in a Sunday evening Mass-with-homily at his cathedral of Notre-Dame.

World Youth Day-1997 fit snugly into this strategy of reconversion through culture. World Youth Day would not simply happen in Paris. In the strategic vision of Cardinal Lustiger and his associates, shared by John Paul II, World Youth Day would be an integral part, perhaps even a turning-point, in the reconversion of France through the evangelization of culture. Thus the pope's contacts with the French authorities were kept to the minimum required by protocol and good manners; there was a brief welcoming meeting with President Chirac and a brief pre-departure meeting with Prime Minister Jospin. But whenever John Paul appeared in public in Paris it was in an explicitly ecclesial context:

his was not a "Church of power," but a Church of the Gospel whose witness to Christ compelled a defense of the rights of man.

The rhythm of the 12th World Youth Day was deliberately set by a model of pilgrimage that Lustiger had first encountered in his days as chaplain at the Sorbonne. There, Msgr. Maxim Charles, later the rector of Sacre Coeur, was reviving the French tradition of student pilgrimages with a group of young intellectuals who would later become close friends of Father Lustiger and, later, his informal advisors as archbishop. These pilgrimages, first to Notre-Dame, later to Chartres, were inspired by the theology of Louis Bouyer and his teaching that every significant Christian event should, in some fashion, recapitulate the Paschal Triduum, the core of Christian experience. Thus on every student pilgrimage, no matter at what time of the year, the retreatants would "re-live" Holy Week, from Palm Sunday through the Easter Vigil.

The Bouyer-Charles paschal template was adapted to World Youth Day-1997 to great effect. Thus the first official day of the youth festival (which happened to be a Tuesday) "was" Palm Sunday: the Holy Year cross, given by John Paul II to the participants in the first World Youth Day in 1985, was solemnly processed by a dozen youngsters from around the world, through a crowd of perhaps 500,000 young people stretched from the Eiffel Tower along the Champs de Mars to the front lawn of the Ecole Militaire, where a great platform had been built for the opening Mass. Thursday, when John Paul II arrived in Paris and first met the young people, was "Holy Thursday;" the Gospel read during the welcoming ceremony was John 13:1–15, the washing of the disciples' feet, which the pope explicated to the youngsters in a text read in their language-based catechetical groups the next day. On Friday, hundreds of thousands of teenagers and young adults relived Good Friday by making the Way of the Cross at dozens of venues all over Paris. On Saturday night, a candlelight baptismal vigil was celebrated by a congregation of 750,000 at the Longchamps racecourse, as the pope baptized twelve young catechumens from every continent. And then, after this re-creation of the Easter Vigil, came the closing Eucharist on Sunday morning, which turned out to be the largest Mass in French history, with more than a million in attendance at Longchamps.

The massive turnout far exceeded the expectations of the event's planners who, as things got underway, were anticipating perhaps 250,000 youngsters all week, and a crowd of 500,000 for the closing Mass. At least twice that number of young people turned out, and the outpouring of interest from French teenagers stunned the Parisian press, which spent the better part of the week editorially wondering what on earth was going on. One also had the sense that it stunned those French bishops who, having internalized a sense of their own marginality, were unsympathetic to Lustiger's pastoral strategy and its forthrightly evangelical approach to the keepers of the French cultural flame.

When John Paul II visited Reims in September 1996, similar skepticism about public interest was expressed but another massive turnout ensued. Then, the focus was on the Christian roots of the French nation, the occasion being the 1500th anniversary of the baptism of Clovis. At World Youth Day, the two "icons" proposed for reflection were drawn from the modern history of French Catholicism: St. Thérèse of Lisieux, and Frederic Ozanam, founder of the worldwide St. Vincent de Paul societies, whom the pope beatified at Notre-Dame on August 22. This choice of patrons for the papal pilgrimage to Paris was not accidental. Both were young Catholics (Thérèse died at 24, Ozanam at 40). Thérèse, perhaps the most popular of modern saints, was a contemplative, a woman who made original contributions to theology. Ozanam was an intellectual in an age of radical skepticism, a democrat detached from the ancien régime fantasies of many of his co-religionists, a servant of the poor, a devoted husband and father, and an original thinker whose writings on the just society prefigured and influenced the birth of modern Catholic social doctrine in Leo XIII's *Rerum Novarum*. The message being sent through this iconography was unmistakable: sanctity is possible in modernity; youthful enthusiasm can be drawn to Christ; Catholic faith can nurture a free society (liberty), human dignity (equality), and human solidarity (fraternity). Cardinal Lustiger drove this point home on French national television the night World Youth Day concluded. Asked by a middle-aged interviewer how he explained such an extraordinary response to World Youth Day, the cardinal suggested that it was a question of generations. The reporter belonged to a generation that had grown up in the Church, had lost its faith (c. 1968), and had been fighting its parents, so to speak, ever since. These young people, the cardinal said, grew up empty; they have found Jesus Christ; they want to explore all that that means. Do not, he concluded, read their lives through your experience. They do not think that being Christian and being engaged, intelligent, compassionate, dedicated people are antinomies.

Or, as the pope put it to the young in his closing homily at Longchamps: "Go forth now along the roads of the world, along the pathways of humanity, while remaining ever united in Christ's Church. Continue to contemplate God's glory and God's love, and you will receive the enlightenment needed to build the civilization of love, to help our brothers and sisters to see the world transfigured by God's eternal wisdom and love." In the capital of a particularly skeptical and anticlerical Enlightenment, a new enlightenment of culture, leading to a new concept of the free society, was being proposed. The response suggested that World Youth Day-1997 may, one day, be remembered as a turning-point in the modern history of France.

IV.

Professor Stefan Swiezawski, the distinguished Polish historian of philosophy who was instrumental in bringing young Father Karol Wojtyla to the faculty of the Catholic University of Lublin, once said that the post-Conciliar Church was "living in a new epoch. Vatican II was not just one Council; it marked the end of the Constantinian epoch, thank God. Now the Church has no army, no state. It is a quite different situation." Working out the implications of this post-Constantinian ecclesiology with an eye toward the third millennium of Christian history has been one of the principal leitmotifs of the pontificate of John Paul II, who played such an important role in drafting *Gaudium et Spes*, the Council's Pastoral Constitution on the Church in the Modern World.

In some respects, of course, the Church will always be engaged with "power," as the world defines power. Vatican diplomacy continues; the Holy See exchanges diplomatic representatives with 166 states and is an active participant in international legal and political institutions. What the pontificate of John Paul II has done, in fulfillment of the promise of Vatican II and its seminal Dogmatic Constitution on the Church (*Lumen Gentium*), is to locate this inevitable engagement with the principalities and powers in an explicitly evangelical context. The Church's defense of human rights (and especially the first human right of religious freedom), like its groping toward an ethic of "humanitarian intervention" in the post-Cold War world, its efforts to mediate ethnic and nationalist conflict in the Middle East and elsewhere, and its proposals for securing the moral foundations of the free society, cannot be understood merely as the Church's dealings with the "real world." In the ecclesiology and social doctrine of John Paul II, the witness of the "public Church" is an expression of the Church's essential task, which is the proclamation of the Gospel of Jesus Christ—a Gospel with many things to say about the nature of man, of human community and human destiny.

The "real world" is the human universe that has been redeemed and transformed by the atoning death of the Son of God. The Church is not "here" and the "real world" there; the story of the Church is the world's story, rightly understood. This belief is what grounds the public ministry of John Paul II and directs his attention, as teacher and witness, to the realm of culture: that dimension of the human universe in which the self-understanding of individuals and peoples is formed and is transmitted to new generations. Because the Church is first and foremost evangelical, the Church must, in this post-Constantinian epoch, be the evangelizer of cultures.

This steady insistence on the priority of culture is difficult to grasp for those who read John Paul II as another great figure on a world-historical stage whose dramatic action is defined by politics. He has been that, of course. But he is that precisely because, not in spite of, the fact that he is a Christian, a priest, and a bishop who insists that politics is not all there is. Thus there are not two John Pauls: in conventional media terms, the "social progressive" and the "doctrinal conservative." There is only one John Paul II, as there is only one Karol Wojtyla.

Jonathan Kwitny's *Man of the Century* is less woodenheaded in its wrestling with the complex simplicity of the life of Karol Wojtyla than were Tad Szulc and the authorial dyad of Carl Bernstein/Marco Politi. But Kwitny, who deserves full marks for demolishing the Bernstein/Politi "holy alliance" fiction and who avoids the worst of Szulc's gaucheries about the angry old man fighting vainly against the world he helped create, also tries to force Wojtyla's life and accomplishment onto the Procrustean bed of his own political preferences: in this instance, the pope becomes the last great twentieth century exponent of democratic socialism and pacifism.[1] The public accomplishment, Kwitny rightly claims, is a large one: Wojtyla was crucial in the destruction of the totalitarian option, which had caused such immense human suffering throughout the century. But is John Paul II the "man of the century" because of a political achievement?

The crisis of the twentieth century, which gave birth to totalitarianism in its sundry forms, has been in the first instance a crisis of culture: a crisis in the order of ideas and morals. This has been Karol Wojtyla's conviction since he helped lead a clandestine cultural resistance to the Nazi occupation of Poland during World War II. The will-to-power, the hallmark of the politics of this century, was a direct consequence of the collapse of a publicly-available concept of human freedom that was tethered to truth and ordered to an objectively-knowable human good. A modernity that could not give a persuasive account of the truth of its highest aspiration—freedom—was a modernity in which freedom necessarily came to be understood as a neutral faculty of choice. And, absent any agreed and publicly-accessible standards by which the goodness of various choices could be judged and adjudicated, the reduction of social life to a raw contest for power necessarily ensued. Nietzsche, in other words, was right; and seeing what was coming, he went mad.

If there is a plausibility to John Paul II as the "man of the century," it is not because he put paid to one of the epiphenomena of the crisis of late modernity; it is because he has advanced a proposal that cuts to the heart of the modern crisis of truth and freedom. That proposal, which has emerged from the heart of the Church, has been primarily directed toward the realm of culture because it is, first and always, an evangelical proposal: a proposal to consider the possibilities of human freedom in the light of God's freedom, which led to the Cross. To account for the life of Karol Wojtyla, his stewardship of the office of Peter in the Church, and his impact on the history of our time means taking seriously the pope's conviction that reality is cruciform, and that the story of the world is, in the final analysis, the story of the Paschal Mystery.

NOTES

[1] Kwitny traces the intellectual origins of this political stance to what he presents as a hitherto-undiscovered book by Karol Wojtyla, *Catholic Social Ethics*, published underground in 1953. The problem is that the "book" isn't a book, and Wojtyla wasn't its principal author. *Catholic Social Ethics*, as scholars have known for some time, is the text of Wojtyla's lectures for a social ethics course at the Kraków seminary. When Wojtyla was assigned to teach this course, he adapted the lecture notes of his predecessor, Father Jan Piwowarczyk, a distinguished specialist in the field. The notes are a rather conventional exposition of Catholic social doctrine in the period after Pius XI's 1931 encyclical *Quadragesimo Anno*. One of the pope's closest associates has confirmed that Father Wojtyla, for whom social ethics had not been a major intellectual preoccupation prior to his assignment to teach the course, used the Piwowarczyk notes "with some elaborations." But "the material was not his own."

CHAPTER FOUR

John Paul II and
The Gospel of Life

Helen Alvare

"The Church knows that this Gospel of life, which she has received from her Lord, has a profound and persuasive echo in the heart of every person—believer and non-believer alike because it marvelously fulfills all the heart's expectations while infinitely surpassing them" (*Evangelium Vitae*, 2).

ohn Paul II and the gospel of life—the two are nearly inseparable. For not only by words—many words—but in his person, he proclaims this gospel, the good news about human life.

The gospel of life has been a central (perhaps *the* central) teaching of the entire papacy of Our Holy Father. It has been central in his words. How often does he exhort us about "the dignity of the human person"? He proclaims the gospel of life at the United Nations, during his visits to every country, in his reflections and homilies delivered in Rome, and, of course, in the great encyclical, *Evangelium Vitae*, *The Gospel of Life*. In this document—his most complete discourse on the gospel of life—he asserts that this Gospel is at the "heart" of Jesus' message. When Jesus presents the "heart of his redemptive mission," he says "I came that they may have life, and have it abundantly (*John* 10:10)" (*Evangelium Vitae*, 1).

The gospel of life has been central, too, in our Holy Father's deeds. His prolific travels have brought him into personal and joyous contact with millions of people around the globe. You can *feel* the good news about life. You can *see* it in that look he gets on his face when meeting people, especially the children and the young people of the world; it is that look of joy almost too great to bear, joy verging almost on tears. And you can see it on the faces of the people looking back at Our Holy Father, delighting in his presence.

What is this gospel, this good news about life? And what is its real significance for each of us in the United States and for our country as a whole? Is there more to it than proscriptions on abortion and assisted suicide? Why the emphasis on the basic good of "life"? Surely, we hate death and love life? Surely we don't need to be reminded that life is good?

In this essay, I will try to answer these questions. First, I will address the substance of the gospel of life as articulated by Our Holy Father. After that, I will identify its particular resonance and meaning in the context of U.S. culture and our particular abortion and euthanasia problems.

The Gospel of Life

This gospel—so simple and brief when written on a page—is great good news. It is the good news that human beings, created by God from love, are invited to a new and eternal life with God. It is the good news that God is a "living" God who calls us to "profound communion" with himself and a sharing in His very life. It is the good news that, in every single person, we can glimpse the face of Christ, a "trace of his glory" (*Evangelium Vitae*, 34). It is the good news that our mortal lives, being a "fundamental condition" for our eternal life, have immense worth. It is, finally, the news that the path to authentic freedom and happiness lies in living as Jesus lived, loving as Jesus loved, *e.g.* making a "sincere gift of self" to God and to others (*Evangelium Vitae*, 2, 37–39, 51).

The gospel of life also includes the consequences that flow from it. Flowing directly from the sacredness of human life is its inviolability. Therefore, it is wrong to directly kill, including by abortion and assisted suicide. Society must "respect, defend and promote the dignity of every human person, at every moment and in every condition" of life. All social institutions, all science and technology, all political institutions, must serve life (*Evangelium Vitae*, 40–43).

Pope John Paul II teaches that this good news is richly illustrated throughout both the Old Testament and the New. In *Evangelium Vitae*, Our Holy Father lavishes attention—and not without emotion—on the stories of God's personal care for human life. By virtue of these stories, he calls the gospel of life "something concrete and personal." It is the "proclamation of *the very person of Jesus*," of his words, his actions and his person (*Evangelium Vitae*, 29–30, italics original).

The fullness of this proclamation was prepared for in the Old Testament. It first appears in the story of God's creation of humans who have the unique potential to attain truth and freedom (*Evangelium Vitae*, 34). Again it is present when Israel learned the "preciousness of its life" in God's eyes. It is expressed in the literature of *Wisdom* and *Job* as the Chosen People grappled with the problem of suffering.

In the New Testament, Jesus proclaims the "meaning of his mission" in these concrete and personal terms: "The blind receive their sight, the lame walk, lepers are cleansed, and the deaf hear, the dead are raised up, the poor have good news preached to them" (*Luke* 7:22). The message is clear: God cares about their human lives, particularly the lives of the poor, the sick and the outcast. By the example of his own life, Jesus demonstrates that God affirms the value of human life in the very midst of constant threats to it. Life is a value so great, in fact, that Jesus could take it up and make it the "instrument of the salvation of all humanity" (*Evangelium Vitae*, 33).

But the gospel of life is always also about eternal life. Eternal life means more than "a perspective which is beyond time." It is eternal in the sense of participating in the life of knowing and accepting the mystery of the one true God. The dignity of every human person, in other words, flows not only from our origin, but from our ultimate destiny—"fellowship," "knowledge" and "love" of God (*Evangelium Vitae*, 38).

What are the consequences of this gospel? First, we are never solely our own. Our lives are subject to God. As God said to Noah: "For your own lifeblood, too, I will demand an accounting . . . and from man in regard to his fellow man I will demand an accounting for human life (*Genesis* 9:5). The sacredness of human life, in other words, leads directly to its *inviolability* (*Evangelium Vitae*, 40). The Old Testament commands: "you shall not kill" (*Exodus* 34:28). The New Testament reveals the positive commands flowing from this inviolability of human life: "You shall love your neighbor as yourself" (*Romans* 13:9–10).

Finally, in the death and resurrection of Jesus Christ, Sacred

Scripture reveals to us one final and ultimate facet of the gospel of life: *"[L]ife finds its centre, its meaning and its fulfillment when it is given up"* (*Evangelium Vitae*, 51).

The American Context

And now from the sublime to the local. From a consideration of the gospel of life as expressed by Our Holy Father to its application in the American context. Clearly, the gospel of life is a message for all times and all peoples. But an American observer might be forgiven —especially upon a close reading of *Evangelium Vitae*—for thinking it is written just for us. The document addresses with uncanny accuracy the specific way America has come to terms with socially accepted killing. The document's description of a "culture of death" that celebrates some forms of killing as "rights," canonizes majority rule, and reduces "freedom" to "choosing" strikes very close to home. There is no doubt that many, inside and outside the Catholic Church in the United States, reacted to *Evangelium Vitae* as akin to a personal address. An editorial on *Evangelium Vitae* in the *Chicago Tribune* put it this way: "He caught us with our rationalizations down and our contradictions showing."

There are four particular aspects of John Paul II's message about the gospel of life which speak directly to our American situation: 1) The necessary relationship between our country's founding principles and the gospel of life; 2) the use of euphemisms to justify intentional killing; 3) the identification of the roots of the culture of death; and 4) the situation of women in the abortion debate. I will consider each of these below.

"We hold these truths to be self evident"

Pope John Paul II spoke directly to American bishops about the gospel of life during an *ad limina* visit in Rome in October 1998. He urged the Church in America to draw attention to "the relationship of the moral law to constitutional and positive law in your society." He concluded, "What is at stake here is nothing less than the indivisible truth about the human person on which the Founding Fathers staked your nation's claim to independence." (John Paul II speech October 2,

1998 to Bishops from California, Nevada, and Hawaii on *ad limina* visit to the Holy See).

In any country, Our Holy Father has not been sparing in condemning the enormous gulf that exists between lofty national and international declarations of human rights, and their actual practice:

> On the other hand, these noble proclamations are unfortunately contradicted by a tragic repudiation of them in practice. This denial is still more distressing, indeed more scandalous, precisely because it is occurring in a society which makes the affirmation and protection of human rights its primary objective and its boast (*Evangelium Vitae*, 18).

One of the specific failings he identifies is the growing tendency in democracies, such as ours, to equate majority opinion with what is right:

> Democracy can't be idolized to the point of making it a substitute for morality or a panacea for immorality. Fundamentally, democracy is a 'system' and as such is a means, and not an end. Its 'moral' value . . . depends on the morality of the ends which it pursues and of the means which it employs (*Evangelium Vitae*, 70).

This is a message desperately needed in our political and legal culture today where abortion is allowed precisely by denying and subverting our founding principles; where elected politicians profess the deepest concern for children while repeatedly voting to allow the killing of unborn and even mostly born infants; and where assisted suicide, when it is legalized, is justified by majority vote.

Euphemism

"Perhaps nothing has been so damaging to our cause as the advances in technology which have allowed pictures of the developing fetus, because people now talk about the fetus in much different terms than they did 15 years ago. They talk about it as a human being, which is not something I have an easy answer on how to cure" (Harrison Hickman, pollster for the National Abortion Rights Action League, promoting the

slogan "Who Decides" at NARAL's 20th Anniversary, Washington D.C., October 13–15, 1989).

Campaigns to promote abortion and euthanasia in the United States employ a significant amount of semantic dodging. Reacting to the natural abhorrence of death, advocates for abortion and assisted suicide hired the best public relations minds money could buy to find more pleasing ways to speak of killing the very young, very old or very sick. And so they came upon the empty slogans of "choice" and "Who decides?"

This is not a small problem for the pro-life movement. The language of choice is a considerable obstacle for the pro-life activist trying to make logical headway in any debate. It pits her in a boxing match with a shadow whose outlines are never well defined. She is forced, preliminarily, to both define what's really at stake *and* to overcome all good feelings about "choice" (a word loaded with enormous good will in the United States) before beginning even to make her precise case. This regularly allows the abortion advocate to avoid the real subject entirely, while pretending to wave the flag, stand in solidarity with the Statue of Liberty, and make all manner of ridiculous assertions about "choice" *defining* the American experiment.

But John Paul II cuts through this entirely with his description of the unique problems that are abortion and euthanasia.

"Here though, we shall concentrate particular attention on *another category of attacks*, affecting life in its earliest and in its final stages, attacks which present *new characteristics with respect to the past and which raise questions of extraordinary seriousness*. It is not only that in generalized opinion these attacks tend no longer to be considered as 'crimes'; paradoxically they assume the nature of 'rights,' to the point that the State is called upon to give them *legal recognition and to make them available through the free services of health-care personnel*. Such attacks strike human life at the time of its greatest frailty, when it lacks any means of self-defense. Even more serious is the fact that, most often, those attacks are carried out in the very heart of and with the complicity of the family—the family which by its nature is called to be the 'sanctuary of life'" (*Evangelium Vitae*, 11, italics original).

In other words, what we have in abortion and euthanasia is killing members of our own families, at the most vulnerable times in their lives in the name of "rights," and accompanied by demands of state support. (In their document welcoming *Evangelium Vitae*, published in 1995, the Bishops of the United States pointed out that, in the United States, *only* family members can be killed with legal impunity. Kill a stranger—then you're in trouble (*Faithful for Life: A Moral Reflection*, p. 10)). Now this is a true, and not inflammatory, description of the abortion and euthanasia problems. It completely sidesteps the traps into which such discourse can fall, traps set when the movements for abortion and euthanasia self-consciously align themselves with certain wings of feminism and party politics. Our Holy Father models a way to speak of abortion and euthanasia that points directly to necessary solutions.

The Roots of the Culture of Death

For citizens of the United States, perhaps the most chilling aspect of Our Holy Father's teaching on the gospel of life is his reading of the "roots" of a "culture of death." He identifies the culture of death as a "conspiracy against life" that is larger than the individuals involved. The culture of death is a "veritable *structure of sin*," fostered by "powerful cultural, economic and political currents which encourage an idea of society excessively concerned with efficiency," a "*war of the powerful against the weak*" (*Evangelium Vitae*, 12, italics original).

For laborers in the pro-life vineyard, the pope's message about the roots of the culture of death brilliantly describe the beating heart at the center of the pro-death movement we have encountered—one person and one institution at a time—over many years in the United States. Rarely does a disagreement about abortion or euthanasia stop at the precise boundaries of these topics. Almost always, fundamental disagreements about the nature of real freedom arise. The pope speaks brilliantly to these in his reflections on the culture of death.

First, the pope identifies as a preeminent source of the culture of death a "notion of freedom which exalts the isolated individual in an absolute way, and gives no place to solidarity, to openness to others and service of them" (*Evangelium Vitae*, 19). In this understanding, freedom is as "all about me." Americans have been tender of conscience about this for some time, but without significantly changing their ways. There have been times of useful public discussion of our problem, such as on the publication of the celebrated *Habits of the Heart* (1985). This book, at once both scholarly and popular, described our difficulty with sustained devotion to the common good and even helped prompt a new movement dubbing itself "communitarian." But the language of our marketing and our politics hasn't moved decisively away from an individualistic conception of freedom. And the consequences, particularly for the unborn, the sick and the dying, are, as Our Holy Father, predicted: this freedom ends up by becoming "the freedom of 'the strong' against the weak who have no choice but to submit" (*Evangelium Vitae*, 19).

A second root of the culture of death the pope identifies is a notion of freedom as untethered to the truth, of freedom "made absolute in an individualistic way." In this understanding, "any reference to common values and to a truth absolutely binding on everyone is lost, and social life ventures on to the shifting sands of complete relativism. At that point, everything is negotiable, everything is open to bargaining: even the first of the fundamental rights, the right to life" (*Evangelium Vitae*, 19–20). If anything, I judge that this second flawed notion of freedom is even more entrenched in the United States than the first. The idea that there are truths we can all know is rejected by an astonishing number of Americans. Here is one very telling barometer: in 1995 the *Wall Street Journal* (with the largest national circulation of all U.S. newspapers) published an editorial entitled "No Guardrails." It asked the rhetorical question why U.S. citizens professed to continue to be shocked by assorted horrible killings that had recently happened in America (a terrorist bombing, an abortion clinic shooting), while tacitly accepting an idea propounded by the elites in charge that there is really only one rule: express yourself. According to the editors, this editorial generated the angriest and most prolific response ever received by the newspaper in its history. One very telling reply came from a woman who declared that she was so angry at the editorial that she simply threw up while reading it!

Here is another example of the widespread belief in individualistic freedom cut off from concern for truth. There are continual denials that our sexual mores are off-track while sexually transmitted diseases, abortion rates and out-of-wedlock births hang at epidemic levels. This awful notion of "freedom" is indeed deeply entrenched in the United States.

A third important source of the culture of death as described by our Holy Father is the "eclipse of the sense of God and of Man":

> "But when God is forgotten the creature itself grows unintelligible. Man is no longer able to see himself as 'mysteriously different' from other earthly creatures. . . . Enclosed in the narrow horizon of his physical nature, he is somehow reduced to being a 'thing.' . . . Life itself becomes a mere 'thing,' which man claims as his exclusive property, completely subject to his control and manipulation. . . . He is concerned only with 'doing,' and using all kinds of technology, he busies himself with programming, controlling and dominating birth and death. Birth and death, instead of being primary experiences demanding to be 'lived,' become things to be merely 'possessed' or 'rejected.'"

In such a worldview, ideas about suffering and sexuality become terribly warped. Suffering is "censored," rejected as useless. And when it becomes unavoidable, "then life appears to have lost all meaning and the temptation grows in man to claim the right to suppress it." Sexuality becomes "depersonalized and exploited" as the body is no longer seen as in relationship with God, but as a thing to be "used according to the sole criteria of pleasure and efficiency." In both cases, Our Holy Father has managed to describe, in chilling detail, the prevailing winds driving the movement to legalize suicide, and to depersonalize sexual relations and the children conceived thereby.

In such a situation, the gospel of life exhorts us to evangelize! Conversion to the person of Jesus Christ will make men and women again intelligible to themselves and accepting of the mysteries of human sexuality and suffering.

Women and Abortion

Prior to writing *Evangelium Vitae*, Pope John Paul II convened a special consistory of cardinals from all over the world to seek their guidance about the threats to human life in the world today. At this time, and on other occasions, the pope heard from a number of American bishops on the matter of women and abortion. When John Paul II reflects on these matters in connection with the gospel of life, he brings together clear Catholic thinking about the evil of abortion with a personal approach to women that is likely to gain a hearing in the United States.

First, our Holy Father clearly distinguishes between the certain evil of abortion, and the culpability of the woman who has one. While never demurring regarding the evil of the act of abortion, he recognizes that some mothers who abort may believe they are acting to protect "important values such as her own health or a decent standard of living." He also recognizes that the father of the child may be to blame for putting extraordinary pressure on the mother, as might her family, the movement for abortion and even the legislatures which have allowed abortion (*Evangelium Vitae*, 59). In the United States, while even these clear distinctions can be difficult to communicate publicly, they are absolutely necessary for drawing post-aborted and pro-abortion women to listen to the pro-life message. When they are successfully communicated, they make an enormous difference for the good.

Second, Our Holy Father juxtaposes the need for an aborted woman to "face . . . honestly" what she has done, with the moving promise: "The Father of mercies is ready to give you his forgiveness and his peace in the Sacrament of Reconciliation. You will come to understand that nothing is definitively lost and you will also be able to ask forgiveness from your child, who is now living in the Lord" (*Evangelium Vitae*, 99). I'm not sure even the Holy Father can gauge how much solace this last promise provides to post-aborted women! In Project Rachel programs across the United States, counselors continually encounter women who feel that they are completely beyond such mercy, such forgiveness. At some point after the abortion—usually not sooner than 5 to 10 years post-abortion—when they acknowledge that they have killed their own helpless child, despair is too small a word for what they feel. Yet here is the pope himself telling them, "nothing is definitively lost." This is indeed good news that restores life! In this case, it restores the life of the woman herself.

Conclusion

The gospel of life is one of the great themes of the papacy of John Paul II. He has devoted a great deal of his considerable intellect and his considerable public appeal to putting it across. He has preached it in simple terms and in complicated theological terms; in philosophical terms and in social terms; in short speeches and in lengthy encyclicals;

in person, and in writing. A great number of people all over the world are familiar with its outlines, if not with its details. They have heard it many times. In all this, Our Holy Father has accomplished one thing for certain: he has made it very difficult to take this message lightly. It is difficult for a conscientious listener to make a casual decision whether or not to accept this gospel. The gospel of life contains too many ideas that appeal to the human heart and mind as necessarily true, too many insights that illumine the deepest mysteries of life, and too many claims that answer our hearts' deepest longings for us to respond casually. The gospel of life must either be accepted or outright rejected. It cannot be ignored.

CHAPTER FIVE

John Paul II and Non-catholics

Jerram Barrs

𝔍n responding to the request to write on the subject of John Paul II and non-Catholics I felt it was necessary to attempt two things: first to reflect on what John Paul II has written and spoken about non-Catholics; second to consider the response of non-Catholics to the thought of John Paul II. I recognize that this second part may be more difficult for Catholics to read, but I believe it is important for Catholics celebrating the legacy of John Paul II to understand how his words are seen by non-Catholics.

John Paul II has from the beginning of his papacy made greater and more far-reaching steps towards non-Catholics than any of his predecessors in the Roman see. His passionate commitment to build bridges to non-Catholics is evident in his meetings with non-Christians (Muslims, Jews, Hindus, Buddhists and others) as well as his involvement in ecumenical dialogue with Orthodox and Protestant Christians. Simply to make a list of every such meeting with non-Catholics, or of every statement the pope has made about non-Catholics or of each document he has issued relating to this subject during his papacy, would more than fill a lengthy chapter.

As of the first days of October 1998, John Paul II has made eighty four journeys outside of Italy, and on many of these he has made an effort to meet with non-Catholics, both Christian and non-Christian. In addition, he has invited many non-Catholics to visit him at the Vatican. As we draw closer to the year 2000, he seems more and more eager to see Christian unity become a reality, and more ready than ever to reach out his hand to non-Christians. He has said of himself that the Jubilee celebrations of the year 2000 provide a kind of hermeneutical key for understanding his pontificate.

> Since the publication of the very first document of my Pontificate, *I have spoken explicitly of the Great Jubilee*, suggesting that the time leading up to it be lived as "a new Advent." This theme has since reappeared many times, and was dwelt upon at length in the encyclical *Dominum et Vivificantem*. In fact, preparing for the *year 2000 has become as it were a hermeneutical key of my Ponitificate*. It is certainly not a matter of indulging in a new millenarianism. . . . Rather, it is *aimed at an increasing sensitivity to all that the Spirit is saying to the Church and the churches* (*Celebrate 2000*, 234).

Here, John Paul II ties this celebration of the new Advent to the Spirit's work, as He, the Spirit, speaks to all of God's people, Catholic and non-Catholic today. There seems to be a deep longing within him to try to realize significant steps towards unity by or in the Year 2000, to present a growing ecumenical movement to the Lord as a kind of Jubilee gift in honor of His "new Advent" and in fulfillment of His high priestly prayer:

> May all of them be one, Father, just as you are in me and I am in you. . . . May they be brought to complete unity to let the world know that you sent me and have loved them even as you have loved me (*John* 17:21,23).

Dialogue with Non Christians - Jews

What are some of the more remarkable steps John Paul II has taken while on this particular pilgrimage of his pontificate? How has he reached out to non-Catholics? We turn first to the Jews whom he has referred to many times as "our elder brothers in the faith of Abraham" (*Spiritual Pilgrimage*, 100, 187). He has spoken also of "our common spiritual patrimony with Abraham's stock, our Jewish brothers and sisters" (*Spiritual Pilgrimage*, 132).

From these brief statements, which he has used many times, we see that, towards Jews, John Paul II has followed the lead of Vatican Council II in its statement on non-Christian religions. He has continued and deepened the dialogue that was encouraged by that Council's documents *Lumen Gentium* and *Nostra Aetate*. In addition to this respectful dialogue, he has made many declarations and gestures of sorrow for the events of the Holocaust, the Shoah. These climaxed with the visit of Prime Minister Rabin to the Pope on March 17th 1994, the establishment of diplomatic relations at the level of apostolic nunciature and embassy between the Holy See and the State of Israel on June 15th 1994, and on a more personal level at a concert held at the Vatican for the commemoration of the Shoah in the presence of John Paul II and the Chief Rabbi of Rome, Elio Toaff, on April 7th of the same year.

More significant even than these ceremonial occasions are the laments the pope has expressed for the past persecutions of Jews and for the involvement of Christians in these events.

> There is no doubt that the sufferings inflicted upon the Jews are also for the Catholic Church a reason for deep sorrow, especially if we think of the indifference and sometimes the resentment that in particular historical situations have divided the Jews and Christians. Certainly this calls for yet stronger resolutions to cooperate for justice and true peace (Accattoli, 118).

In his address on Sunday January 14th, 1996, the pope came close to a formal apology and request for forgiveness. He spoke of the common heritage of Christians and Jews in sharing the Old Testament Scriptures, of the Hebrew people's religious experience providing the origin for Christianity, and then he added these words:

> The inauguration of the new age established by him with a new and eternal Covenant, does not destroy the ancient foundation but opens it up to universal fruitfulness. Considering all that, the remembrance of the tensions that have so often marked the relationship between Christians and Jews cannot help but arouse great sorrow (Accattoli, 119).

In many other contexts John Paul has formally asked forgiveness for the sins of the past, and it may be that he is moving towards such an apology to the Jewish people, an apology which would add greatly to the steps he has already taken to the Jewish people. Such an apology would be a recognition that the Catholic Church as a Church has been guilty of sins towards the Jews in its past. This is more difficult, of course, because the Roman Church as a Church believes that its leadership represents Christ, and that as a Church it is Christ's Body here on earth. However, John Paul II has done this in other contexts, and as Luigi Accattoli has written:

> No one can silence the pope, and only the pope can really say mea culpa for the Catholic Church. To bring up its own past against the Church, or simply to confront the Church with its past, could be equivalent to opposing popes of the past; and only a pope can contradict another pope (xxii).

Dialogue with Non Christians - Muslims

Similarly with Muslims John Paul II has made an effort to have many official and unofficial meetings with Muslim leaders. There has been a deep commitment throughout his years in office to reach out the hand of brotherhood to Muslims and to try to move forward to the peaceful coexistence of Muslims and Christians together. The book published by the Pontifical Council for Inter-religious Dialogue, *Recognize The Spiritual Bonds Which Unite Us*, has an extensive record of meetings between the pope and Muslims and excerpts from many of the speeches he has given and prayers he has offered on these occasions. He has repeatedly addressed Muslims as 'brothers' (the first pope to use this form of greeting); as "our brothers in faith in the one God" (29); or "your God and ours is one and the same, and we are brothers and sisters in the faith of Abraham" (72).

John Paul II has also taken a step with Muslims which is controversial to some of his fellow Catholics, for, just as with the Jews, there has been a series of public acknowledgments that Christian behavior towards Muslims has not always been what it should. For example, in an address to young Muslims in Casablanca, Morocco, August 19th 1985, he said:

> Christians and Muslims, in general we have badly understood each other, and sometimes, in the past, we have opposed and even exhausted each other in polemics and in wars. I believe that, today, God invites us to change our old practices (Accattoli, 186).

A message by Cardinal Arinze given at the close of Ramadan in 1996 speaks even more clearly about forgiveness, and this message was sent out to Muslims in the name of the pope:

> The time has come to free our memories of the negative consequences of the past, however painful they may be, and look resolutely toward the future. The one who has given offense must repent and ask for pardon. We need mutual pardon. Without true reconciliation we cannot commit ourselves together on behalf of our fellow believers and for the good of the whole world (Accattoli, 187–188).

Emboldened by the pope's lead in acknowledging wrongdoing in the past by Christians, Archbishop Cascante of Tarragon, Spain confessed the sins of Christians towards Muslims:

> There is no doubt that what the Christians did to the Muslims and Jews in Spain in 1492 is completely contrary to that which they should have done in accordance with the principles of our Christian faith (Accottali, 189).

Salvation without Explicit Faith in Christ?

In calling Muslims 'brothers in the faith' (just as he does with Jews) John Paul II uses a title that traditionally has been reserved for other baptized Christians. This form of address or way of describing Muslims is intended, of course, to be a mark of respect and a means of building bridges where, for so much of the past, there has been distance and enmity. But, more is intended than this. In using this language John Paul II is speaking in the tradition of Vatican II which made it clear in *Lumen Gentium*, 1 that Muslims may be saved without coming to faith in Christ:

> The plan of salvation also includes those who acknowledge the Creator, among whom are, in the first place, the Muslims. These profess to hold the faith of Abraham, and together with us they adore the one, merciful God, judge of humankind on the Last Day.

John Paul II has referred to both this statement and the affirmative words about Islam in *Nostra Aetate*, 3 on many occasions. He has made it explicit that he accepts this view. For example, in his address to the Bishops of Tanzania in 1987, he said:

> The truth that the plan of salvation includes all who acknowledge the Creator offers us a solid basis for dialog and for peaceful coexistence with Muslims (*Recognize the Spiritual Bonds that Unite Us*, 47).

This conviction, that salvation comes to people in other religions without the explicit knowledge of Christ, is evident in many of John Paul II's statements. He frequently appeals to the belief that there are *semina Verbi,* the seeds of the Word, in all religions. He argues that these "constitute a kind of *common soteriological root present in all religions*" (*Crossing the Threshold of Hope*, 81). In the context John Paul II is answering a question about the variety of religions.

> The Church seeks to identify the *semina Verbi* present in the great traditions of the Far East. . . . The Church is guided by the faith that *God the Creator wants to save all humankind in Jesus Christ,* the only mediator between God and man, inasmuch as He is the Redeemer of all humankind. The Paschal Mystery is equally available to all, and, through it, the way to eternal salvation is also open to all (*Crossing the Threshold of Hope*, 81).

Later in the same chapter of *Crossing The Threshold Of Hope* he answers the question as to how people may be saved who do not hear and respond to the Gospel of Christ, for example indigenous peoples of a land like Australia whose ancient religions existed before the time of Abraham.

> He (Christ) redeemed them all and has His own ways of reaching each of them in the present eschatological phase of salvation history. In fact, in those regions, many accept Him and many more have an implicit faith in Him (83).

The idea of the *semina Verbi* goes back to the thinking of Justin Martyr and Clement of Alexandria who were seeking to explain the wisdom found in the philosophy of the Greeks, particularly in the Platonic tradition. Their answer to this was that there were seeds of the

Word, the *Logos spermatikos,* to be found in Greek philosophy. God, they suggested, made a Covenant, *diatheke,* with the Greeks, a Covenant of Wisdom, just as he had made a Covenant of Law with the Hebrews. The purpose of these two Covenants was to lead the Greeks and Jews to Christ, and both Covenants found their fulfillment in Christ. This meant, therefore, that Plato, for example, was a 'Christian before Christ.'

It is clearly this tradition to which John Paul is referring, but from an Evangelical and Reformed perspective, I would have to say that this tradition does not go back far enough, that is, it does not go back to Scripture itself. It is certainly appropriate to acknowledge that the Light of the Word gives knowledge and wisdom to every one who is in the world (*John* 1:9; *Proverbs* 8:1–4,15–16). We ought to receive gladly the biblical teaching that all men and women are made in God's image, and are to be treated with respect and honor for the dignity they bear (*Psalm* 8; *James* 3:9–10). We know too, therefore, that every man or woman to whom we go with the Gospel, is living in a world where they face the daily revelation of God's eternal power, divine nature and moral perfection through the glory of creation and through their own human nature (*Psalm* 19; *Romans* 1:18–2:15).

However, the Word teaches us that this universal general revelation is not sufficient to bring people salvation, but rather renders them inexcusable (*Romans* 1:18–25). Such revelation provides us with bridges for communicating the good news about Jesus Christ, but it does not give a saving knowledge of Him. Neither does Scripture support the teaching of salvation through implicit faith, but rather it demands that people come to an explicit response to the message of Jesus Christ (*Romans* 10:9–10). "Salvation is found in no one else, for there is no other name under heaven given to men by which we must be saved" (*Acts* 4:12).

John Paul II has done a work of great value in the world and to the Church of Jesus Christ by building the bridges towards Jews, Muslims, Hindus and many others, by his courage in acknowledging the failures of Christians in the past, by his readiness to meet with non-Christians and to greet them with the genuine honor and respect which is so evident in all his encounters. However, the Word of God is clear when it teaches us that Jews and God-fearers must believe in Jesus Christ in order to be saved. Nicodemus, the devout Jew who came to Jesus at night (*John* 3), and Cornelius, the God-fearing centurion to whom Peter went with the gospel of Jesus (*Acts* 10), were not saved because of their devout hearts, nor because of their prayers or charitable gifts. They received salvation when they heard the message of Christ and, being born again by the Spirit, believed in that message.

Dialogue with other Non Christians

Just as with Jews and Muslims there have been bridges built by the pope to those in other non-Christian religions: Hindus and Buddhists, for example. (See the chapter 'Why So Many Religions?' in *Crossing the Threshold of Hope*. For a very critical Buddhist response to John Paul II's words about Buddhism, see Thinley Norbu's *Welcoming Flowers From Across the Cleansed Threshold of Hope*.) Almost always when he addresses the issue of other religions he quotes extensively from *Lumen Gentium* and *Nostra Aetate,* for he is clearly committed to following the lead of Vatican II with its concern to provide a positive evaluation of all religious traditions.

In this he has sought to set an example to his fellow Catholics and to fulfill his teaching responsibility to direct Catholics to treat their fellow men and women with respect and honor whether or not they are in agreement with them about the nature of God, the human condition, salvation and other basic issues of the faith. This is clearly in accord with Scripture, which challenges believers to do good to all men, to speak the truth in love, to let your conversation always be gracious, to love your neighbor as yourself whoever that neighbor is, and even, if there are those who have evil intentions towards believers, as the Lord himself says, to "Love your enemies, do good to those who hate you, bless those who curse you, pray for those who mistreat you" (*Luke* 6:27–28). The pope has demonstrated this kind of forgiving love even towards the man who sought to assassinate him.

John Paul II and Fellow Christians

What about fellow Christians who are not members of the Catholic Church; how has John Paul II spoken, written and acted towards those who are not in the particular flock of which he is the head? Again, he has followed the lead of Vatican Council II with regard to other Christians. His speeches, letters and books refer constantly to "members of Churches and Ecclesiastical Communities not in full communion with the Catholic Church." It is clear from reading these that Christian unity is one of the passions that motivates his heart.

Nowhere is this clearer than in his encyclical letter *Ut Unum Sint.* The encyclical opens with these stirring words:

> *Ut unum sint!* The call for Christian unity made by the Second Vatican Ecumenical Council with such impassioned commitment is finding an ever greater echo in the hearts of believers, especially as the year 2000 approaches. . . . The courageous witness of so many martyrs of our century, including members of Churches and Ecclesial Communities not in full communion with the Catholic Church, gives new vigor to the Council's call and reminds us of our duty to listen and put into practice its exhortation . . . *Christ calls all his disciples to unity.* . . . Believers in Christ, united in following in the footsteps of the martyrs, cannot remain divided. . . . They cannot fail to meet this challenge. Indeed, how could they refuse to do everything possible, with God's help, to break down the walls of division and distrust, to overcome obstacles and prejudices (1–2).

John Paul then mentions the 'doctrinal differences needing to be resolved,' the 'mutual misunderstandings and prejudices,' the 'indifference and insufficient knowledge of one another.' He recognizes that there can be no movement forward without the conversion of hearts and prayer. He calls for mutual forgiveness and reconciliation in what are, perhaps, the most moving words of this encyclical.

> All together, they are invited by the ever fresh power of the Gospel to acknowledge with sincere and total objectivity the mistakes made and the contingent factors at work at the origins of their deplorable divisions. *What is needed is a calm, clear-sighted and truthful vision of things,* a vision enlivened by divine mercy and capable of freeing people's minds (2).

This plea is followed by a frank admission of sin among Catholics in the past towards other Christians:

> The Catholic Church acknowledges and confesses *the weakness of her members,* conscious that their sins are so many

betrayals and obstacles to the accomplishment of the Savior's plan (3).

From the perspective of Protestants, and I am sure this would be true of the Orthodox as well, this call to conversion, to confession, is very welcome, particularly when it is supported by such an example of confession from the lips of the pope.

There have been, in fact, numerous occasions when John Paul II has made personal confession for the past. (See the book *When the Pope Asks for Forgiveness* for a comprehensive account of these occasions.) An example of such confession towards Protestants comes from his words on the occasion of the canonization of a Catholic martyr, Jan Sarkander, in the Czech Republic, May 21,1995.

> This canonization must in no way reopen painful wounds, which in the past marked the Body of Christ in these lands. On the contrary, today I, the pope of the Church of Rome, in the name of all Catholics, ask forgiveness for the wrongs inflicted on non-Catholics during the turbulent history of these peoples (Accattoli, 146).

In Salzburg, Austria, June 26,1988, John Paul II spoke of the "unjust expulsion of Protestants from this place in the eighteenth and nineteenth centuries, in accordance with the principle, *'cuius regio eius religio,'* which was legally applicable in former times." He then went on to speak of asking for pardon, of forgiveness and reconciliation (Accattoli, 149). He has set an example himself, which, it is to be hoped, will be followed by his fellow Catholics and by Protestant and Orthodox leaders also.

In referring specifically to the *cuius regio eius religio* principle, John Paul is asking all Catholics to turn away from that past of forced attempts at conversion and, instead, to acknowledge the principles of freedom of religion and tolerance for other convictions. Furthering this commitment to teach and to demonstrate respect for the religious and Christian convictions of others, he has made a consistent effort to speak with praise about the great figures of Protestant history. Speaking of Calvin and Zwingli at the Federation of Protestant Churches in Kehrsatz, Switzerland, June 14th 1984, he said:

> We find the historical influence of their witness not only in the

area of theology and ecclesial structure, but also in the cultural, social and political fields. The legacy of the thought and convictions particular to each of these two men continues to be forcefully and dynamically present in various parts of Christianity . . . elements in the theology and spirituality of each one of them maintain deep ties between us . . . each wanted to make the Church more faithful to the will of the Lord (Accattoli, 154–155).

In a similar vein John Paul spoke warmly of Martin Luther during his 1980 trip to Germany. Having recalled Luther's pilgrimage to Rome, he said of himself: "Today I come to you, to the spiritual heirs of Martin Luther. I come as a pilgrim." He then referred to Luther's words about Paul's Letter to the Romans and concluded by saying: "We all need conversion. . . . 'Let us no longer pass judgment on one another' (*Romans* 14:13). Let us rather recognize our guilt" (Accattoli, 197/"The Pope in Germany," 1216).

John Paul II and Church Unity

This changed attitude to Protestants of the past is matched by John Paul's readiness to seek unity with Protestant Churches today. He sees all of us as united by baptism and a common faith in Jesus Christ, and so he has traveled many times to meet with Protestant Church leaders, joined in united services of worship, and invited leaders to Rome.

What is difficult for Protestants, and also for the Orthodox, is John Paul's insistence that the Roman Catholic Church is the one true Church. However affirmative he may be about the faith and spirituality of other believers, in the end we are expected to acknowledge that his view of the Catholic Church ought to be ours as well.

This becomes clear when John Paul quotes Vatican II: "The Church of Christ 'subsists in the Catholic Church, which is governed by the Successor of Peter and by the Bishops in communion with him'" (*Ut Unum Sint*, 10); or again, writing about the way God has manifested the Church "*already* in her eschatological reality": "The elements of this already-given Church exist, found in their fullness in the Catholic Church and without this fullness in the other Communities" (14). Elsewhere, he argues that the efficacy of ministry in "separated Churches and Communities" is derived from "the very fullness of grace and truth entrusted to the Catholic Church" (10).

It is encouraging to be recognized as a Christian as John Paul II does of other believers. It is affirmative to be told that there are "elements of sanctification and truth" in one's personal life, or in one's Ecclesial Community. But, it is not encouraging to be told that one's salvation arises from an invisible bond with the Roman Church, or that any efficacy of one's ministry derives from the grace and truth entrusted to Peter and his Successors in Rome. What is distressing about *Ut Unum Sint* to the non-Catholic reader is the appearance of such statements as those above, which (in my estimation) demean other Churches and other Christians, alongside such statements as the following:

> God calls us to give thanks: the knowledge that the Spirit is at work in other Christian Communities, the discovery of examples of holiness, the experience of the immense riches present in the communion of saints, and contact with unexpected dimensions of Christian commitment. In a corresponding way, there is an increased sense of the need for repentance: an awareness of certain exclusions which seriously harm fraternal charity, of certain refusals to forgive, of a certain pride, of an unevangelical insistence on condemning the "other side," of a disdain born of an unhealthy presumption. . . . Christ summons the Church, as she goes on her pilgrim way, to that continual reformation of which she is always in need. . . . No Christian Community can exempt itself from this call (15,16).

As a member of a Reformed church, I want to applaud this call to *all Christian Communities* to be *semper reformandum*. However those statements that suggest that these words apply in a deep way to every Church but the Catholic Church do not serve the cause of unity. In reading the encyclical, it sometimes seems that Catholics are called to reform their attitudes; Protestants are called to reform their attitudes, their theology and their ecclesiology.

The encyclical has sections on the Orthodox Churches which John Paul II is now able to recognize as 'Sister Churches.' This is possible because each Church acknowledges the validity of the other's ministry, "apostolic succession is fundamental for the sanctification and unity of the people of God," and because "the Catholic Church and the Orthodox Church can already profess together that common faith in the mystery of the Church and the bond between faith and sacraments" (59). There is still, however, considerable distance to travel before the realization of full communion between the two Churches. It has to be said that the most difficult issue for the Orthodox is the requirement for them to acknowledge the primacy of the Roman see. (See, for example *Protestations Orthododoxes*, for a critique of the visit of the Patriarch of Constantinople to the pope in December 1987.)

In a similar vein *Ut Unum Sint* makes warm statements about the fruitful dialogue there has been with other Ancient Churches of the East: the Coptic Orthodox Church, the Syrian Orthodox Church, the Ethiopian Church, the Assyrian Church. John Paul has met with the leaders of each of these Churches, "the Bishop of Rome has been able to converse with them as with brothers who, after a long time, joyfully meet again" (62), and they have issued joint declarations affirming a shared faith and apostolic ministry.

With regard to the Protestant Churches, John Paul II has also sought progress in relationship. He visited Canterbury for a joint service in the Cathedral with then Archbishop Runcie, Anglican Primate, in 1982 (Parker, 7,9,12). More recently he has welcomed the present Primate, George Carey, to the Vatican for discussion about unity between the two Churches (*A New Spirit*). However, considerable difficulties remain in moving forward in this relationship. There has been no withdrawal of the statements by Pope Leo XIII in 1896 that Anglican orders were "absolutely null and utterly void," and that "the Anglican Church is not regarded by Rome as a schismatic church but as a heretical church." To withdraw these papal condemnations would show the mutual honor and respect of which John Paul II speaks and writes so eloquently; just as with the Orthodox the mutual excommunications of the past have been "removed from memory and from the midst of the Church" (*Ut Unum Sint*, 52) and "consigned to oblivion" (42).

Other problems which make the way forward problematic from the pope's side are the commitment to ordain women to the priesthood in the Anglican Church; though George Carey acknowledged that the Anglican Church itself is still deeply divided over this issue. From the Anglican position, one of the most difficult barriers to any way forward is the apparent stalling of the Anglican-Roman Catholic International Commission (ARCIC) dialogues (Tavard).

This commission appointed by the two Churches has produced statements which suggest ways to resolve differences between the Churches. The theologians on both sides have found ways to commend one another and to express the convictions of their Churches in mutually acceptable words. Each time, however, John Paul and the Vatican authorities have found these statements unacceptable. In other words, there has not been from the Papacy the willingness to move at all to accommodate the Anglicans, though there has been considerable movement by the Anglicans and by the Catholic theologians on the ARCIC panels.

In addition, John Paul II used language on his visit to Britain, which, at best, could be regarded as insensitive to British Christians who know their history. In Wembley stadium in London, he referred to England as the "Dowry of Mary," words attributed to King Richard II in 1339: "This is thy Dowry, O Loving Virgin, wherefore rule it"; in Scotland, (a country which was committed to the Calvinistic Reformation) he referred to the nation as the "Special Daughter of the Roman Church"; in Wales, he proclaimed that the "seed of God's Word first came to you from Rome," ignoring the centuries old history of Celtic Christianity flourishing in Wales before the arrival of Augustine in Britain in 597 AD (North 12). These and other statements John Paul II made on his trip to Britain can only be read, even with a charitable heart, as a reaffirmation of the claim to Papal primacy over British Christians and a rejection of both the history of early Christianity in Britain, and of the Churches of the Reformation as valid expressions of the faith once delivered to the saints.

The concern expressed by some in Britain has more recently surfaced in Latin America. In many parts of Latin America, evangelical churches have been growing rapidly, sometimes at the expense of the Catholic Church. On his trips to Mexico in 1990 and to Guatemala, Nicaragua, El Salvador and Venezuela in 1996, John Paul II has urged straying Catholics to return to the fold, referring to all evangelicals as "sects." *The New York Times* reported:

> He urged his listeners to seek "a more solid training in the truths of our Catholic faith so as to form a front against the sects and groups that try to pull you away from the true fold of the good pastor." This afternoon at an open-air mass here, the pope again noted that some Catholics had "broken the link of

saving grace, joining the sects." He said "no Catholic in Mexico can consider himself exempt" from the obligation to bring defectors back to the church. "I would like to meet with you one by one to tell you: come back to the church, your mother," he said (Rochter).

In 1996, he made similar appeals, complaining, according to the report in *Christianity Today*:

> That Indians and peasants are being led astray by "sects and new religious groups, who sow confusion and uncertainty among Catholics." . . . "All those who have at some time prayed to the Most Holy Virgin, even though they may have strayed from the Catholic church, conserve in their hearts an ember of faith which can be revived," he said. "The Virgin awaits them with maternal arms open wide" (Symulka, 94).

Earlier we saw how the pope acknowledged the sin of the *cuius regio eius religio* principle in past times, and affirmed religious tolerance and respect. It is important, if he desires the good will of evangelical Protestants, and if he is to apply his own insight about European history to the present, that he recognize that the Latin America situation needs the same respect and tolerance. In some parts of Mexico, for example, evangelicals are still persecuted by Catholics, and some of the Catholic hierarchy in Latin America are still acting as if *cuius regio eius religio* were in force today (Symulka). Some of the pope's words on his trips to Latin America further that view. The faith of evangelical believers ought to be respected in every part of the world. Despite these problems it should be gladly acknowledged that in *Ut Unum Sint* there are many positive words about Protestant believers by John Paul II. He commends the theological dialogue, the times of prayer between Catholics and Protestants together, the organizations committed to the relief of spiritual and bodily distress, the joint translations of Scripture, above all the witness of Protestant martyrs, and many other "trustworthy signs of genuine faith and spirituality."

Towards the end of the encyclical John Paul writes:

> We can now ask how much further we must travel until that blessed day when full unity in faith will be attained and we can

celebrate together in peace the Holy Eucharist of the Lord. The greater mutual understanding and the doctrinal convergences already achieved between us, which have resulted in an effective growth of communion, cannot suffice for the conscience of Christians who profess that the Church is one, holy, catholic and apostolic. The ultimate goal of the ecumenical movement is to re-establish full visible unity among all the baptized (77).

Areas Needing further Discussion

Having made this noble and encouraging declaration, and having repeatedly called himself and all Christians and Churches to repentance, continual conversion and reformation, he lists the areas which are important for ongoing discussion:

It is already possible to identify the areas in need of fuller study before a true consensus of faith can be achieved: 1) the relationship between Sacred Scripture, as the highest authority in matters of faith, and Sacred Tradition, as indispensable to the interpretation of the Word of God; 2) the Eucharist, as the Sacrament of the Body and Blood of Christ, an offering of praise to the Father, the sacrificial memorial and Real Presence of Christ and the sanctifying outpouring of the Holy Spirit; 3) Ordination, as a Sacrament, to the threefold ministry of the episcopate, presbyterate and diaconate; 4) the Magisterium of the Church, entrusted to the pope and the bishops in communion with him, understood as a responsibility and an authority exercised in the name of Christ for teaching and safeguarding the faith; 5) the Virgin Mary, as Mother of God and Icon of the Church, the spiritual Mother who intercedes for Christ's disciples and for all humanity (79).

Justification

These five points are a useful summary of the issues that led to the Reformation in the sixteenth century, with the exception of the central matter which concerned all the reformers: justification through faith alone, by grace alone, *sola fide* and *sola gratia*. As will be shown several of these points relate to *sola fide*, but, it is surprising that this major cause of the division between the Churches is not listed. Is this because justification is no longer seen as an issue of disagreement? Two documents, "Evangelicals and Catholics Together" (May 1994) and "The Gift of Salvation" (October 1997), drawn up and signed by a group of Roman Catholics and evangelical Protestants from several different Churches, have moved the discussion of common theological ground between evangelicals and Catholics a considerable distance forward. "The Gift of Salvation" expresses the matter thus:

> The New Testament makes it clear that the gift of justification is received through faith. 'By grace you have been saved through faith; and this is not your own doing, it is the gift of God' (*Ephesians* 2:8). By faith, which is also the gift of God, we repent of our sins and freely adhere to the Gospel, the good news of God's saving work for us in Christ. By our response of faith to Christ, we enter into the blessings promised by the Gospel. Faith is not merely intellectual assent but an act of the whole person, involving the mind, the will, and the affections, issuing in a changed life. We understand that what we here affirm is in agreement with what the Reformation traditions have meant by justification by faith alone (sola fide) ("The Gift of Salvation," 20–23).

This is a remarkable statement. If John Paul II could affirm that it were indeed the official position of the Catholic Church, it would constitute a very large step forward in improving relationships and clearing away evangelical suspicion towards Rome. Apparently there is such a move by the pope. After the discussions of thirty years between Lutheran and Catholic theologians on the subject of justification, a document has been produced. It was reported that on June 25th 1998, the Vatican said:

> That it would sign a joint declaration with most of the world's Lutherans affirming that Roman Catholics and Lutherans now share a basic understanding of how human beings receive God's forgiveness and salvation ("Repentance or Ruse," 1–2).

Significantly some of the more conservative and evangelical Lutherans are unhappy with this joint declaration, which more liberal Lutherans have gladly signed. However, it seems clear that there is truly substantial progress on this particular and central question which has been at the heart of evangelical criticism of Rome for almost 500 years. "The Gift of Salvation" acknowledges that there are still some major differences keeping evangelicals and Catholics apart; the document mentions baptism, the Eucharist, sacramental grace, Marian devotion and several other issues. This list is similar to the five points in John Paul II's summary of areas needing discussion, quoted above. For Reformed evangelicals the pope's five points capture the problem areas well, and the heart of each of these is the bearing these matters have on the two issues central to the Reformation: justification through faith alone and the unique authority of Scripture (*sola fide* and *sola Scriptura*).

Scripture and Tradition

Reformed Churches have willingly acknowledged that tradition can be valuable but have always rejected its authority being raised to the level of Scripture. (Calvin said that 'tradition is a good guide, but a poor master' and Luther 'that one book is enough, but a thousand books are not too many'). I do not see how it would ever be possible for Reformed or any other evangelicals to say that "Sacred tradition is indispensable to the interpretation of the Word of God," or to acknowledge that the "Magisterium of the Church, entrusted to the pope and the Bishops of the Church" should be regarded as "an authority exercised in the name of Christ for teaching and safeguarding the faith." Equally, is there any way for the Catholic Church to soften its view of tradition and affirm instead the *sola Scriptura* of the Reformation? Neither position seems amenable to a change that might bring them closer. However, the movement on the doctrine of justification is cause for encouragement.

Apostolic Succession and Valid Ministry

Another question which arises is whether John Paul II will ever be able to acknowledge the validity of the ordination of the ministry of evangelical Churches when apostolic succession is understood by them to be a matter of faithfulness to Scripture rather than lineal inheritance from the New Testament apostles? Equally, how can evangelicals betray (this is not too strong a word to express how seriously this matter of authority is regarded) their understanding of authority by submitting to the ongoing claim of supremacy by John Paul II? After his summary of the five areas of difference, the pope has in *Ut Unum Sint* a long section defending the apostolic succession and also the primacy of the Roman Church and of himself as Peter's heir. This defense comes in the strongest possible words:

> Among all the Churches and Ecclesial Communities, the Catholic Church is conscious that she has preserved the ministry of the Successor of the Apostle Peter, the Bishop of Rome, whom God established as her "perpetual and visible principle and foundation of unity" and whom the Spirit sustains in order that he may enable all the others to share in this essential good (88).

> With the power and authority without which such an office would be illusory, the Bishop of Rome must insure the communion of all the Churches. . . . This primacy is exercised on various levels, including vigilance over the handing down of the Word, the celebration of the Liturgy and the Sacraments, the Church's mission, discipline and the Christian life. . . . When circumstances require it, he speaks in the name of all the Pastors in communion with him. He can also . . . declare *ex cathedra* that a certain doctrine belongs to the deposit of faith. By thus bearing witness to the truth, he serves unity (94).

> The Catholic Church, both in her *praxis* and in her solemn documents, holds that communion of the particular Churches with the Church of Rome, and of their Bishops with the Bishop of Rome, is—in God's plan—an essential requisite of full and visible communion. . . . This function of Peter must continue in the Church so that under her sole Head, who is Jesus Christ, she may be visibly present in the world as the communion of all his disciples (97).

These statements of the authority of the pope are so strong that they stand as obstacles in the path of any ecumenical discussion. They seem to concede not one inch of the highest statements of papal supremacy made at Vatican I in the last century. John Paul II sees the pontiff as the guarantor and means of unity, but these claims of authority are, I am afraid, the guarantor and surety of disunity.

In the New Testament, which John Paul II extensively quotes in this section of the encyclical, Peter is presented not only as the leader of the apostles, but also as a boaster who did not see his own weaknesses (*Luke* 22:33; *Mark* 15:27–31); as one of Jesus' closest friends who could not stay awake to watch and pray with Jesus in his hour of need in Gethsemane (*Mark* 15:32–42); as one who disowned Jesus three times (*Luke* 22:54–62); as one who was very slow to obey Jesus' command to go to the Gentiles (*Acts* 10); as one who, years after he had been dragged to Cornelius' home by the Lord, was still struggling with the status of Gentiles and broke the unity of the Church by refusing to eat with them in Galatia so that it was necessary for the Apostle Paul to rebuke him publicly (*Galatians* 2:11–14).

If Peter himself was sinful and weak in these ways, both before and after the resurrection of Christ and the Pentecostal reception of the Spirit, how much more will this have been true of every other church leader in history, including the bishops of Rome? These words are not intended to be churlish, nor to suggest that the bishop of Rome has a monopoly on sin and weakness. Rather, it is a basic tenet of a Reformed and evangelical faith to recognize that all believers, including those ordained to the ministry, continue to be weak and sinful and need to repent of their errors in teaching and life. John Paul II acknowledges this in principle repeatedly in *Ut Unum Sint,* but fails to apply it to the doctrinal and practical issues that are at the heart of the continued division between the Churches.

The other problem which seems insurmountable from a Reformed perspective is that the issues which John Paul II identifies as needing further discussion are matters which bear on the central issue of justification through faith alone in the once offered death of Christ alone, *sola fide:* the Eucharist defined by the encyclical as "the sacrificial memorial and Real Presence of Christ"; and the status of the Virgin Mary, "the spiritual Mother who intercedes for Christ's disciples and for all humanity."

Eucharistic Sacrifice

A repeated sacrifice of Christ undermines for Reformed evangelicals the statements about the complete sufficiency of Christ's death which Scripture makes repeatedly: "Unlike the other priests, he does not need to offer sacrifices day after day, first for his own sins, and then for the sins of the people. He sacrificed for their sins once for all when he offered himself' (*Hebrews* 8:27); "Nor did he enter heaven to offer himself again and again, the way the high priest enters the Most Holy Place every year with blood that is not his own. Then Christ would have had to suffer many times since the creation of the world. But now he has appeared once for all at the end of the ages to do away with sin by the sacrifice of himself" (*Hebrews* 9:25–26); "We have been made holy through the sacrifice of the body of Jesus once for all. . . . By one sacrifice he has made perfect forever those who are being made holy" (*Hebrews* 10:10,14).

While we treasure the Eucharist, and recognize, as did Calvin and Cranmer, that Christ is truly and spiritually present when we participate in the body and blood of the Lord, while we believe that we are spiritually nourished by Christ in our hearts as we eat and drink with faith and thanksgiving, it is, for us, a denial of the clear words of Scripture on the sufficiency of his atoning death, to regard the Lord's Supper as a sacrifice for sin.

John Paul II and Marian Devotion

Similar and even more serious problems are raised by John Paul II's teaching on the Virgin Mary. We gladly call her 'blessed' and acknowledge that she was highly favored by the Lord, but the present pope's emphasis on Mary's role in our salvation and Christian life seems, to us, to undermine Scripture's teaching that there is only 'one mediator between God and men, the man Christ Jesus' (*1 Timothy* 2:5).

In answer to a question about the motto he chose for his papacy, *Totus Tuus,* John Paul II replies in *Crossing The Threshold Of Hope*:

> In regard to Marian devotion, each of us must understand that such devotion not only addresses a need of the heart, a sentimental inclination, but that it also corresponds to the objective truth about the Mother of God. Mary is the New Eve, placed by God in close relation to Christ, the new Adam. . . .
> The Mother of Christ the Redeemer is the Mother of the Church (213).

Writing of the shrine of Jasna Gora with its icon of the Black Madonna, he comments further on his motto:

> Our Lady of Jasna Gora has been venerated for centuries as the
> Queen of Poland. . . . The Polish nation has sought for
> centuries, and continues to seek, support and strength for
> spiritual rebirth from its lady and queen. . . . I think what I
> have said sufficiently explains the Marian devotion of the
> present pope and, above all, his attitude of total *abandonment
> to Mary*—his *Totus Tuus* (215).

Discussing the numerous private revelations and apparitions of Mary
that have taken place 'especially in the last two hundred years,' John
Paul II again refers to the impact on his own life of shrines to Mary, and
places where Mary is said to have appeared:

> On October 22, 1978, when I inherited the Ministry of Peter in
> Rome, more than anything else, it was this experience and
> devotion to Mary in my native land which I carried with me.
> . . . *Mary's participation in the victory of Christ became clear
> to me above all from the experience of my people. . . .* On this
> universal level, if victory comes it will be brought by Mary.
> *Christ will conquer through her, because He wants the
> Church's victories now and in the future to be linked to her*
> (220–221).

John Paul II then refers to the appearance at Fatima in Portugal in
1917 when an apparition claiming to be Mary requested:

> . . . that the pope and all the bishops in the world shall
> consecrate Russia to the Immaculate Heart on one special day.
> If this is done, she will convert Russia and there will be peace
> (Kauffman, 144–145 ff).

John Paul II makes it clear that he believes that the attempt on his life
on May 13, 1981, bore a direct relationship to the Fatima vision and
request:

> At first, I did not pay attention to the fact that the assassination
> attempt had occurred on the exact anniversary of the day Mary
> appeared to the three children at Fatima in Portugal and spoke
> to them the words that now, at the end of this century, seem to
> be close to their fulfillment (*Crossing the Threshold of Hope*,
> 221).

Subsequent to his recovery from the attempt on his life John Paul carried out the wish of the apparition on March 25th 1984 in St. Peter's Square in Rome, consecrating Russia, and along with Russia all the world, to the Immaculate Heart of Mary, and then added these words:

> The act requested at Fatima is now accomplished, but now it is necessary for every bishop to consecrate his diocese, every pastor his own parish, every father and mother their own family (Kauffman, 145 ff).

In addition to Fatima, John Paul II has clearly accepted as valid the apparition at Knock in Ireland, visiting the site there, and presenting a gold rose to the shrine in memory of the gold rose Mary was said to have worn when the apparition was seen. Of one of the most recent of these apparitions in Medjugorje in Bosnia and Herzegovina the pope is reported to have stated: "If I wasn't a pope I'd be in Medjugorje already" (Kauffman, 144 ff).

It might be possible to pay little attention to this acceptance of such apparitions if John Paul II's views were not so widely disseminated and were less influential. But he is the pope, and his every word about Mary fuels and encourages the devotion to Mary which seems to be growing so rapidly. It has become an item of widely reported news that there is a popular movement urging John Paul II in petition after petition to make an *ex cathedra* statement of infallible dogma proclaiming Mary as Coredemptrix, Mediatrix of all graces, and Advocate.

In his encyclical *Redemptoris Mater,* John Paul II spells out his theology of Mary. He repeatedly refers to Mary's cooperation in her Son's work of redemption, to her unceasing intercession for believers and for the world, to her work of protection of God's people and of nations, to her absolute purity and sinlessness, to her bodily assumption into heaven and her present reign as Queen of the Universe. A few passages from the encyclical give the flavor of the whole:

> Mary's motherhood continues unceasingly in the Church as the mediation which intercedes, and the Church expresses her faith in this truth by invoking Mary "under the titles of Advocate, Auxiliatrix, Adjutrix and Mediator" (39).

> The Church draws abundantly from this cooperation, that is to say from the maternal mediation which is characteristic of

Mary, insofar as already on earth she cooperated in the rebirth and development of the Church's sons and daughters (44).

We believe (here he is quoting Paul VI from 1968) that the Most Holy Mother of God, the new Eve, the Mother of the Church, carries on in heaven her maternal role with regard to the members of Christ, cooperating in the birth and development of divine life in the souls of the redeemed (47).

Mary, present in the Church as the Mother of the Redeemer, takes part, as a mother, in that "monumental struggle against the powers of darkness" which continues throughout human history. And by her ecclesial identification as the "woman clothed with the sun" (*Revelation* 12:1) it can be said that "in the Most Holy Virgin the Church has already reached that perfection whereby she exists without spot or wrinkle. Hence, as Christians raise their eyes with faith to Mary in the course of their earthly pilgrimage, they "strive to increase in holiness." Mary, the exalted daughter of Sion, helps all her children, wherever they may be and whatever their condition, to find in Christ the path to the Father's house (47).

She is also the one who, precisely as the "handmaid of the Lord," cooperates unceasingly with the work of salvation accomplished by Christ, her Son (49).

Elsewhere John Paul II describes Mary as: "The living and concrete guarantor of this salvific presence of God" (*Lift Up Your Hearts*, 85), as the one who gives "Motherly protection of the Church (203), as the one "the church venerates as queen of all saints" (271), as

Immaculate one!
Mother Of God and of men!
You are the light of the first Advent!
You are the morning star which precedes the coming of the Messiah. . . .
be for us the light of this new Advent,
be its morning star,
so that darkness will not overcome us! (303).

He also refers to Mary as "The meeting place of the Old and New

Covenants . . . she is the last and perfect expression of the children of God born of Abraham under the Old Covenant and the first and highest expression of the new children of God born of Christ" (305).

As if all these honors and titles bestowed on Mary were insufficient, John Paul II has also on several occasions referred to Mary as Coredemptrix:

> Mary, though conceived and born without the taint of sin, participated in a marvelous way in the sufferings of her divine Son, in order to be Coredemptrix of humanity (Miravalle, 122).

John Paul II appears to believe that this emphasis on Marian devotion and on "Mary's role in the work of salvation" will help the divided churches on their path towards unity.

> By a more profound study of both Mary and the Church, clarifying each by the light of the other, Christians who are eager to do what Jesus tells them—as their Mother recommends (cf. *John* 2:5)—will be able to go forward on "this pilgrimage of faith." Mary, who is still the model of this pilgrimage, is to lead them to the unity which is willed by their one Lord and so much desired by those who are attentively listening to what "the Spirit is saying to the Churches" today (*Revelation* 2:7,11,17) (*Redemptoris Mater*, 30).

The sober and sad reality is that this high view of Mary will prevent the Churches coming to unity rather than assist them. In an article entitled 'Reactions to *Redemptoris Mater*' an Evangelical Lutheran, Ulrich Wilckens, writes, after severely criticizing the way the pope goes far beyond the Biblical record and even contradicts it in some of his understanding of Mary:

> Thus, unification of our churches will not happen by looking at Mary, but only by looking at Jesus Christ, "the pioneer and perfecter of our faith" (*Hebrews* 12:2) (Koch, 13).

Damaskinos Papandreou gives an Orthodox reaction in which he criticizes the doctrine of the Assumption of Mary and in particular the doctrine of the Immaculate Conception, insisting that:

> The dogma . . . is not part of the patristic tradition of the unseparated church, nor of Western theology (Augustine, Bernard of Clairvaux, Thomas Aquinas, Albertus Magnus, *et al.*). . . . The Encyclical . . . Adheres to the dogma of the Immaculate Conception and thus does not help ecumenical dialog (Koch, 13).

One of the Catholic reactions to the encyclical also regards its Marian devotion as unbiblical:

> Everything that is said about the Marian dimension of faith and the church can also be expressed without direct reference to Mary. One can believingly accept God's word in the spirit of Jesus' mother, follow Christ, and witness to him without talking about Mary. Where this kind of freedom is not present, Marian devotion is no longer biblical, no longer Marian (Koch, 15).

From a Reformed evangelical perspective it is necessary to add that in this encyclical, and in much of what John Paul II has written and spoken about Mary, he appears to have taken the attributes and saving work of Jesus, the Son of God, and also the Holy Spirit and applied them to Mary. Many of the titles he gives her—from Mediator to Morning Star, from Advocate to Adjutrix, from Protector to Perfect Model—are properly titles of Christ Himself or of the Holy Spirit. There is no biblical warrant for applying them to Mary, the Mother of Jesus. The only effects this multiplying of titles, of honor, of Christological attributes, to Mary can possibly have are 1) to diminish the uniqueness of the saving work of God's Son in the minds and hearts of believers; 2) to weaken the sense of immediate access to Christ that is the birthright of every Christian; 3) to replace this confidence of access to Christ with a sense of needing to turn to his mother who is more likely to gain a hearing with him than I myself could hope for; and 4) to undermine the *sola fide* of the Reformation—justification through faith alone in Christ alone.

This criticism may seem severe, but John Paul II's Marian devotion does severe damage to the cause of Christian unity to which he is so evidently committed.

Despite this, there is much that ought to be said in appreciation of John Paul II. His strong and clear stand on so many moral issues, in particular all that he has said about the sacredness of human life is something for which I, as a non-Catholic Christian, thank God. His challenge to the moral relativism of our secularized society needs to be taken up and heralded around the world. His critique of the arid rationalism of the enlightenment is like medicine to the soul. His respectful welcoming of non-Catholics, both Christian and unbeliever, sets an example to be admired and imitated. His passionate summons to unity is one for every Christian to heed if we wish to be obedient to the prayer of Christ.

Bibliography

A New Spirit. Anglican Communion Publications: London, 1997.

Accattoli, Luigi. *When A Pope Asks Forgiveness.* Alba House: New York, 1998.

Accattoli, Luigi. "Pope's Change of Direction: Pardon Us!" *Religion in Western Europe,* Vol. 15, October 1995.

Beckwith, Roger. "Ut Unum Sint." *Churchman,* 1997.

Boer, Harry R. "An Authoritative Voice." *Reformed Journal,* Vol. 37, October 1987.

"Canterbury and Rome Discuss Differences." *Christian Century,* Vol. 114, January 1–8, 1997.

"Evangelicals and Catholics Together." *First Things,* May 1998.

Harrison, Barbara Grizzuti. "My Eve, My Mary." *Newsweek,* August 25, 1997.

"Highlights Of the Life Of His Holiness Pope John Paul II." *Internet Document.* June 29, 1998.

Kauffman, Timothy F. *Quite Contrary.* White Horse Publications: Huntsville, AL, 1994.

Kezmos, Heidi Schulmpf. "Top Evangelicals Confer With Pope." *Christianity Today,* Vol. 39, November 13, 1995 .

Koch, Kurt. "The Marian Encyclical and the Marian Year." *Theology Digest,* Vol. 35 (1), Spring 1988.

Lergand, Herve. "Announcing the Gospel in Europe: Facing The Challenges of Cultural Changes and Religious and Ethnic Divisions." *Melita Theologica,* Vol. 47 (1), 1996.

Mary Coredemptrix, Mediatrix, Advocate. Theological Foundations. Towards a Papal Definition? Queenship Publishing Company: Santa Barbara, 1995.

Mary Coredemptrix, Mediatrix, Advocate. Theological Foundations II. Papal, Pneumatological, Ecumenical. Queenship Publishing Company: Santa Barbara, 1996.

"Mary in the Bible." *Newsweek,* August 25, 1997.

Meyer, Harding. "Différence Fondamentale, Consensus Fondamental: Esquisse d'un projet d'étude du Centre d'Études Oecumeniques de Strasbourg." *Irenicon,* Vol. 58, No. 2, 1985.

Miravalle, Mark I. *The Dogma and the Triumph.* Queenship Publishing Company: Santa Barbara, 1998.

Norbu, Thinley. *Welcoming Flowers From Across the Cleansed Threshold of Hope.* Jewel Publishing House: New York, 1997.

North, J.E. *The Papal Visit weighed and found waiting.* Bushey Mead Press: Sussex, 1983.

Owens, Virginia Stem. "A Well-Versed Pope." *Books and Culture,* November/ December 1995.

Papandreou, Damaskinos. "Orthodox Reactions." *Theology Digest,* Vol. 35(1), Spring 1988.

Parker, Dorothy Mills. "The Dean of Canterbury on the Papal Visit." *The Living Church,* July 11, 1982.

—. "John Paul at Canterbury." *The Living Church*, July 4, 1982.

Pope John Paul II. *Celebrate 2000!* Servant Publications: Ann Arbor, 1996.

—. Encyclical Letter *Ut Unum Sint.* May 25, 1995.

—. *Crossing the Threshold of Hope.* Alfred A. Knopf: New York, 1994.

—. *Lift Up Your Hearts: Daily Meditations.* Servant Publications: Ann Arbor, 1995.

—. *Spiritual Pilgrimage.* The Crossroad Publishing Company: New York, 1995.

Pope John Paul II and the Archbishop of Canterbury. "The Common Declaration" of May 29, 1982. *The Living Church,* July 4, 1982.

Pope John Paul II, J. R. Crumley. "Lutheran, Catholic Leaders Exchange Letters of Hope." *Ecumenical Trends,* Vol. 15, January 1986.

Protestations Orthodoxes. Fraternité Orthodoxe Saint Gregoire Palamas: Paris, 1988.

Recognize the Spiritual Bonds Which Unite Us. Pontifical Council for Interreligious Dialogue: Vatican City, 1994.

"Repentance or Ruse." *Religion and Society Report,* Vol. 15, No. 9, September 1998.

Rochter, Larry. "Pope, In Mexico, Faces Rising Protestant Tide." *New York Times,* Vol. 139, May 12, 1990.

Symulka, Stephen R. "John Paul Woos Straying Flock." *Christianity Today,* April 8, 1996.

"The Augsburg Confession and the Catholic Church." *AFER.,* Vol. 22, October 1980.

"The Gift Of Salvation." *First Things,* January 1998.

"The Pope in Germany." *Christian Century,* Vol. 97, December 10, 1980.

Tavard, George H. "The Anglican-Roman Catholic Agreed Statements and Their Reception." *Theological Studies,* Vol. 41 (1), 1980.

Van Leeuwen, Mary Stewart. "How the Vatican Spells Sex." *Books and Culture*, November/ December 1995.

Vatican. "Events In The Pontificate Of His Holiness Pope John Paul II." *Internet Document. WWW.VATICAN.VA.* June 29, 1998.

Voss, Gerhard. "Marian Spirituality." *Theology Digest,* Vol. 35 (1). Spring 1988.

Wilckens, Ulrich. "Evangelical Lutheran Agreement and Criticism." *Theology Digest.* Vol. 35 (1), Spring 1988.

Woodward, Kenneth L. "The Meaning of Mary." *Newsweek,* August 25, 1996.

CHAPTER SIX

John Paul II and The Family

The Family: A Communion of Persons

Janet E. Smith

𝒜 mong the thematic concerns of Pope John Paul II's pontificate have been the restoration of Christian Unity and the fall of communism, and increasingly a plea to the West to abandon its materialistic ways. He has been working actively to advance these goals. Indeed, he played a major role in the fall of Communism, progress has been made in various ecumenical endeavors and, arguably, World Youth Days have begun to direct the youth of the world away from consumerism to supernatural realities.

A concern of seemingly equal importance for John Paul II has been the promotion of the Christian understanding of the family. He has expressed repeatedly that "at [this] moment in history, . . . the family is the object of numerous forces that seek to destroy it or in some way to deform it" (*Familiaris Consortio*, 3). Thus, he seeks to fortify the family to withstand these attacks so that it can perform its vital role for the good of the individual, society, and the Church. John Paul II's numerous and profound writings on sexuality, marriage, and the family are shaped by theological, philosophical, and political perspectives. From his pre-pontifical years, we have the philosophical, incomparable *Love and Responsibility*, and from the early years of his pontificate we have his elaborate theology of the body set out in a series of Wednesday audiences. The family is comprehensively treated in *Familiaris Consortio* and his *Letter to Families*; these are complemented by lengthy

85

passages in his writings on women and also his writings on the laity and social justice. There are few portions of his thought that are not touched by concern for the family.

The first portion of this paper presents in a sketchy form some of the philosophical principles that undergird John Paul II's thought on the family. A brief history of competing views of the family and of the human person will serve to set those views in high relief. The second portion of the paper lays out John Paul II's particular vision of the Catholic understanding of the family.

Part I

Views on the Family

Here let us take a brief look at a few other views of the family. While the necessary simplification may involve some distortion, nonetheless this exercise should allow us to construct a sharper and clearer picture of the views of Pope John Paul II.

The view of the family in the Old Testament is one of the nation, tribe, or clan. One belongs to a body of individuals who have a corporate destiny. While God communicates with particular individuals, He does so to direct His chosen people. Sons carry on the project of their fathers, and the sins of the fathers are visited upon the heads of the sons. In the New Testament, salvation extends to all, to Gentiles as well as Jews, and we now speak of the brotherhood of all mankind. This view of the family, of course, remains in the thought of John Paul II, especially when he calls upon particular families to extend their apostolate of love, when he calls upon them to have a preferential option for the poor. But I am getting ahead of the story.

Plato's view of the family has disturbed many. In the fifth book of the *Republic*, he argues (one wonders how seriously) for a dissolution of the family for the aristocratic class. He proposes that "wives and children" be held in common. That is, the highest quality warriors will mate with the highest quality women—not in a monogamous way—and their children will be raised in a group fashion without knowing who their parents are. This proposal was made not because of a suspicion about the value of the family; rather it was made so that the rulers of the state would think of themselves as one big family and have the love and unity which characterize a family.

Aristotle in his *Politics* rejects this proposal as being totally incompatible with human nature. Among other objections, he notes that human beings care much more for what is their own, and if they can identify no spouse or children as their own they will not be able to show the proper care for them (*Politics*, 1261b35). Aristotle believed that the family was a natural institution; in the *Nicomachean Ethics* he states, "The friendship between husband and wife is thought to exist by nature; for men by nature tend to form couples more than to be political, and they do this to the extent that a household is prior and more necessary than a state . . ." (1162a17).[1] Aristotle recognized that the relationship between family members was one of love and friendship: "parents love their children as they love themselves . . . and children love their parents as being born of them . . . brothers love each other by having been born of the same parents . . ." (1161b28). The family provides for the physical, psychological, and social needs of the individual who then has a base from which to serve the common good.

Aquinas, of course, built much upon Aristotle but went beyond him. He shares Aristotle's understanding of the naturalness of marriage and family and holds that love is the proper bond between the members of a family. Marriage was established as a natural institution before original sin. After the Fall, marriage served as sacrament of the Old Law as a remedy for the sin of concupiscence. Under the New Law it serves as a sacramental sign of the mystery of Christ's Union with the Church and provides spouses with the graces enabling them to perform the good works proper to marriage (*Summa Theologica* II–II, Q. 42, a. 2–3).

With the Enlightenment, however, there came to be a radical challenge to the understanding of marriage and family as natural unions, let alone sacramental unions. Many examples can be given, but perhaps that of Rousseau suffices for our purposes. As he writes, "Man is born free, and is everywhere in chains."[2] He sees the family as a natural society, but one that serves largely to meet the temporary needs of the human being. Once a child no longer needs a father for survival, "the children are released from the duty of obeying the father, he is released from the duty of taking care of them, and they all become independent."[3] All future association is simply voluntary. The state is much like the family; it is a union required by needs of survival, but it is legitimate ultimately only if it is a voluntary association. Even at their best, in many respects the family and the state are destructive to the human being since they require a conformity of the human being to corporate rather than individual goods.

With the acceptance of the theory of evolution, the malleability of the family has become a constant theme. The family is "natural" in the sense that it has served certain purposes of survival of the human species, but it, along with all institutions, is still evolving. There is nothing to prevent other means of nurture and education from performing the functions of the family and in fact from performing them better. There is no reason to envision the family as a basic unit of father, mother, children and other related persons; rather it can be constituted by any collection of people living with and caring for each other. Hence we now have calls for recognition of homosexual unions as marriages and any grouping of individuals as families.

Over time the individual rather than the family has become the focus of legal protection and public policy.[4] The individual now is largely seen as an atomistic entity in need of a maximal opportunity for the actualization of his or her preferences without interference from others, including the family. General enthusiasm for an ever-proliferating set of rights[5] seeks to protect individual rights threatened by such institutions as the family. This shift from focus on the family to focus on the individual is not as much actuated by respect for the rights of the individual as one might hope; rather it is accompanied by a desire to transfer power from the family to some other group. Mary Ann Glendon has observed:

> In one sense, the current attacks on the family represent a new version of a story that is as old as politics itself. Those who seek power have always known that the more that individuals can be detached from families and other mediating groups, the more easily they can be subjugated, and their allegiances shifted to the state, the party, or the charismatic leader. Contemporary movements to "deconstruct" and delegitimate the family thus have implications for human freedom far different from those imagined by hardline feminists and homosexual activists naïve enough to believe they would be better off without strong families and vibrant religious groups.[6]

It is against this background that John Paul II's understanding of the family should be seen.

Views of the Person

Still, in expounding John Paul II's understanding of the family and its importance, one should not begin with the family. Indeed, one cannot speak of any elements of the thought of John Paul II without reference to his personalism, and that is particularly true in respect to his understanding of the family. It is as impossible to do a full review of the many views of the human person that have been proposed throughout the history of philosophy as it is of the family. Yet we must provide a least a sketch of various views, for they also constitute a background and a useful foil to the thought of John Paul II.

As a philosopher, Karol Wojtyla[7] has shown a keen awareness of the philosophical challenges to the Christian understanding of the human person. He has formulated much of his own philosophy in the context of a response to Marxism with its utterly utilitarian evaluation of the human person; for Marx, individual persons could and would certainly be sacrificed to the march of history. Karol Wojtyla was no less cognizant of the reduction of the horizon of the human person produced by Enlightenment philosophers. They valued man largely for his rational capacities, capacities in their view to be exercised within the limits either of the material world or within the limits of the contents of the human mind, that is, without reference to anything supernatural.

For Wojtyla, of course, the human person has an inviolable dignity and a transcendent destiny. These features of the human person are knowable both through the discoveries of reason and through revelation. Yet, while Wojtyla accepts the scholastic definition of the human person as an individual substance of a rational nature, his analysis of the human person does not focus so much on man's cognitive capacity, on his ability to understand universal truths. Rather, he concentrates primarily upon the person's powers of self-determination, hence his book *The Acting Person*.[8] Indeed, Wojtyla does not take as his point of departure the Aristotelian-Thomistic movement from sense data to universal truths. Rather, he begins his analysis of the human person, with the very modern vantage point of the contents of the human mind, most particularly the experience of self-consciousness and particularly the consciousness of a self that knows itself to be a self-determining entity. (This does not mean, of course, that Wojtyla rejects a role of experience in ethics. Indeed, he objects to all ethical systems that do not make experience a starting point for the ethical act).[9]

One might suspect that this emphasis on the self-determining powers of the person would suggest that Wojtyla has a highly individualistic understanding of the human person. After all, as we have noted, much of modern philosophy places rather extreme emphasis on the human person as a free individual with inalienable rights. Indeed, John Paul II has taken care to express repeatedly his affinity for the modern commitment to freedom and the modern doctrine of fundamental human rights. He was reportedly one of the driving forces behind the Vatican II document, *Dignitatis Humanae,* which argued for a freedom in religious matters that some find nearly radical. In *Veritatis Splendor*, he acknowledges that "the right to religious freedom and to respect for conscience in the journey towards the truth is increasingly perceived as the foundation of the cumulative rights of the person" and speaks of this "heightened sense of the dignity of the human person and of his or her uniqueness, and of the respect due to the journey of conscience" as one of the "positive achievements of modern culture" (31).[10]

In *Evangelium Vitae*, John Paul II praises the growth of the modern understanding and commitment to universal fundamental human rights. There he states:

> . . . the various declarations of human rights and the many initiatives inspired by these declarations show that at the global level there is a growing moral sensitivity, more alert to acknowledging the value and dignity of every individual as a human being, without any distinction of race, nationality, religion, political opinion or social class (18).

In spite of all his admiration for the modern concern with the rights of conscience and with other inalienable rights, John Paul II detects dangerous trends regarding both.

John Paul II's fears concerning the modern doctrine of fundamental, inalienable, universal rights are 1) that there has been a "tragic repudiation of them in practice" (*Evangelium Vitae*, 35) and even worse 2) that attacks against life "tend no longer to be considered as 'crimes'; paradoxically they assume the nature of 'rights.' What were once considered crimes, such as abortion and assisted suicide, have now come to be considered fundamental human rights. John Paul II finds the roots of these problems to be in a "perverse idea of freedom":

> When freedom, out of a desire to emancipate itself from all

forms of tradition and authority, shuts out even the most obvious evidence of an objective and universal truth, which is the foundation of personal and social life, then the person ends up by no longer taking as the sole and indisputable point of reference for his own choices the truth about good and evil, but only his subjective and changeable opinion or, indeed, his selfish interest and whim (*Evangelium Vitae*, 19).

He finds that this same perverse idea of freedom corrupts the modern emphasis on the primacy of conscience insofar as it tends to give an absoluteness to freedom, a freedom to be exercised without submission to the demands of objective truth. He observes:

> . . . the inescapable claims of truth disappear, yielding their place to a criterion of sincerity, authenticity and "being at peace with oneself," so much so that some have come to adopt a radically subjectivistic conception of moral judgment (*Veritatis Splendor*, 32).[11]

The exercise of freedom detached from the truth is a misuse of freedom. As *Veritatis Splendor* also states:

> Although each individual has a right to be respected in his own journey in search of the truth, there exists a prior moral obligation, and a grave one at that, to seek the truth and to adhere to it once it is known (50).[12]

It would be difficult to find a modern thinker who has a higher regard for the dignity of the human person than John Paul II, but that regard is predicated on the power of the human person to know and to act freely in accord with the truth.

Relationality

The human person's freedom does not make him free from the obligations and demands of truth, nor does it make him free from the obligations and demands of his relationships with others. When defining human nature, Karol Wojtyla stresses not only the human person's rationality and freedom, but also his relationality or his need for being in solidarity with others. This relationality is not simply defined by the need of the human person for others to supply his physical needs nor by the need of the human person for others to help him accomplish his other goals. Rather, Wojtyla finds man's need for others to be deeply constitutive of his very being.[13] He argues that the human person can discover himself fully only by the "sincere giving of himself."[14] *Evangelium Vitae* states that

> . . . God entrusts us to one another. And it is also in view of this entrusting that God gives everyone freedom, a freedom which possesses an inherently relational dimension. This is a great gift of the Creator, placed as it is at the service of the person and of his fulfillment through the gift of self and openness to others; but when freedom is made absolute in an individualistic way, it is emptied of its original content, and its very meaning and dignity are contradicted (19).

John Paul II argues for this understanding of the person as essentially a relational entity, both philosophically and theologically. It surprises and troubles some that Karol Wojtyla cites regularly the Enlightenment philosopher Kant for the philosophical grounding of his understanding of the person. The understanding of the person that Wojtyla shares with Kant is not so much metaphysical as it is anthropological and ethical.[15] While Wojytla acknowledges that anthropology and ethics require a metaphysics and while he acknowledges the basic truth of an Aristotelian/Thomistic metaphysics, again, he does not use such a metaphysics as the point of departure for his anthropology and his ethics. What he adopts from Kant seems perfectly compatible with Aquinas' view of the human person, but one suspects he begins with a Kantian principle rather than a Thomistic one for pedagogical as much as philosophical purposes. In Kant we have a "pure philosopher," one who eschews revelation as a source of philosophical insight and one who rejects nature as a source of norms. (Needless to say, Wojytla does not accept these limitations).[16]

The dictum of Kant that Wojtyla most often cites is his claim that one should always treat persons as ends and never use anyone solely as a means to an end.[17] In *Love and Responsibility* he explains what he considers to be the foundation for this principle:

> . . . a person is a thinking subject, and capable of taking decisions: these, most notably, are the attributes we find in the inner self of a person. This being so, every person is by nature

capable of determining his or her aims. Anyone who treats a person as the means to an end does violence to the very essence of the other, to what constitutes its natural right. Obviously, we must demand from a person, as a thinking individual, that his or her ends should be genuinely good, since the pursuit of evil ends is contrary to the rational nature of the person. This is also the purpose of education, both the education of children and the mutual education of adults; it is just that—a matter of seeking true ends, i.e., real goods as the ends of our actions, and of finding and showing to others the ways to realize them.[18]

A person is an "end" and not a "means" because a person is not determined to be this or that, like a cow is determined to be a cow and a tomato plant is determined to be a tomato plant. Certainly, a human being is determined to be rational, free, and relational, but this very freedom allows the human person to be self-determining in the way that is unique and the source of his dignity; the human person determines his or her self to be morally good or morally evil. The human person's greatest achievement is to make moral choices that give him or her a good moral character, that align him or her with what is good and true. This is to become perfect as one's heavenly father is perfect; this is how the human person shares in the divine. Wojtyla makes the important observation that not even God uses a person as a means; he states,

God allows man to learn His supernatural ends, but the decision to strive towards an end, the choices of course, is left to man's free will. God does not redeem man against his will.[19]

Wojtyla claims that there are two ways to treat things; to use them as means, or to honor them as ends. He elaborates on this distinction at considerable length in *Love and Responsibility*. In his *Letter to Families*, Pope John Paul II distinguished the Christian view of the person and marriage from the more prevalent contemporary one by speaking of a contrast between a "civilization of use" and a "civilization of love." There he states:

Utilitarianism is a civilization of production and of use, a civilization of "things" and not of "persons," a civilization in which persons are used in the same way as things are used. In the context of a civilization of use, woman can become an object for man, children a hindrance to parents, the family an institution obstructing the freedom of its members (13).

The family has as its mission the creation of a civilization of love. But, again, this is to get ahead of the story. Let us continue to explore the pope's personalism.

While Wojtyla draws a great deal upon Kant's imperative forbidding the use of persons, he goes beyond Kant not only in counseling against maltreatment of the person as means, but also in stating that the person requires more; the person requires "affirmation of the person as a person."[20]

His ethics is based upon what he calls the personalistic principle that the person is "the kind of good which does not admit of use and cannot be treated as an object of use and as such the means to an end."[21] Again, he gives a positive cast to the norm derived from this principle; he formulates the personalist norm as: "the person is a good towards which the only proper and adequate attitude is love."[22] Wojtyla speaks of this norm as a requirement of justice; love is what we owe other persons.

This being just to other persons, this loving others, is not only demanded of us because of the needs of others, because of their good; it is demanded of us because of our needs and our good. We must love, we must be self-giving in order to actualize fully our being.

Here, perhaps, the point is best made not so much through Wojtyla's philosophical deliberations (though this can be done) but through John Paul II's meditations on scripture, most particularly *Genesis*. John Paul II has developed what he calls a "theology of the body." One of his most striking phrases and terms is the "nuptial meaning of the body." By this he means that the very make-up of the human body, the very fact that we are all creatures of one sex or the other, indicates that we are "made for union with another." This is so both physically and spiritually. John Paul II has spoken movingly of the human person's "existential loneliness" that is eased by the relationship of marriage. He observes the deep joy and satisfied longing that is expressed in Adam's utterance upon seeing Eve: "Here at last is bone of my bone and flesh of my flesh." We are made to give ourselves to another and to receive another; our very physiological make-up demonstrates that. And this mutual giving and receiving is to issue forth in new life. Thus we are all, in the depths of our being, beings that require a spouse and children for the fulfillment of our being, whether that spouse be a flesh and blood spouse and the children be biological children, or whether the spouse be the Church, the bride of Christ, and one's parenthood be a spiritual parenthood.

For John Paul II the body is the visible expression of the human person. Our need for another is not simply physiological. Here we move to an even more transcendent level of revelation. He speaks of the human person being made in the likeness and image of God not only in our possession of rationality and free will, but, again, in our relationality. God is not only rational and free; God is a trinity; God is a loving family. Thus the human person images God in being a part of a family, in being made to love and be loved.

Part II

As we shift to consideration of John Paul II's understanding of the family, let us briefly summarize John Paul II's understanding of the human person. The human person is a rational, self-determining, relational entity whose dignity resides in his ability to choose freely in accord with the truth. The human person who does so will fulfill his nature as a self-giving loving being. As *Familiaris Consortio* states, "Love is . . . the fundamental and innate vocation of every human being" (11). Later in *Familiaris Consortio* he cites a passage from *Redemptor hominis*:

> Man cannot live without love. He remains a being that is incomprehensible for himself, his life is senseless, if love is not revealed to him, if he does not encounter love, if he does not experience it and make it his own, if he does not participate intimately in it (18).

With this background, we can begin to see why the family assumes a position of such importance in the thought of John Paul II. The family is the natural school of love and thus is essential to enabling human persons to achieve the fulfillment of their fundamental dignity. In *Familiaris Consortio* he describes the family in many ways, beginning with a phrase from *Gaudium et Spes*: the family is an "intimate community of life and love" (*Familiaris Consortio*, 17; *Gaudium et Spes*, 48).

Sexuality

The family is clearly the outgrowth of the love between spouses. Thus, of course, a few things must be said about marriage and the sexual union from which children issue. In his *Love and Responsibility*, Karol Wojtyla carefully describes what must be true about the sexual relationship for it to be raised to the level of the person. He explains how only an exclusive, indissoluble commitment properly expresses love of the person; any other type of sexual relationship involves an element of using the other, not of respecting the other. Wojtyla constantly counsels how the human person must always act in accord with the truth, and a fundamental truth about the sexual union is that it may result in a new human life. To act without regard for that possibility is to use another and to allow oneself to be used.

One must regard one's spouse, one's sexual partner, as the possible parent of one's future children. In *Love and Responsibility*, Wojtyla states:

> [the sexual union] is raised to the level of the person only when it is accompanied in the mind and the will by the acceptance of the possibility of parenthood. This acceptance is so important, so decisive that without it marital intercourse cannot be said to be a realization of the personal order.[23]

Without this ordination, the sexual union tends towards bilateral enjoyment rather than towards unification. Wojtyla states that the "willingness for parenthood" serves to break down egoism and opens spouses to the creative power of love.[24] Further we read "Responsibility for love . . . is very closely bound up with responsibility for parenthood."[25]

These claims appear in a chapter entitled "Justice Towards the Creator." Wojtyla maintains that since God is a personal being, He has certain rights and man has certain duties in respect to Him. "Man is just toward God the Creator when he recognizes the order of nature and conforms to it in his actions."[26] But even more, man is a *particeps Creatoris*, that is, he is a participant in the very creative work of God. Through the act of becoming a parent, spouses become participants in God's creation in a most incredible way; they become cocreators with God in the bringing forth of a new human person, of an immortal entity.

In *Evangelium Vitae*, John Paul II cites a portion of his *Letter to Families*:

> In affirming that the spouses, as parents, cooperate with God the Creator in conceiving and giving birth to a new human being, we are not speaking merely with reference to the laws of biology. Instead, we wish to emphasize that *God himself is present in human fatherhood and motherhood* quite differently than he is present in all other instances of begetting 'on earth.' Indeed, God alone is the source of that 'image and likeness' which is proper to the human being, as it was received at Creation. Begetting is the continuation of Creation (43; citing *Letter to Families*, 9).

As Wojtyla states, *"Man must reconcile himself to his natural greatness."*[27]

It is a matter of philosophic truth that God must be present at the conception of each and every human being, because only God can create an immortal soul; the human parents provide the matter necessary for human life and God provides the immortal soul. Scripture takes this insight further and through story after story stresses the loving attentiveness of God to each new soul. Perhaps this is best said in *Jeremiah* 1:5 "Before I formed you in the womb I knew you, and before you were born I consecrated you" (cited in *Evangelium Vitae*, 44). Spouses, then, are persons who cooperate with God in bringing forth new persons. As parents, they are to be symbols of God's unconditional love for those whom He has called into existence.

Tasks of the Family

Perhaps now it is easy to understand why John Paul II teaches that the family plays a key role in the economy of salvation. In his *Letter to Families*, he speaks of the family as "the first and most important path" on our way to Christ. He realizes that it is within the family that human persons are first schooled in virtue. In fact, he calls the family "the school of social virtues" (*Familiaris Consortio*, 42). He also speaks of it as "a school of deeper humanity" (*Familiaris Consortio*, 21), "a school of social living" (*Familiaris Consortio*, 13), and "a school of following Christ" (*Familiaris Consortio*, 39).

We must note that John Paul II not only speaks of the family as a school for the children but also as a school for the parents. As his says in the *Letter to Families*, "While [parents] are teachers of humanity for their own children, they learn humanity from them" (16). Indeed, it is through giving of themselves to each other and their children that spouses grow in virtue and holiness (*Familiaris Consortio*, 34).

In *Familiaris Consortio*, John Paul II identifies four tasks for the family:

1. forming a community of persons;
2. serving life;
3. participating in the development of society;
4. sharing in the life and mission of Christ (17).

Forming a Community of Persons

We have already spoken to some extent about how the family is a community of persons. Perhaps here it would be appropriate to speak somewhat of the role of women in the family, for women, as persons with what John Paul II calls a special "genius,"[28] make a unique contribution. While John Paul II clearly recognizes that women have the full range of abilities and talents as men, and while he promotes their right to access to a role in the public realm, he mourns that modern culture has tended to devalue the important, indeed irreplaceable and indispensable, work of wives and mothers in the home. The "genius" of women of which he speaks is a genius that is linked to the female capacity to bear children. He speaks of the love that a woman has for the child in her womb which gives rise to a special attitude "not only towards her own child, but every human being." He states,

> It is commonly thought that *women* are more capable than men of paying attention *to another person*, and that motherhood develops this predisposition even more. The man—even with all his sharing in parenthood—always remains "outside" the process of pregnancy and the baby's birth; in many ways he has to *learn* his own *'fatherhood' from the mother.*[29]

This passage reflects several of John Paul II's themes concerning women. In his *Letter to Women*, he identifies the special "genius" of women as being a readiness to engage in services of love (10). In the above passage he maintains that this readiness is rooted in the maternal nature of women and flows from the love they have for their own children extended to others. He also makes the interesting point that in many ways the man must learn fatherhood from the mother. Moreover, he speaks about how the burden of parenthood is greater for the mother and draws the conclusion that this creates a "special debt to the woman" and says "No program of 'equal rights' between women and man is valid unless it takes this fact fully into account." There he implies almost mischievously that equality between the parents weighs out in favor of the mother!

We recall that Pope John Paul II holds that the ultimate achievement for the human person, the human person's fulfillment, comes from being self-giving. Here we learn that parenthood, both motherhood and fatherhood, because of the instinctive love that parents have for their very needy children, is designed by nature to foster selflessness in the parents, and clearly selflessness is essential to the ability to be self-giving.

In his *Letter to Families*, John Paul II cites the words of the apostle Paul, "I bow my knees before the Father, from whom every fatherhood and motherhood is named 'that he may grant you to be strengthened with might through his Spirit in the inner man" (*Ephesians* 3:16). He then states, "The family is the first human setting in which is formed that 'inner man' of which the Apostle speaks. The growth of the inner man in strength and vigour is a gift of the Father and the Son in the Holy Spirit" (23). Karol Wojtyla's philosophic thought greatly emphasizes the "subjectivity" of the human person, the sense that the human person has of his own unique unrepeatability and of himself as a self-determining, responsible agent. The family is the first place where the human person begins to develop this sense of himself or herself. This development is essential to the full flowering of personhood.

Serving Life

The second task that John Paul II identifies for the family is "serving life." We have already spoken about the tremendous privilege and responsibility spouses have in being cocreators with God of a new human person. This in itself is an element of human dignity that is of inestimable value; as the opening line of *Humanae Vitae* states, "God entrusts to spouses the extremely important mission of transmitting human life" and all the responsibilities of parenthood that come with it.

In *Evangelium Vitae* John Paul II bemoans the fact that man has lost "sight of the mystery of God, [and] also the mystery of the world and the mystery of his own being" (21). He goes on to say that this loss of the sense of mystery has led to a *"practical materialism*, which breeds individualism, utilitarianism and hedonism" (23). Here we find the marvelous phrase "The values of *being* are replaced by those of *having*." The service of the family to life includes loving persons primarily and simply for the fact that they exist rather than for how useful they may be to us. It is only the natural love that arises in the family, supplemented by that appreciation of the supernatural destiny of all souls that will enable us to resist the forces of the culture of death.

The family by God's design is meant to be the "sanctuary of life." Our culture has earned the title "culture of death" precisely because the crimes against life in our society are often "carried out in the very heart of and with the complicity of the family" (*Evangelium Vitae*, 9). That is, it is because abortion is had by a mother (and often abetted by the father if only in his abandonment of the mother) and because assisted suicide is frequently performed in accord with the wishes of the family, that *Evangelium Vitae* calls ours a "culture of death."

Education in Human Sexuality

In the service of life, one of the primary tasks of the family is to teach children the truth about human sexuality and to prepare them well for marriage. The Vatican has issued several documents in recent years attempting to lay down guidelines for education in sexuality and in preparation for marriage. John Paul II insists that, in accord with the principle of subsidiarity, schools must respect the principle that parents are the first and foremost educators of their children and that all sex education must be education in chastity. Moreover, parents must be attentive to the three states of marriage preparation. Remote preparation takes place in the home as the child from a very young age observes how his or her parents interact. Proximate preparation takes place as young people learn about the various sacraments and vocations. Immediate preparation is that which takes place in the months and weeks prior to the wedding ceremony as the couple come to appreciate how their marital relationship must be lived in a Christian way. Given that so much dysfunctionality in our culture comes from divorced households, preparation for marriage assumes a very great importance, for intact households give children the stability and self-confidence they need to be leaders in solving the world's problems.

Participating in the Development of Society

The Christian way of life is a way that is open to life, not only to the life brought forth from the love of the parents but also to all human life. The family is the "first cell of society" (*Familiaris Consortio*, 42) and is the "school of the social virtues" (*Familiaris Consortio*, 44). The reach of the family is to be an extended one:

> Families . . . either singly or in association, can and should devote themselves to manifold social service activities, especially in favor of the poor, or at any rate for the benefit of all people and situations that cannot be reached by the public authorities' welfare organization (*Familiaris Consortio*, 69).

The family is called to a special "hospitality" for the needy; it is to have a "special concern for the hungry, the poor, the old, the sick, drug victims and those who have no family" (47).

The family is also called to work for the rights of the family. *Familiaris Consortio* presents a fairly lengthy "Charter of Family Rights" (46). In a day when many social and political forces are destroying the family, John Paul II finds it ever more imperative to implore families to fulfill the unique charisms of families and to work to form societies and governments that make this possible.

Sharing in the Life and Mission of Christ

The fourth task belongs to the family in its dimension as the Domestic Church. It is as a community of love that the family participates in the prophetic, priestly, and kingly mission of Christ (*Familiaris Consortio*, 50).

It fulfills its participation in the prophetic mission by being a school of evangelization; the parents are to grow in their knowledge of their faith, they are to catechize their children in the faith, and the family is to be "animated in its own inner life by missionary zeal" for those who do not live by the gospel (*Familiaris Consortio*, 54).

The family participates in the priestly mission of Christ by aiding all its members in responding to the universal call to sanctity

(*Familiaris Consortio*, 56). Families are to develop a reverence for the Eucharist, to make ample use of the sacrament of reconciliation and to participate in family prayer. In his comments on prayer in his *Letter to Families* Pope John Paul II returns to his concern for the development of the inner person. He states, "It is significant that in and through prayer, man comes to discover in a very simple and yet profound way his own subjectivity: in prayer the human 'I' more easily perceives the depth of what it means to be a person. This is also true of the family, which is not only the basic 'cell' of society, but also possesses a particular subjectivity of its own" (4). This talk of a "particular subjectivity" of the family achieved through prayer is fascinating; John Paul II is saying that the family gets a sense of its own identity, its own uniqueness, its own blessedness by God through family prayer. As the individual person gets a sense that he or she is individually beloved by God and has a special unique calling, so too does the family as a unit get that sense.

As we can see, John Paul II's philosophy and his understanding of the family stem from and continually return to his understanding of the human person. Ultimately, achieving full personhood means becoming Christ-like, for "Christ reveals man to himself." It is because it is a community of persons, a community of love and life, that the family is a "school of following Christ."

John Paul II recognizes this as an age when there is a near obsession with the value of the individual and of individual rights, and an age when those rights are depicted as even extending to the mastery over life and death. He has judged that the proper antidote to this situation is an emphasis on the dignity of the human person as made in the image and likeness of God, on the dignity of marriage as a symbol of the relationship of Christ and His Church, and on the dignity of the human family as the image of the Holy Trinity and Holy Family. It may be impossible to overstate the importance of these themes to his pontificate.

NOTES

[1] *Aristotle's Nicomachean Ethics* trans. by Hippocrates G. Apostle (Peripatetic Press, 1984).

[2] "The Social Contract" in the *The Essential Rousseau* trans. by Lowell Blair, (Mentor, 1974), p. 8.

[3] *Ibid*, p. 9.

[4] For an excellent brief survey of how and when this happened see Mary Ann Glendon, "The Family and Society: International Organizations and the Defense of the Family," in *La Famiglia: Dono e Impegno Speranza dell'Umanita: Atti del Congresso Internazionale* (Libreria Editrice Vaticana, 1998) pp. 30–47.

[5] For an excellent analysis of the dangers of "rights" language, see Mary Ann Glendon, *Rights Talk: The Impoverishment of Political Discourse* (The Free Press, 1991).

[6] *Ibid*, p. 39.

[7] I shall refer to Pope John Paul II frequently as Karol Wojtyla to emphasize that his philosophical views were developed as a professional philosopher prior to his pontificate.

[8] See also his "Thomistic Personalism" in Karol Wojtyla's *Person and Community: Selected Essays* trans. by Theresa Sandok, OSM (Peter Lang, 1993), pp. 165–75.

[9] Among other essays, see "The Problem of the Separation of Experience from the Act in Ethics," in *Person and Community: Selected Essays*, pp. 23–44.

[10] For passages from papal writings, I am using the approved Vatican translation used in nearly every published edition.

[11] John Paul II also observes that there is a curious denial of freedom side by side with the excessive exaltation of freedom, based on a view that all of reality is determined (*Veritatis Splendor*, 33).

[12] See also, for instance, *Evangelium Vitae*, 19.

[13] See his "The Person: Subject and Community," in *Person and Community*, pp. 219–261.

[14] His Holiness John Paul II, *Crossing the Threshold of Hope*, (Alfred A. Knopf, 1994), 201.

[15] See his "The Problem of Experience in Ethics," in *Person and Community*, pp. 107–27.

[16] See his "Human Nature as the Basis of Ethical Formulation," in *Person and Community*, pp. 95–100.

[17] E.g., *Love and Responsibility*, pp. 28, 37, 41, *Crossing the Threshold of Hope*, p. 201.

[18] Karol Wojtyla, *Love and Responsibility*, (Ignatius Press, rpt. 1993), pp. 26–7.

[19] *Ibid*, p. 27

[20] *Crossing the Threshold of Hope*, p. 201.

[21] *Love and Responsibility*, p. 41.

[22] *Ibid*, p. 41.

[23] *Ibid*, p. 228.

[24] *Ibid*, p. 230.

[25] *Ibid*, p. 236.

[26] *Ibid*, p. 246.

[27] *Ibid*, p. 236.

[28] *Letter to Women*, 10.

[29] *On the Dignity and Vocation of Women*, 18.

CHAPTER SEVEN

John Paul II and Economics

The Pope and the Free Economy

Robert A. Sirico

I. Introduction

The moral test of any social or governmental policy is whether it is consistent with a rigorous concern for the life, liberty, and dignity of the human person, a right that each person has been given by God. Along with that dignity, God gives to each of us a rightful expectation that our liberties be respected and that justice be pursued on our behalf, so that we may work for our own personal and familial fulfillment as a means for achieving the common good as well as our spiritual salvation. It is the goal of Catholic social teaching, especially under the pontificate of John Paul II, to articulate this moral vision of the free and virtuous society.

In his encyclicals touching on economic systems, the pope has made remarkable contributions to religious thought concerning public policy and free economic systems. In what follows, I will not attempt to present the fullness of his very complex, subtle, and developing thought on these matters. Rather I intend to provide a brief overview of a specific and especially notable dimension of the pope's social teaching, namely its intersection with a tradition of classically liberal economic ideas. I will elaborate on the implications of the liberal tradition for the social order and draw connections between papal social teaching and market economics generally.[1] My commentary will not and cannot be restricted to economic subjects, since, in the pope's mind, economics impacts a whole range of human problems linked with the issue of the dignity of the human person.

II. Economic Systems

It would be an error to characterize the thought of the pope by exclusive reference to a system of economics we observe at work in the world today. Instead, the pope is calling for a wholly different approach that rises above the materialism of Western capitalism, the bureaucratization of European welfare states, and the mercantilist tendencies of Latin American economies. It would also be incorrect to associate the pope's thought with the calls for a "third way" between laissez-faire and state planning. The pope writes,

> The Church's social doctrine is not a 'third way' between liberal capitalism and Marxist collectivism, nor even a possible alternative to other solutions less radically opposed to one another: rather, it constitutes a category of its own. Nor is it an ideology, but rather the accurate formulation of the results of a careful reflection on the complex realities of human existence, in society and in the international order, in the light of faith and of the Church's tradition. Its main aim is to interpret these realities, determining their conformity with or divergence from the lines of the Gospel teaching on man and his vocation, a vocation which is at once earthly and transcendent; its aim is thus to guide Christian behavior. It therefore belongs to the field, not of ideology, but of theology and particularly of moral theology.[2]

The pope further writes, "the Church has no models to present; models that are real and truly effective can only arise within the framework of different historical situations, through the efforts of all those who responsibly confront concrete problems in all their social, economic, political and cultural aspects, as these interact with one another."[3]

Nonetheless, it remains true that this pope's major contributions to social thought are inspired by the recognition of the profound failures of socialism, the key social-political doctrine of the twentieth century, which collapsed into rubble with the fall of the Soviet Union and its satellites in Eastern Europe. "The fundamental error of socialism," writes the pope, "is anthropological in nature."

> Socialism considers the individual person simply as an element, a molecule within the social organism, so that the good of the individual is completely subordinated to the functioning of the socioeconomic mechanism. Socialism likewise maintains that the good of the individual can be realized without reference to his free choice, to the unique and exclusive responsibility which he exercises in the face of good or evil. Man is thus reduced to a series of social relationships, and the concept of the person as the autonomous subject of moral decision disappears, the very subject whose decisions build the social order. From this mistaken conception of the person there arise both a distortion of law, which defines the sphere of the exercise of freedom, and an opposition to private property. A person who is deprived of something he can call "his own," and of the possibility of earning a living through his own initiative, comes to depend on the social machine and on those who control it. This makes it much more difficult for him to recognize his dignity as a person, and hinders progress towards the building up of an authentic human community.[4]

The pope rightly rejects the politically charged term "capitalism"; the phrase means too many things to too many people, as Rocco Buttiglione has pointed out.[5] Instead, and with some reluctance, he embraces the phrases "free economy" and "business economy." "The modern business economy has positive aspects," he writes.

> Its basis is human freedom exercised in the economic field, just as it is exercised in many other fields. Economic activity is indeed but one sector in a great variety of human activities, and like every other sector, it includes the right to freedom, as well as the duty of making responsible use of freedom. But it is important to note that there are specific differences between the trends of modern society and those of the past, even the recent past. Whereas at one time the decisive factor of production was the land, and later capital—understood as a total complex of the instruments of production—today the decisive factor is increasingly the person, that is, one's knowl-

edge, especially one's scientific knowledge, one's capacity for interrelated and compact organization, as well as one's ability to perceive the needs of others and to satisfy them.[6]

Again, "it would appear that, on the level of individual nations and of international relations, the free market is the most efficient instrument for utilizing resources and effectively responding to needs."[7]

Within the free market economy, however, a juridical setting is needed to protect the requisite institutions of property, exchange, entrepreneurship, and the rule of law. Secular attempts to disregard these essential institutions, especially during this century, possibly the most secular since time has begun, have resulted in material deprivation and human impoverishment. It is not only through sentiment, but also through careful analysis, that political, sociological, and economic insights can be gained and applied to real-world situations. To be sure, religious and spiritual concerns are primary to the pope's analysis. At the same time, as the pope believes, we disregard the insights of economic science and history only at our peril. The good intentions of political ideas must always be checked by a reasonable understanding of the results of ideas.

III. Exchange, Association, and Enterprise

The aim of economic policy should be to expand the production and availability of goods and services, to increase the quality of life for individuals and the community, and to do so in a manner consistent with the rights of individuals and the common good. These goals are not incongruous. Respect for human liberty and the increase in the quality of life are both features of the exchange economy. In this form of economy, people are left free to improve their lot through cooperative efforts.

Economic theory teaches that the institution of economic exchange is the primary means of increasing overall prosperity. When an economic exchange takes place, each person trades something subjectively regarded as having lower value for something subjectively regarded as having higher value. If two people voluntarily trade eggs and milk, for example, each is made better off than before, else the trade would not have occurred. If everyone in the economy is free to perform these types of exchanges, and to plan for exchanges in the future, a vast network of human cooperation arises to form a market. To have a market requires free persons who come to a meeting of minds.[8] The market is a constantly changing and developing process because people's values change, as does the availability of resources.

The introduction of money into this exchange process does not change the essential cooperative nature of the market. Money makes it possible for the parties in the economy to have a common unit of value, further facilitating the opportunities for trade as well as efficiency. In a money economy, the unit of exchange becomes the common measure by which people can communicate with each other about their respective talents and needs.

Money's significance as the most economically desirable commodity is precisely in its use as a means of exchange. The creation of a network of human cooperation that permits rising prosperity is impossible to achieve without economic exchange. Even with exchange, third-party interruption in the market puts barriers between cooperation that can limit its abilities to make possible the improvement of the human condition.

As much as possible, then, freedom and "right of association"[9] should be permitted so that people can seek out others who desire to engage in voluntary cooperation and exchange. Through this kind of contact, the market process allows people the opportunity to realize material fulfillment; and by finding ways to agree on exchange, the market process increases contact and understanding between people and therefore the sense of community, even internationally. The more diverse the cultural values of the people, the more freedom of association through exchange becomes an essential means of bringing people together and making their well-being dependent on each others' talents and willingness to trade.

This is why the pope took special mention of the political and economic institutions in the United States, where such freedoms are a primary element of the political culture and the driving force behind economic life, during his 1987 visit:

> Among the many admirable values of this nation there is one that stands out in particular. It is freedom. The concept of freedom is part of the very fabric of this nation as a political community of free people. Freedom is a great gift, a great blessing of God.

From the beginning of America, freedom was directed to forming a well-ordered society and to promoting its peaceful life. Freedom was channeled to the fullness of human life, to the preservation of human dignity, and to the safeguarding of all human rights. An experience of ordered freedom is truly a part of the cherished history of this land. This is the freedom that America is called to live and guard and to transmit. She is called to exercise it in such a way that it will also benefit the cause of freedom in other nations and among other peoples.[10]

The market economy and its requisite institutions are not only highly desirable in the market for goods and services. In the labor sector, where people offer their talents to others in return for the payment of wages and salaries, free exchange and free association are also crucial components of healthy community. All people are called to work for their own well being as well as society as a whole. As the pope writes, "The church's teaching has always expressed the strong and deep conviction that man's work concerns not only the economy but also, and especially, personal values. The economic system itself and the production process benefit precisely when these personal values are fully respected. In the mind of St. Thomas Aquinas, this is the principal reason in favor of private ownership of the means of production."[11]

This work can take many forms, and its ultimate value is obtained when it is offered to the glory of God under His value system, regardless of remuneration. In a free economy, however, wages and salaries reflect the contribution an individual worker makes to the community of workers in the business firm and to the overall wealth of society. The freedom of employees to change jobs, and the freedom of employers to make unhampered and enforceable contracts with workers, insures that each individual can find opportunity for work. "As a person," the pope writes, "man is therefore the subject of work. As a person he works, he performs various actions belonging to the work process; independently of their objective content, these actions must all serve to realize his humanity, to fulfill the calling to be a person that is his by reason of his very humanity."[12]

Market competition for labor works to make sure that workers are paid a wage that corresponds to their talents and contributions. A thriving exchange economy for labor requires more than a commitment to equality, for even in the most homogeneous society, people are radically different from each other, a reflection of the diversity of God's creation. No two members of society will have identical interests and talents. An economic system should make it possible for everyone who so wishes to participate in the common task of building prosperity. Fortunately, the cooperative nature of the market economy makes this possible so long as there are no unnecessary barriers to entering existing particular markets for goods, services and labor. And yet the labor market can easily be discoordinated through an ill-advised policy of making all wages and salaries the same (labor equality or parity), through inhibiting the free movement of laborers from one firm to another, or through seeking equality of outcome rather than equality of rules. The result of such policies is a displacement of human resources, a limiting of opportunities, and a decline in overall standards of living.

Employees should be treated with the dignity and respect to which their nature as human beings entitles them. This obligation should be considered binding because it grows out of Christ's commandment to love our neighbor. In addition, the same Gospel that would have workers treated with respect also binds employees to treat their employers with respect for their inherent dignity. In a free market, the relation between the two is characterized by both parties coming together on terms of common agreement. Their contracts should be honest and their commitments to each other should be kept. As *Proverbs* says, "Wealth obtained by fraud dwindles, but the one who gathers by labor increases it" (13:11). The well-being of society depends on workers not to mislead employers, for workers have a special obligation to be conscious of the risks employers undertake in their roles as entrepreneurs.

An unfortunate feature of much modern religious thought on economics is its characteristic lack of appreciation of the entrepreneurial function. Because the world is not static, and people's needs and values are constantly changing, an economic system requires some means of adjustment. The person who invests himself or herself, and the resources he or she owns, is choosing to assist the economy by keeping up with changes and serving others in the process. The entrepreneur must constantly be aware of the needs of others, sometimes even before others have become conscious of those needs, and apply resources to see that they are met. He or she must have an alertness and innovativeness of mind. To be sure, entrepreneurs can never be certain that a particular investment or project will ultimately work out. But he takes a risk, and even chooses to meet a payroll, before he is certain of what the future holds. Sometimes his assessment of the future turns out well, and sometimes it does not. In either case, the entrepreneur's courage to face an uncertain future is a commendable virtue and a worthy calling.

It is a triumphant contribution of John Paul II to have introduced the "right of economic initiative" into the vocabulary of religious thinkers. "It should be noted," writes the pope, "that in today's world, among other rights, the right of economic initiative is often suppressed."

> Yet it is a right which is important not only for the individual but also for the common good. Experience shows us that the denial of this right, or its limitation in the name of an alleged "equality" of everyone in society, diminishes, or in practice absolutely destroys the spirit of initiative, that is to say the creative subjectivity of the citizen. As a consequence, there arises, not so much a true equality as a "leveling down." In the place of creative initiative there appears passivity, dependence and submission to the bureaucratic apparatus which, as the only 'ordering' and 'decision-making' body if not also the 'owner' of the entire totality of goods and the means of production, puts everyone in a position of almost absolute dependence, which is similar to the traditional dependence of the worker-proletarian in capitalism. This provokes a sense of frustration or desperation and predisposes people to opt out of national life, impelling many to emigrate and also [bringing about] a form of "psychological emigration."[13]

When entrepreneurs are successful, they advance the cause of growing prosperity by providing the goods and services that people need and want. They discover new ways of undertaking old tasks; they rediscover old ways to undertake new tasks. They find more efficient ways of producing, which is another way of saying that they demonstrate to us ways that God's resources can be put to use more wisely. By providing jobs, moreover, they do so in a way that is respectful of human dignity. "Man's principal resource is man himself," the pope writes. "His intelligence enables him to discover the earth's productive potential and the many different ways in which human needs can be satisfied. It is his disciplined work in close collaboration with others that makes possible the creation of ever more extensive working communities which can be relied upon to transform man's natural and human environments."[14]

Planned economies that have lacked an appreciation for the economic innovator and denied the innovator a chance to act out his vocation have stagnated because they failed to keep up with changes in public values and create new technologies. Market economies that provide opportunities and rewards for entrepreneurs, as well as cultures that afford them appreciation and respect, generate wider prosperity.

The entrepreneurial function is often associated with high profits. Yet in the market, the only way that high profits can come about is when a seller provides products or services at fair prices that the public purchases. "When a firm makes a profit," the pope writes, "this means that productive factors have been properly employed and corresponding human needs have been duly satisfied."[15] That in no way suggests that the products the public chooses are the best ones or are the ones virtue would most recommend; it is the task of religious leaders, not economic institutions, to direct consumer tastes towards good ends. It is only to say that entrepreneurs successfully profit only to the extent they serve the public.

The entrepreneur is an obvious example of a person who uses his creative talents, given to him by the Ultimate Creator, to the good of others. Others in the market-based division of labor should also exercise the virtues of enterprise and creativity in as many ways as possible. Workers can discover better ways to accomplish tasks, and owners and employers are wise to be open to their suggestions. The freedom to change jobs and locations also provides institutional assurance that those with new ideas and new talents can discover the best way to put them toward the service of others.

The pope writes:

> A person who produces something other than for his own use generally does so in order that others may use it after they have paid a just price, mutually agreed upon through free bargaining. It is precisely the ability to foresee both the needs of others and the combinations of productive factors most adapted to satisfying those needs that constitutes another important source of wealth in modern society. Besides, many goods cannot be adequately produced through the work of an isolated individual; they require the cooperation of many people in working towards a common goal. Organizing such a productive effort, planning its duration in time, making sure

that it corresponds in a positive way to the demands which it must satisfy, and taking the necessary risks—all this too is a source of wealth in today's society. In this way, the role of disciplined and creative human work and, as an essential part of that work, initiative and entrepreneurial ability becomes increasingly evident and decisive.[16]

The freedom of enterprise is the best institutional setting for the lessons of the Parable of the Talents to be realized (*Matthew* 25: 14–30). In that parable, Christ tells the story of three men who are given three unequal talents. Two men invest their talents and double their value. They receive praise and added trust and responsibility. The third buries his talent and is scorned as a result. The lesson points to personal development as a spiritual virtue and to its economic effect of growing wealth as being praiseworthy as well.

IV. Ownership and Stewardship

The central aim of economic policy—increasing the quality of life for individuals and the community in a manner consistent with the dignity of persons—is impossible unless the economy rests on a foundation of privately owned property. With the Psalmist, we should affirm that "the earth is the Lord's, and all it contains, the world, and those who dwell in it" (24:1), and as stewards of that property, we must use it according to God's laws and values. "The earth," the pope writes,

> by reason of its fruitfulness and its capacity to satisfy human needs, is God's first gift for the sustenance of human life. But the earth does not yield its fruits without a particular human response to God's gift, that is to say, without work. It is through work that we, using our intelligence and exercising our freedom, succeed in dominating the earth and making it a fitting home. In this way, one makes part of the earth one's own, precisely the part which one has acquired through work; this is the origin of individual property. Obviously, one also has the responsibility not to hinder others from having their own part of God's gift; indeed, one must cooperate with others so that together all can dominate the earth.[17]

Property should not become a source of conflict, but rather be used to improve the human condition. As the pope writes:

> It is obvious that when we speak of opposition between labor and capital, we are not dealing only with abstract concepts or 'impersonal forces' operating in economic production. Behind both concepts there are people, living, actual people: On the one side are those who do the work without being the owners of the means of production, and on the other side those who act as entrepreneurs and who own these means or represent the owner. Thus the issue of ownership or property enters from the beginning into the whole of this difficult historical process.[18]

Many societies have experimented with the idea of collective ownership, but have discovered that the entire concept is a misnomer. All property must be owned by someone or something, so when we speak of collective ownership, we are really talking about ownership by the state or government. Not the least problem with that concept is that it concentrates power and influence too heavily in one sector. Privately held property, on the other hand, tends to diffuse power and influence throughout society.

"In the church's teaching," writes the pope, "ownership has never been understood in a way that could constitute grounds for social conflict in labor."

> [P]roperty is acquired first of all through work in order that it may serve work. This concerns in a special way ownership of the means of production. Isolating these means as a separate property in order to set it up in the form of "capital" in opposition to "labor"—and even to practice exploitation of labor—is—contrary to the very nature of these means and their possession. They cannot be possessed against labor, they cannot even be possessed for possession's sake, because the only legitimate title to their possession—whether in the form of private ownership or in the form of public or collective ownership—is that they should serve labor and thus by serving labor that they should make possible the achievement of the first principle of this order, namely the universal destination of goods and the right to common use of them.[19]

The incentive structure too is different under privately held, as versus collectively held, property. When property is in private hands, it must be cared for and used to serve others. With a market process for private property, resources will flow in the direction of people who can care for it best and use it to serve others. On the other hand, publicly owned property can easily fall into disrepair because no one in particular is responsible for its upkeep and use.[20]

The proper distribution of private property generates controversy because there are no possible human circumstances under which it can be perfectly equal. Nor should that be the goal in a humane society. Rather, it should be our primary concern that those who own and acquire property have done so justly, for as the *Proverbs* tells us, "ill-gotten gains do not profit, but righteousness delivers from death" (10:2). Property should be owned by virtue of free contract and voluntarism, not through confiscation, force, or fraud. If we can be certain that titles to property—whether those assets are in money, property, or businesses—are justly acquired, the demands of formal justice are therefore satisfied without reference to equality in the distribution of that property.

The moral injunction against theft—common to most all religions—implies a moral injunction against violating the established barriers of property ownership, and, logically, the moral legitimacy of property ownership to begin with. The most bitter and even bloody struggles in world history have come about because of a failure of some, whether private criminals or public magistrates, to respect the biblical commandment against theft (*Exodus* 20:15). A similar struggle ensues when society's essential resources are controlled exclusively by public hands, which leads to tragedies of its own sort. To reiterate, social peace and cooperation are not advanced through struggles over resources but rather through trade and exchange. That requires that the boundaries of property be well defined and well respected.

It is commonplace, even in market economies, for certain goods and services to be owned and controlled collectively, that is, by the state. Often, however, the efficient provision of these goods and services can be increased when they are owned by people who have stronger stake in proper and wise use of the resources. The pope's reasoning therefore implies that it may be a worthy idea to consider ways to put increasing amounts of social resources in the private economy precisely so that it can better serve the public. Industrialized nations have successfully experimented with privatizing indus-tries—and even placing in private hands some goods and services usually thought to be best kept outside of the market process.

V. Prices and Profits

Every society must have a guide for allocating its resources because the unlimited nature of human wants always outpaces the scarce resources required to meet them. Even economies where most or all property is held in private hands must have a tool for making sure those resources are used in ways that the community finds most valuable. It is not automatically clear which of the many possibilities of resource use are the best. We must have some way of knowing whether water is best used for drinking, bathing, or irrigation, or if iron ore is best used making cars or building tractors. The same is true for all social resources. Even the resource of time, which is also scarce, requires some tool for efficient allocation.

The best guide for wise allocation is the network of prices which arises naturally from the buying and selling by acting individuals. Here the laws of economics come into play. When the price of a good is lower, it signals abundance and people can buy more of it. When it is higher, it signals a relatively higher level of scarcity, and people must economize their use of the good. Through the price system, which is constantly in flux, consumers know how much of a good they can purchase and use, and producers know how much of a good they can produce and sell. Prices serve as more than signals for consumption and production; they also allow us to consider costs. They help us determine whether a good or service is being wasted and therefore should not be in production, or if it is highly desired and therefore its production should be increased.

The idea of profit is simply the name that accounting and bookkeeping attaches to the condition of income outpacing costs. When a company is making a profit, it is given a signal that it is performing its tasks properly in the eyes of the public. But when it makes a loss, the price system is informing the managers and owners that they need to turn to other pursuits so that social resources are not wasted. The social obligations of the business do not stop there; business must deal honestly, keep contracts, serve the community in the broadest sense, and be attentive to the moral dimension of the investment process. Nonetheless, the signaling devices of profit and loss serve an irreplaceable economic function.

The pope writes forthrightly:

> The Church acknowledges the legitimate role of profit as an indication that a business is functioning well. When a firm makes a profit, this means that productive factors have been properly employed and corresponding human needs have been duly satisfied. But profitability is not the only indicator of a firm's condition. . . . Profit is a regulator of the life of a business, but it is not the only one; other human and moral factors must also be considered which, in the long term, are at least equally important for the life of a business.[21]

Often, we hear complaints about "excess" profits, but in a market economy even these serve an essential function. They signal other entrepreneurs that the public is demanding more of a particular good or service than is being produced at some price. When businessmen notice the high profits of others, new investors and creators enter the market to meet the demand. It is precisely this inflow and outflow of investors and producers in various markets that makes high profits a possibility. But the competitive bidding for resources and public attention means no one can find himself in an automatically profitable position. This process also sets conditions for increasingly efficient modes of production.

From a moral point of view, we cannot say whether the "profit motive" is always a good motive. Indeed, a person motivated by the pursuit of profit alone may be seeking a material gain to the exclusion of his primary duty to family, community, and God. Yet is it not the "motive" to make profits which makes the existence of prices, profits, and loss essential for any just economy; it is their function as signals to production and consumption that makes prices, profits, and losses essential to wise resource use. In absence of prices, there is literally no way to tell if resources are serving the public or are being wasted. With prices determined by market conditions, we have the ability to calculate rationally, and information about scarcities is made always available.

The benefits of the price system are innumerable. Consumers rely on prices every day to make decisions about activities they take for granted. The price system allows businessmen to think far into the future. It allows the public to partake in the ownership of companies through an active market for capital and to try a hand at entrepreneurship. It grants to everybody the incentive to work and better themselves in the pursuit of living holy lives. But mostly, the price system protects God's world from being abused through waste and ignorance, as has happened wherever prices are not allowed to float freely.

A religious leader may call on every businessman to give up his profits so that the businessman may repair his soul. Whether that is sound advice is to be determined by the individual affected. What this religious leader cannot and should not do is call for an economic system without profits, papal teaching implies, for in doing so he would eliminate the best way people have of being good stewards and wisely using God's resources.

When the price system is fixed or distorted through various third party interventions—whether price control, inflation,[22] or excessive regulation—the production that it governs similarly becomes distorted. When the prices of goods are held at some level by the force of law, producers can no longer recover costs in production and shortages inevitably ensue. Economic reasoning suggests that when wages, which reflect a price for labor, are fixed at a high level, they shut the most marginal workers out from the division of society's essential tasks. When inflation makes the price system unreliable, which is a form of tampering with weights and measures (*Leviticus* 19:35–36), it causes grave miscalculations, removes the reason to save and invest in future economic growth, and makes the cost of living rise for everyone.

VI. Charity and Welfare

The welfare of the vulnerable members of society should be a central concern of any society. Some members of society will always require the care of others, including children and the aged. We have an absolute moral obligation that these people be watched over, cared for, and loved.

The major question for social policy is not whether these individuals should be taken care of, but how should people in their capacities as parents and relatives be responsible? Or should they be relieved of that responsibility through social insurance schemes and laws that hand over to bureaucracies the role of primary caretaker? The best insurance of the well-being of the vulnerable is the intact family unit, because the family knows their needs best. The second option, giving responsibility away, has grave consequences for the family, for it tells those whom Christ commanded to love others that they no longer need to provide care because others will do so (*Luke* 10:33–37). The system of old-age insurance in no way relieves the obligation to care for one's parents in old age, but it sets up incentives that are more likely to tempt people to forget their obligations.

The pope has heavily criticized the inhumane aspects of the welfare state with these sentences:

> In recent years the range of such intervention has vastly expanded, to the point of creating a new type of state, the so-called "Welfare State." This has happened in some countries in order to respond better to many needs and demands, by remedying forms of poverty and deprivation unworthy of the human person. However, excesses and abuses, especially in recent years, have provoked very harsh criticisms of the Welfare State, dubbed the "Social Assistance State." Malfunctions and defects in the Social Assistance State are the result of an inadequate understanding of the tasks proper to the State. Here again the principle of subsidiarity must be respected: a community of a higher order should not interfere in the internal life of a community of a lower order, depriving the latter of its functions, but rather should support it in case of need and help to coordinate its activity with the activities of the rest of society, always with a view to the common good.[23]

When the state becomes the primary caretaker of children through well-intentioned laws designed to enhance their welfare, it tragically reduces the responsibility of parents and the value of children to parents. A particular problem occurs when the state subsidizes behavior that should be discouraged if we want to retain strong families. An example is out-of-wedlock births, which have dramatically increased anywhere the state has chosen to give an excess of money to women in this position. When the state intervenes in this manner it sends a signal to fathers that it is not necessary for them to stay in their roles as husbands and fathers, resulting in an increase of single parents (usually female).

Also among the vulnerable in any society are the poor, whether in our own families and communities or in society at large. When this issue is usually discussed, the issue of inequality of wealth inevitably arises. But it is not the issue of inequality of wealth that should concern us primarily; for inequality can also be reduced by making everyone equally poor. The issue is poverty itself and the human suffering that accompanies it, and, more foundationally, the rights that are violated along with the denial of economic opportunity and other rights of the poor. The pope writes,

> The denial or the limitation of human rights as for example the right to religious freedom, the right to share in the building of society, the freedom to organize and to form unions, or to take initiatives in economic matters—do these not impoverish the human person as much as, if not more than, the deprivation of material goods? And is development which does not take into account the full affirmation of these rights really development on the human level?[24]

The best solution to poverty is a growing economy. It provides jobs, better pay, better working conditions, more opportunities, and a chance for everyone to achieve. A growing economy requires that the market economy be allowed to function without the kind of excessive interruption and intervention that diminishes overall wealth. There are cases when even a growing economy, and all its requisite institutions, leave some out. The causes can be manifold, including personal misfortune or lack of initiative (In *2 Thessalonians* 3:10, St. Paul identifies this latter situation). A note of caution, however: so long as trade is voluntary, the state remains limited, and people can freely contract with each other, the cause of poverty cannot be the wealth of others as Marxian political philosophy would have us believe. That is why the temptation toward mere redistributionism in the name of charity should be entirely avoided. No benefit accrues from this policy to anyone but the radical egalitarian, whose impulses should not be allowed to drive public policy in a good and just society. We should strive to always make the pie expand rather than fight over the various ways in which the pie can be sliced up.

In thinking about ways to help the poor, we must consider the costs and benefits of various strategies. If we turn to the government, particular dangers arise. Government policies can create impersonal forces with which the poor will be forced to deal, which can be demeaning. In addition, bureaucracies have a tendency to expand their own payrolls rather than their ability to serve others. They can take a greater and greater share of private wealth, instead of staying within fiscal constraints. The benefits of aid to a specific group might be outweighed by indirect and longer term costs to the whole community.

State bureaucracies have illustrated a lack of ability to fully understand the nature of the problem of poverty. The targeting of assistance within the context of bureaucracy tends toward imprecision. Public agencies cannot make the necessary distinctions between legitimate need and illegitimate demands, and they tend to impose heavy burdens of debt on future generations, which are best avoided.

John Paul explains:

> By intervening directly and depriving society of its responsibility, the Social Assistance State leads to a loss of human energies and an inordinate increase of public agencies, which are dominated more by bureaucratic ways of thinking than by concern for serving their clients, and which are accompanied by an enormous increase in spending. In fact, it would appear that needs are best understood and satisfied by people who are closest to them and who act as neighbors to those in need. It should be added that certain kinds of demands often call for a response which is not simply material but which is capable of perceiving the deeper human need. One thinks of the condition of refugees, immigrants, the elderly, the sick, and all those in circumstances which call for assistance, such as drug abusers: all these people can be helped effectively only by those who offer them genuine fraternal support, in addition to the necessary care.[25]

Even the worker in the bureaucracy himself is given attention by the pope:

> [Dignity] is extinguished within him in a system of excessive bureaucratic centralization, which makes the worker feel that he is just a cog in a huge machine moved from above, that he is for more reasons than one a mere production instrument rather than a true subject of work with an initiative of his own. The church's teaching has always expressed the strong and deep conviction that man's work concerns not only the economy but also, and especially, personal values.[26]

Long-term poverty is more than a condition of lacking material goods; it is a condition that involves deeper and more structural problems that require personal attention. This kind of attention is best given by individuals, families, and churches rather than by agents of the state, which have often proven not to be the friend of the poor but rather their oppressor. That is why the assertion of rights—to a job, to health care, to a good living—is such serious business. Special care should be taken to prevent open conflicts between rights. For example, a right to a job implicitly requires the obligation on the part of those in a position to hire to act in a way that violates the potential employer's claim to liberty. The idea of an absolute material entitlement, provided by force or threat of force, has no basis in Holy Scripture.

Jesus commands his followers to be charitable. This must be exercised in accordance with His will, and nowhere does He suggest this obligation can be passed on to public employees. Neither can the obligation be discharged by lobbying the government to take on new social welfare functions. Although it may tempt some, the existence of the welfare state and various forms of social regulation in no way fulfills Christ's commandment to care for the poor. Indeed, forms of charity that keep people in an unnecessary dependency relationship to the state are actually doing more harm than good. In this case, a person following the Gospel of Christ might have an obligation to speak out against the system or program that is the source of the problem.

The most charitable societies in the world have been the wealthiest, and the richest societies have also been the most free. When people have more disposable income, they can contribute more to charitable causes. Only a free economy can generate this kind of wealth, and it requires humane virtues, not selfishness, to give of oneself regardless of economic conditions. Prosperity permits people to spend more time in leisure rather than work, which allows them to spend more time volunteering for community activities and service to the poor. Only a free economy allows for growing levels of voluntary leisure time to make this possible. It is these facts that have led free societies to be the most attentive to the needs of the most vulnerable.

We should remember that even the most competent helper of the poor does not discharge his or her whole duty to God because the poor are made better off. The option for the poor is not the whole of the Gospel, and may never be construed as a legal preference for one class over another (*Leviticus* 19:15). In understanding assertions regarding the supposed inherent moral superiority of one class, we must remember the call to universal salvation issued by the same Gospel. As religious men and women, love and service of God should always be our primary focus, and the obligation to others follows from that. When charity and concern for others become secularized and taken over by the state, they thereby becomes less of an instrument in the service of God.

VII. Subsidiarity and Solidarity

The whole of society is made of spheres of sovereignty, which are both distinct and intertwined. The state is distinct from society, society from locality, locality from community, community from church, church from family, and family from individual. Each is essential and each has a function to fulfill. The function is best fulfilled by staying within its own domain as much as possible. For example, we should not want the state to assume the task of facilitating religious conversion or spiritual renewal, for that is the task of the Church. Correspondingly, we should not want the Church to assume the task of secular law enforcement, for that would represent an equal corruption of proper purpose.

We do well to consider, then, which social functions are best addressed by which sphere and to establish protections for that domain. This is not to say that the spheres cannot overlap. Business, for example, is the place for enterprise, but a family business can be among the most efficient. The community can engage in charitable work that complements the work of the Church. But we err if we forget that each institution has a primary function often exclusive of others.

The primary purpose of the state is the enforcement of the rule of law and the administration of justice. With regard to other social and individual human problems, we should not regard the government as the problem solver of first resort. Establishing that a moral obligation exists—to help the poor for example—does not also establish that government should be charged with fulfilling that obligation. Allowing for the encroachment of one function on another should be carefully thought out, but a special danger exists when the state is made to interfere with functions that are not its own. Power tends to corrupt precisely because the state has a legal monopoly in its use of coercion.

Just as the social functions should be distinguished among institutions, the principle of subsidiarity must be brought to bear for the common good of the community. This principle says that social issues are best addressed by those closest to the problem, and that higher orders should be enlisted only in cases of obvious failure. The care of the aged and poor, for example, is best left to the lower order of the family, church, and community, and not the higher orders of the nation and state. Subsidiarity also warns the higher orders against intervening unnecessarily in the affairs of the lower order.

"The principle of subsidiarity must be respected," the pope insists.

A community of a higher order should not interfere in the internal life of a community of a lower order, depriving the latter of its functions, but rather should support it in case of need and help to coordinate its activity with the activities of the rest of society, always with a view to the common good.[27]

Moreover, "the principle of subsidiarity is opposed to all forms of collectivism. It sets limits for state intervention. It aims at harmonizing the relationships between individuals and societies."[28]

The principle itself is not satisfied unless the lower orders themselves take care to address the needs that most closely and directly fall within their purview. The unfortunate spiritual temptation raised by the existence of centralized charity provision is that these responsibilities may be shoved aside. The principle also establishes an ordering of responsibilities, so that we understand our primary ones are to God, our families, immediate and extended, and to our community of faith. The state can easily weaken lower orders, and hinder their ability to manage their own affairs through unnecessary intervention.

This manner of approaching social issues ensures that governments consider carefully what powers legitimately belong to them and whether their exercise would increase or reduce the capacity for responsible decision making at lower levels. Governments, and those who seek to advise them, need to recognize the considerable limits of governments to address human problems. Government can be effective as an instrument of coercion—indeed that is its institutional definition and distinction—but not usually as a force for compassion or social justice.

The principle of solidarity is not intended as a countervailing force to that of subsidiarity, but rather its compliment. If subsidiarity represents the distinctions among spheres of society and the proper chain of social command, solidarity represents the interdependence of all of society's individuals and institutions. "Today perhaps more than in the past," the pope says,

> people are realizing that they are linked together by a common destiny, which is to be constructed together, if catastrophe for all is to be avoided. From the depth of anguish, fear and escapist phenomena like drugs, typical of the contemporary world, the idea is slowly emerging that the good to which we are all called and the happiness to which we aspire cannot be obtained without an effort and commitment on the part of all, nobody excluded, and the consequent renouncing of personal selfishness.[29]

The free economy permits the formation of cooperative associations, business firms, mutually beneficial exchange, charitable actions and institutions, families and civic associations, and also encourages everyone's participation in shaping political institutions consistent with the dignity of the human person. Solidarity, then, presupposes freedom of association, opportunities for exchange and enterprise, and material abundance to ensure that intermediating forces between the individual and the state can form and thrive.

VIII. Conclusion

Serious social and economic issues have confronted the pope during his pontificate, not the least of which was the demise of socialism in the Soviet Union and Eastern Europe, and they have impacted papal social teaching as well. These same issues continue to confront us today. Those issues will continue to be widely discussed and debated in various political circles and campaigns, in books and universities. These comments on morality and economics are offered with the purpose of directing attention to issues concerning the role of government and public policy, which will inevitably arise. I do this as a pastor anxious to apply the pope's concerns to a tradition of economic thought as well as to contemporary social problems.

This discussion has highlighted the importance of free exchange, free association, enterprise, private property, the price system and profits, voluntary charity and welfare provision, and the limited role of the state, both in the pope's thought and the tradition of economic theory generally. This has been done in an ecumenical spirit, in the belief that the flourishing of these institutions is consistent with a rigorous concern for the life, liberty, and dignity of the human person, and in harmony with the moral tradition of a truly Catholic civilization.

NOTES

[1] This connection between classical liberalism and Catholicism will not be explored here, but it is not new in history; it dates from the development of the scholastic tradition in Spain in the sixteenth century. See Laurence S. Moss and Christopher K. Ryan, *Economic Thought in Spain: Selected Essays of Marjorie Grice-Hutchinson* (Brookfield, VT, Edward Elgar, 1993); Marjorie Grice-Hutchinson, *The School of Salamanca: Readings in Spanish Monetary Theory 1544–1605* (Oxford: Clarendon Press, 1962); Raymond de Roover, "Scholastic Economics: Survival and Lasting Influence from the Sixteenth Century to Adam Smith," *Quarterly Journal of Economics* LXIX (2), 1954; Raymond de Roover, *Business, Banking, and Economic Thought in Late Medieval and Early Modern Europe* (Chicago: University of Chicago Press, 1974); Joseph Schumpeter, *History of Economic Analysis* (New York: Oxford University Press, 1954); Alejandro A. Chafuen *Christians for Freedom: Late-Scholastic Economics* by (San Fransico: Ignatius Press, 1986); and Murray N. Rothbard, *Economic Thought Before Adam Smith: An Austrian Perspective on the History of Economic Thought, Vol. I* (Brookfield, VT: Edward Elgar, 1995), pp. 97–134. It is the special virtue of the pope's social teaching to have revived this tradition of thought.

[2] *Sollicitudo Rei Socialis*, No. 41.

[3] *Centesimus Annus*, No. 43.

[4] *Centesimus Annus*, No. 13.

[5] Rocco Buttiglione, "The Free Economy and the Free Man," in George Weigel, ed. *A New Worldy Order: John Paul II and Human Freedom* (D.C.: Ethics and Public Policy Center, 1992), p. 65–66.

[6] *Centesimus Annus*, No. 32.

[7] *Centesimus Annus*, No. 34.

[8] Buttiglione, p. 69.

[9] *Laborem Exercens*, No. 94.

[10] Cited in George Weigel ed., pp. 2–3.

[11] *Laborem Exercens*, No. 94.

[12] *Laborem Exercens*, No. 23.

[13] *Sollicitudo Rei Socialis*, No. 15.

[14] *Centesimus Annus*, No. 32.

[15] *Centesimus Annus*, No. 35.

[16] *Centesimus Annus*, No. 32.

[17] *Centesimus Annus*, No. 31.

[18] *Laborem Exercens*, No. 63.

[19] *Laborem Exercens*, No. 65.

[20] Tom Bethell, *The Noblest Triumph: Property and Prosperity Through the Ages* (New York: St. Martin's Press, 1998).

[21] *Centesimus Annus*, No. 35.

[22] *Centesimus Annus*, No. 19.

[23] *Centesimus Annus*, No. 48.

[24] *Sollicitudo Rei Socialis*, No. 15.

[25] *Centesimus Annus*, No. 48.

[26] *Laborem Exercens*, No. 71

[27] *Centesimus Annus*, No. 48.

[28] *Catechism of the Catholic Church*, (Rome: Urbi et Orbi Communications, 1994), Art. 1885, pp. 460.

[29] *Sollicitudo Rei Socialis*, No. 26.

CHAPTER EIGHT

John Paul II and
The Fall of Communism

Carl Bernstein

On Monday October 16, 1978, ninety–nine cardinals out of one hundred and eight gave the archbishop of Kraków their vote. They had done the unimaginable: They had chosen a pope from a country subject to the Soviet Union, a country with a Marxist and atheist government. He was the first non-Italian pontiff in 450 years, a young pope, at the age of fifty–eight. Outside of Poland and the Sacred College, few knew much about this Slav who had become shepherd to a flock of eight hundred million Catholics.

Amid the silence the voice of the cardinal president could be heard asking: "Do you accept? What name will you take?"

Wojtyla accepted. The tension vanished from his face, which took on a solemn expression. Not only did he say "Yes," as tradition demanded, with a clear voice, but he added: "With obedience in faith to Christ, my Lord, and with trust in the Mother of Christ and of the Church, in spite of the great difficulties, I accept."

Now to express his commitment to the legacy of the last three popes and his affinity to Albino Luciani, he took as his name John Paul II.

* * *

In Warsaw, an officer flung the door open and, ignoring both protocol and discipline, shouted: "Comrade General, sensational news! Wojtyla's been elected pope."

The man at the desk had a pale, almost ghostly white face. Hidden behind dark glasses, his eyes were invisible. The back brace he was snapped into made him sit stiffly. In his olive-green uniform he looked like a mannequin. He thanked the adjutant correctly and acknowledged the message: In two hours members of the Politburo and other state officials would meet in extraordinary session.

Jaruzelski seemed almost overwhelmed with ambiguity: How to handle this news from Rome? Wojtyla as pope meant trouble. Relations between the cardinal of Kraków and the Communist authorities had been strained. Yet the general allowed a wave of patriotism to sweep over him. For the first time in the thousand-year history of Catholic Poland, a son of the motherland was ascending the loftiest throne in the world. It was as if this day—October 16, 1978—had conferred a magnificent prize on the entire nation. Perhaps a bit of the splendor would shine on the government too, undoing the sense of defeat and indignity that scarred the national conscience. Poland had once been a European power, but that had been a long time ago.

The streets of Warsaw were filling up with people on their way to church to pray and light votive candles. Their joy seemed close to rapture—as if Easter, Christmas, and Independence Day had all come at once. Government-controlled Polish radio and television had incongruously broadcast the historic news in the form of a brief bulletin. Since the party hadn't issued any official response, no one had dared flesh out the report with so much as a thumbnail biographical sketch of the new pope.

Yet across the capital the bells were booming like an autumnal cloudburst, as each church rang out in celebration of the news. Jaruzelski thought the choice of a pope from Kraków was a master stroke. From the great cathedral on the Wawel Hill and his episcopal palace, Wojtyla had systematically and ostentatiously ignored the party hierarchy. With philosophical contempt, he had denied any legitimacy to Marxist-Leninist ideology: and with his considerable influence on the Catholic intelligentsia, he had built up a front of spiritual resistance to the country's political leadership. Indeed, Wojtyla's election was dangerous. Jaruzelski was worried that the Polish Church would become a model for all of Eastern Europe, that its influence, hitherto held within the borders of Poland, would now reach Christians in the USSR.

Jaruzelski felt swamped by confusion. He picked up the phone and tried to get some guidance—and commiseration—from the chief Communist overseer of the Catholic Church in Poland, Stanislaw Kania, head of the party's Administrative Department.

"What is there to build on?" Kania asked tentatively. He conceded, of course, that past relations with the archbishop of Kraków offered little ground for optimism. But Communist rhetoric required that every negation be followed by an affirmation. The Church of Rome, he declared, had learned the value of cooperating with the Communist authorities. "We can expect the Holy See to stick to the path of reconciliation, of *Ostpolitik*." But that wasn't enough to calm the assembled leaders, now beset with visions of a grand conspiracy. Was a Polish pope a threat to the socialist system in Poland? That was the crucial question.

"What if the new pope decides to come to Poland?" one of the ministers asked Kania. The weight of the question settled oppressively over the entire room.

The government, warned the minister of internal affairs, has to focus immediately on the risk of a wave of pilgrimages by the Polish faithful to Rome. "Those trips alone might pose a danger to the stability of Poland."

In the very first hours of his pontificate, the election of the first pope from a socialist country had raised the specter of destabilization. Suddenly the Vatican had become an ominous, unknown quantity to the Communist world.

* * *

The first day of John Paul II's triumphant return to his homeland on June 2, 1979, had left the Communist authorities in Warsaw and Moscow shaken. More than a million Poles had converged on the airport road, on Victory Square and in the Old City during the first hours of his visit. Students had taken up the crucifix as the symbol of resistance to the regime. Just as disturbing to the Polish authorities were the pope's words in private to First Secretary Edward Gierek. In the course of their meeting in the Belweder Palace John Paul II had voiced his hopes for the kind of agreement between Church and state that Gierek himself badly wanted. But the pope had laid down a list of conditions designed to convince a Communist power that it would have to make unprecedented concessions if it was to coexist peacefully with the Church.

Gierek had spoken about international detente. The pope replied that "peace and rapprochement among peoples had to be based on the principle of respect for the objective rights of the nation," among which he included its right to "shape its own culture and civilization."

Gierek had spoken about Poland's security obligations and its position in the international community—a clear allusion to the alliances of COMECON (the Council for Mutual Economic Assistance) and the Warsaw Pact, both of which were thoroughly dominated and run by the Soviet Union. John Paul II had responded that "all forms of political, economic, or cultural imperialism contradict the needs of the international order." The only valid pacts could be those "based on mutual respect and on the recognition of the welfare of every nation." His boldness took the Communist leader by surprise. Gierek was disposed to reach a generous settlement on the place to be assigned the Church in Polish society for its religious activities. The pope wanted an acknowledgment that the Church "serves men and women in the temporal dimension of their lives," that is, in the social and political spheres. All this was deeply disturbing to the hierarchy of the Polish Party and—more significant—to the men in the Kremlin.

The next day, Pentecost, June 3, John Paul II arrived in the city of Gniezno like a modern incarnation of the Spirit, by helicopter. The million people who had turned out in Warsaw proved not an exception, just a prelude. Enormous throngs awaited him in the field where his helicopter touched down. "We want God," they chanted, taking up the same cry as the crowds in Warsaw the previous day.

By Sunday evening, June 3, John Paul II had already succeeded, through the prophetic vehemence of his speeches, in challenging the ideology of the regime, the role of the state, the nature of Poland's alliance with the Soviet Union, and the geopolitical arrangements in Europe resulting from the Second World War. General Jaruzelski, who was following the pope's moves from a command center in the Ministry of Defense, could see that his comrades in the Polish Politburo were extremely disturbed, even fearful—both of the responses the pope was eliciting and of reaction from the Kremlin. The party hierarchy didn't like the crowds' attitudes, which struck them as "beyond normal behavior," almost cult-like. Worse, many passages in the pope's speeches went dangerously beyond the expectable tame religious formulas. Gierek, the party secretary, and Premier Piotr Jaroszewicz were already expressing their concerns about "destabilization."

To make matters worse, every gesture, every allusion of the pope was immediately rebroadcast throughout the world by the more than a thousand journalists who had come to Poland to follow the story. In turn, echoes of the trip from the outside world were having negative reverberations in the USSR, Czechoslovakia, and East Germany, whose leaders eyed Warsaw's every move with suspicion and skepticism.

From the third day on, his trip began to look more and more like a triumphant pilgrimage by the pontiff among his people—and an enthusiastic march of millions of Poles toward the pope, their compatriot. All the regime's precautions for limiting the impact of his visit proved futile. On the contrary, every restriction was turned into formidable counterpropaganda against the regime. The roadblocks set up by the police eighteen miles from Czestochowa to screen the pilgrims served only to remind Poles of the vexations inflicted on them by the totalitarian system. The restrictions imposed on television programs —people in Warsaw or Poulah were barred from seeing what anyone in Czestochowa could see—only increased the desire for the free flow of information. The tricks in TV camera coverage, which during religious celebrations tended to show only the pope and persons next to him at the altar, instead of the vast crowds, only added to the drama of his words and the shouted responses from the unseen masses.

An enormous billboard, hung on the walls by the Catholic students of Lublin, summed up the general feeling: "Holy Father, we want to be with you, we want to live a better life with you, we want to pray with you." When the pope met the miners from Silesia, the underground monthly *Glos* commented: "The millions of working people gathered to meet the pope would seem to prove that the official thesis of the natural atheism of the working class and its progressive de-Christianization is utterly false." The dissident journal added prophetically: "At present the authorities are afraid that the pope, who used to be a worker himself, and whose sensitivity to exploitation is well known, might act as a spokesman for the Polish working class." In the face of the intense expectations focused on his person, John Paul II was careful to act with great calm and balance, avoiding confrontational tones. Speaking freely with a group of a thousand university students from Lublin in a closed-door meeting, the pope said: "The cause of Christ can also be furthered or harmed by the choice of a worldview diametrically opposed to Christianity. Everyone who makes this choice with innermost conviction must have our respect." Some students were perplexed by these remarks. By way of explaining his thoughts the pope added: "There is a danger for both sides, both for the Church and for the others, in the attitude of the person who makes no choice at all." Thus, in keeping with his philosophical vocation, John Paul II had returned to preach personal commitment and respect for those who think differently.

On the penultimate day of his trip, the pope chose a meeting with workers near the monastery of Mogila, in the Nowa Huta district, to seize ground traditionally claimed by the Communists and deliver a direct blow to Communist ideology. "Christianity and the Church have no fear of the world of work," he proclaimed. "They're not afraid of any system based on work. The pope isn't afraid of the workers." Many times, of course, popes had feared worker movements. John Paul II recalled his personal experience working in the rock quarry and the Solvay factory during the Nazi occupation; and he extolled the Gospel as a guide for the problems of work in the contemporary world. Amid an ecstatic crowd, waving thousands of flags and banners, the pontiff defiantly declared that people couldn't be demeaned as a mere means of production. "Christ will never approve of it," he exclaimed. "Both the worker and the employer must remember this, both the system of labor and the system of remuneration must remember this. The state, the nation, and the Church must all remember this."

The audience cheered and applauded frenetically. For the workers this was pouring oil on the flames. They were already outraged at the government's latest price increases and eager for higher salaries: and they remembered the regime's violence against the workers' protest in 1976 at Ursus and Radom. Now the Polish leadership took the rebuff, powerless to fight back. In the final analysis the requests made of the pope by the government were having no effect at all. Not on John Paul, not on the people. Monitoring his speeches day by day, General Jaruzelski noted both the force of the pope's words and the subtlety of his approach: John Paul II was not only addressing the present state of affairs, "he was consolidating hope and courage" for future struggles, for the long term.

A similar thought occurred to Wiktor Kulerski, who would join the ranks of Solidarity activists barely a year later. "We're living in a different country," he told himself as the pope traveled around Poland. "Communism doesn't matter anymore, because nobody submits to it." Kulerski felt that the pope's stay in Poland was a moment of relief, a moment to gather one's energies: "The pope is here, and he's beyond the reach of the Communists. He can say and do the things we can't. They can't get him. People repeat the pope's words, and they know that he's their bulwark."

On June 10, more than a million faithful arrived at the meadow at Blonie on the edge of the city. Merely to draw a million people was incredible, even revolutionary in a country of the socialist bloc. That day was chosen to honor St. Stanislaw during the papal trip, and it turned into a celebration of the new power of John Paul II as, brandishing Christ like a battle standard, he announced that the nine-hundredth anniversary of the death of St. Stanislaw would be a turning point for the nation and the Church.

That was all the crowd needed; they understood perfectly. As he left, the pope could bestow a new blessing on his people. He could entrust them with a new mission. "You must be strong, dearest brothers and sisters!" he cried. "You must be strong with the strength that flows from faith! You must be strong with the strength of faith!"

For one last time he addressed—without naming them, but in a way obvious to everyone—the peoples behind the iron curtain. "There is no need to be afraid. The frontiers must be opened. There is no imperialism in the Church, only service." Catching sight of a group of pilgrims from Czechoslovakia, he insisted: "Oh how I would wish that our brothers and sisters, who are united to us by language and the fortunes of history, could also have been present during the pilgrimage of this Slavic pope. If they are not here, if they are not here in this vast expanse, they are surely in our hearts." The pope and the Slavic nations versus the Soviet empire. The battle lines were now drawn. In his native land, almost one out of every three citizens had been able to see him in person.

*   *   *

On Thursday, August 14, 1980, Pope John Paul II spent the day in the papal villa at Castel Gandolfo, twenty miles from the Vatican. The air in the Alban hills was more breathable than in the scorching streets of Rome. Ever since the late 1600s the villa had been a refuge for popes during the hottest months of the year.

That Thursday, the pace at Castel Gandolfo was more languid than usual. It was the eve of the Assumption, *ferragosto*, the summer's most sacred holiday for Italians, when everything stops running, even the buses.

While the pope worked in his study, Lech Walesa, a square-shouldered, unemployed electrician with a distinctive mustache, was clambering up a steam shovel at the Lenin Shipyard in Gdansk, Poland. All summer the workers at the shipyard had declined to join the strikes that were sweeping the country. But on this morning, some of them formed into an unruly procession within the gates, demanding pay raises and the rehiring of the shipyard's crane operator—a defiant critic of management who had been transferred to a job outside Gdansk.

Poland's economy was devastated. Millions of factory workers across Poland were by now thoroughly disgruntled. The spontaneous strikes that had begun in July had spread to more than 150 enterprises. The government was reacting with the usual promises of change and salary increases—so far without violence. This time the protests continued. The sun was setting on the decade of Gierek. The country now found itself mired in debt; productivity was sinking; basic items like spare parts for industrial equipment were in short supply. Bankruptcy loomed.

The workers in the naval shipyard, the most important in Poland, where police in 1970 had killed forty–five striking employees, had shown little enthusiasm for a new confrontation. The director of the Gdansk shipyard, Klemens Giech, was promising a pay raise if workers would go back on the job, and many were ready to agree. But Walesa, who had scaled the yard's twelve-foot high chain-link fence that morning, now stood next to the shipyard manager atop the steam shovel and denounced his offers.

He was a popular figure who had taken part in the uprisings of 1970 that had brought down Gomulka. After the bloody repression of the demonstrations in Radom and Ursus in 1976, he had devoted himself to creating an independent labor union, and he had often been arrested for these activities. Now he called for a sit-down strike: To protect themselves from security forces, workers would lock themselves inside the factory. The crowd heeded his call.

The truth was that the strikes that shook Poland in the summer of 1980 were not merely strikes. They were political insurrections —"counterrevolution," as Brezhnev correctly put it. This movement, like all historic social revolutions, united a constellation of formidable political forces—labor, the intelligentsia, and the Church—that had never before come together so decisively.

In the previous economic crises, which had ended in violence, the workers had been disorganized and had lacked any national forum for expressing their grievances. In 1980, though there was still no centrally organized political opposition, there was a loose alliance of forces prepared to challenge the whims of an imperious state. These were the Workers Defense Committees (known by the acronym KOR) that had been formed by intellectuals to assist workers arrested or fired after the violent crackdown in 1976; the Catholic Intellectual Clubs (KIK); and the bishops who, backed by the Polish pope, now tentatively preached a gospel of human rights as well as of salvation.

On Saturday, August 16, the workers again seemed inclined to call off their strike, in exchange for the promise of a 1,500-zloty raise and a guarantee that a monument would be built at the shipyard to honor the victims of December 1970. But Walesa, emboldened by these concessions, issued a sixteen-point list of demands, the most important of which was government recognition of free trade unions. His proposal was not especially popular, and a day later, when management offered a heftier pay raise, many older workers filed out of the yard, giving up the strike. This was perhaps Walesa's greatest moment: Circling the yard in a small motorized vehicle, he rallied the workers back to the cause. When the strike finally resumed in full force on the 18th, Walesa issued a new, more radical list of twenty–one demands, including alleviation of censorship and the release of political prisoners. It showed the hand of KOR advisers who had infiltrated the shipyard.

All negotiations were broadcast by loudspeaker through the yard, so word of the strike and the workers' audacious new demands spread rapidly across the Baltic seacoast. That day work stopped in 180 more factories from Gdynia, Gdansk, and Sopot on the coast to Tarnow (near Kraków) and Katowice in Silesia. Now the avalanche was unleashed.

At Castel Gandolfo, John Paul II received confidential reports on the events in Poland from Monsignor Dziwisz, his Polish secretary, and from his Secretariat of State, which was in touch with the Polish episcopate. Breaking habit, Wojtyla eagerly watched television reports of the sensational events in his homeland. With him was Sister Zofia Zdybicka, his ex-student who was staying at the summer residence as a guest. Sister Zdybicka, like the pope, was a philosopher, and first as a student, then as a teacher, finally as a friend, she had often discussed such matters as the nature of Marxism and the destiny of man with Karol Wojtyla. "This," she declared as she watched the TV news, "is a lesson for the whole world. Look at the contradiction: The workers are against communism." The pope readily agreed, but at first he seemed less confident, less enthusiastic. "Except that the world doesn't understand anything," he replied. "The world doesn't get it." He said this three times. He didn't seem entirely surprised by the remarkable doings in Poland. Sister Zdybicka remembered being with the pope on another occasion when he had told a visiting professor from the Catholic University in Lublin, "You have to be ready." Ready for what? she and the professor had wondered, but now she thought she understood. This was what the pope had been waiting for.

Walesa, said the pope, had been sent by God, by Providence. On the screen they watched Walesa and the workers praying. "So serious, so young, those intent faces," she noted. In his lapel Walesa wore a pin with a picture of the Black Madonna of Czestochowa. On Sunday and now on Monday, mass was celebrated by the strikers in the shipyard, led by Walesa's parish priest, Father Henryk Jankowski, of St. Brygida's in Gdansk.

Photos of the pope and large pictures of the Black Madonna were posted on the gates of the shipyard. John Paul noted with ironic satisfaction that Western politicians, especially those on the left, were amazed that throngs of strikers were flocking on bended knee around improvised outdoor confessionals and that they had chosen religious symbols for their battle standards. Sister Zdybicka sensed that the pope saw the hand of God lifted up against the Communists, as the workers turned their rulers' weapons against them.

Spontaneous demonstrations were now breaking out along the coast under the leadership of the Inter-Factory Strike Committee in solidarity with the strikers at the Lenin Shipyard. Workers all over the country, spurred into action by KOR, were joining forces with the Catholic intelligentsia, while secular-minded intellectuals too were making common cause with the Church.

John Paul II kept silent for a week. Like the heads of the European community who cautioned Gierek and the Polish leadership not to take repressive measures, like U.S. President Jimmy Carter, and like Moscow, which was trying to figure out how the Polish Communist Party could maintain control of the country, the pope was prudent.

On Wednesday, August 20, as the strike movement threatened to provoke long-term political paralysis, the pope said two brief prayers with a group of Polish pilgrims in St. Peter's Square: "God, grant through the intercession of Mary that religion may always enjoy freedom and that our homeland may enjoy security. . . . Lord, help this people, and always defend it from every evil and danger."

"These two prayers," said the pope, "show that all of us here in Rome are united with our compatriots in Poland, with the Church in Poland, whose problems are so close to our heart."

Thus did the pope do something that old Cardinal Wyszynski couldn't and wouldn't do: He publicly blessed the strike. This was a turning point. Now the bishop of Gdansk, Lech Kaczmarek, presented Walesa and the other fourteen members of the strike committee with medals of Pope John Paul II.

Walesa, in turn, sent a reassuring message to Moscow and the Polish Communists: "Our struggle is about unions; it's not a political effort. . . . We have no intention of calling into question Poland's international alliances."

With the world's attention focused on the extraordinary events in Poland, President Carter privately wrote to the pope that the United States shared the aspirations of the Polish workers and that it would use its diplomatic channels to urge Soviet restraint.

On August 23, the pope sent the primate of the Polish Church a delicately nuanced letter: "I am writing these brief words to say how especially close I have felt to you in the course of these last difficult days." Then, after the affectionate flourishes and invocations of the Madonna, the letter gave a precise political order: "I pray with all my heart that the bishops of Poland . . . can even now help this nation in its difficult struggle for daily bread, for social justice, and the safeguarding of its inviolable rights to its own life and development." Bread, social justice, independent development. With these words the pope gave his complete support to the strikers' goals. The Church, observed the Catholic writer Stefan Kisielewski, with only a touch of oversimplification, was managing the first democratic strike in the history of Poland.

That evening the government made a historic concession, agreeing to enter into direct negotiations with the strike committees in Gdansk, Gdynia, and Szczecin.

With the beginning of negotiations, which turned into a dramatic weeklong test of strength, a group of advisers made an appearance alongside Lech Walesa. The group included intellectuals, professors, and members of the Polish Academy of Sciences. Two of its leaders were closely associated with Wojtyla: Tadeusz Mazowiecki, editor of the Warsaw Catholic periodical *Wiez*, and historian Bronislaw Geremek. With the arrival of this group, the strategic leadership of the movement—eventually to be known as Solidarity—passed largely into the hands of the Church. Now the Black Madonna in Walesa's lapel was a sign that Solidarity had taken its inspiration directly from Karol Wojtyla.

On August 27, at the pope's instigation, the Polish bishops approved a document that explicitly claimed "the right to independence both of organizations representing the workers and of organizations of self-government." The pope's will had become the national will. Now the government had little choice but to give in. Walesa knew he had the pope's backing.

On August 31, the historic Gdansk accords were signed, ratifying the establishment of the first independent union behind the iron curtain. The accords set the standard for subsequent agreements that would be made throughout Poland as the Solidarity movement swept the land. Free trade unions, wage increases, health care improvements, curtailment of censorship, release of political prisoners—virtually everything was now negotiable.

At the signing ceremonies for the accords, Walesa dramatically pulled an oversized, brightly colored pen out of his pocket. TV cameras recorded the moment: The pen was a souvenir from John Paul's trip to Poland, and on it was a picture of the pope.

* * *

The attempt to murder the pope on May 13, 1981 remains one of this century's great mysteries. The pope's response to the shooting and its aftermath has only deepened the mystery.

Nonetheless, many of the pope's closest aides and acquaintances became convinced that the Soviets or their allies, notably the Bulgarian regime, were behind the attempt. An informal group meeting in the Vatican, which included Secretary of State Casaroli, argued secretly that the Soviets wanted the pope killed because his death seemed to be the only way to decapitate Solidarity. With the pope dead, this reasoning went, Solidarity could have been smothered by the Polish authorities without the Soviets incurring the lasting international opprobrium that military intervention by the Warsaw Pact would have brought.

"Surely the assassination was not an isolated attack," Casaroli stated publicly in January 1995.

Cardinal Achille Silvestrini, who was Casaroli's deputy at the time, says, "It was clear to us that it was not a random accident . . . not simply the act of a madman. It was something aimed at a goal, there was something behind the killer. . . . We have to keep in mind the situation in Poland and Eastern Europe at that time. If the assassination attempt had succeeded, it would have been the gravestone for Poland and for those who were challenging the control of the [Soviet] system." But Silvestrini is skeptical about the Bulgarian scenario and believes the trail heads somewhere else in the former communist East.

No illuminating documents relating to the assassination attempt have been found in either Bulgaria or Moscow since the fall of communism—though Western intelligence professionals ridicule the notion that a paper trail to the Kremlin might exist.

Many facts about the attempt on the pope's life are contradictory or open to interpretation, and the failure of intelligence agencies around the world to tackle the case immediately and pool their knowledge has helped make it impossible to piece together a definitive record.

*   *   *

On May 17, 1981, four days after the shooting of Wojtyla, President Reagan, who had only partially regained his strength but seemed in the midst of a vigorous recovery, made his first trip since being shot: to deliver a long-scheduled commencement address at the University of Notre Dame—*Our Lady*—in South Bend, Indiana.

By now, Reagan's speechwriters knew his priorities: As on the day he was shot, Reagan again turned his thoughts to the pope and the Evil Empire. Wearing a black academic gown and a black mortarboard with a yellow tassel, the president looked out over a vast audience; he could see that it included a small number of students wearing white armbands and white mortarboards to protest administration policies in El Salvador and budget cuts that hurt the poor. Then the president of the United States made his own prophecy:

The years ahead will be great ones for our country, for the

cause of freedom and for the spread of civilization. The West will not contain communism, it will transcend communism. We will not bother to denounce it, we'll dismiss it as a sad, bizarre chapter in human history whose last pages are even now being written.

He was deadly serious, though the reporters traveling with him mistook his words for mere rhetoric and blind hope. But he had confided to his wife and his closest aides that he was certain this was why he and the pope had been spared.

The previous day, in Kraków, 300,000 people had attended an open-air mass to pray for their former archbishop John Paul II and for the recovery of Cardinal Wyszynski, whose grave illness had been announced by the episcopate the day after the pope was shot. Reagan continued:

> It was Pope John Paul II who warned last year, in his encyclical on mercy and justice, against certain economic theories that use the rhetoric of class struggle to justify injustice: that "in the name of an alleged justice the neighbor is sometimes destroyed, killed, deprived of liberty or stripped of fundamental human rights." For the West, for America, the time has come to dare to show to the world that our civilized ideas, our traditions, our values are not—like the ideology and war machine of totalitarian societies—a facade of strength. It is time the world knew that our intellectual and spiritual values are rooted in the source of all real strength—a belief in a supreme being, a law higher than our own.

Not only had he quoted the pope, but in the religious cadences of his rhetoric, Ronald Reagan had begun to sound like the pope.

*   *   *

By mid-October of 1981, the situation in Poland was on the brink of chaos. No one seemed to be in control of the country; uncompromising factions in both the Polish Communist Party and Solidarity were demanding harsh, almost apocalyptic action. Riots and clashes between civilians and security forces were spreading. The Polish economy was in ruins, and the crisis was aggravated by hundreds of strikes, by everyone from coal miners to transport workers. In the stores, even toothpaste and soap had disappeared from the shelves.

At the stroke of midnight, tanks and soldiers stationed across the country moved into the streets and forests as Operation X got under way. At six a.m., Jaruzelski addressed the nation on television.

"Citizens and lady citizens of the Polish People's Republic! I turn to you as a soldier and chief of government! Our motherland is on the verge of an abyss." By the time he read his prepared statement, thousands were already in jail. The prisoners, he said, were guilty of "growing aggressiveness and an attempt to dismantle the state. How long will our outstretched hand be met with the fist?" he asked.

For the foreseeable future, the nation would be governed by a Military Council of National Salvation. The new rules of governance, ending sixteen months of hope and excitement, suffering and disappointment, were pasted on lampposts, street corners, and trees throughout the cities and across the countryside. They had been printed months before—in the Soviet Union.

The civil society that Solidarity had been building brick by brick under the protection of the Church was gone. In its place was a declaration of a "state of war." A nightly curfew was in effect indefinitely. Except for those of the military and security forces, every telephone in Poland was dead (even at local Communist Party headquarters) and would remain so for a month. All civilian communications with the outside world were severed. All schools except nursery schools were closed, as were theaters and movie houses. Except for religious services, public gatherings were now illegal. Travel outside one's city of residence could only be undertaken with official permission. All mail was subject to censorship. "Tourism, yachting, and rowing . . . on internal and territorial waters" were forbidden.

During the sixteen months of Poland's great experiment, more than two thousand clandestine books and newspapers had been published, with help from the West. As many as 100,000 Polish citizens had been involved in their preparation, working as printers, writers, or distributors. Now the Military Council of National Salvation forbade the purchase of typewriter ribbons and typing paper without official permission.

The military would henceforth be responsible for running railroads, highways, mail service, broadcasting, distribution of petroleum products, firefighting, importing and exporting, and the manufacture of strategic goods. Polish borders were sealed and the country's airspace, closed. The newscasters on television now wore military uniforms.

Between twenty and thirty people had been killed in the early days of martial law, most of them murdered by security forces. Hundreds of others were injured and arrested at the shipyard at Gdansk, the birthplace of Solidarity, where thousands of workers had rushed when they first heard of the "state of war."

The most serious violence occurred at a coal mine near Katowice, where miners called a sit-down strike.

The violence at Katowice, which was reported by Polish state radio on the next day, Thursday, prompted John Paul II to begin writing a letter that afternoon to Jaruzelski.

> Recent events in Poland since the declaration of martial law on December 13 [wrote the pope] have resulted in death and injury to our fellow countrymen, and I am moved to address this urgent and heartfelt appeal to you, a prayer for an end to the shedding of Polish blood.
>
> During the last two centuries, the Polish nation has endured great wrongs, and much blood has been spilled in the struggle for power over our Fatherland. Our history cries out against any more bloodshed, and we must not allow this tragedy to continue to weigh so heavily on the conscience of the nation. I therefore appeal to you, General, to return to the methods of peaceful dialogue that have characterized efforts at social renewal since August 1980. Even though this may be a difficult step, it is not an impossible one.
>
> The welfare of the entire nation depends upon it. People throughout the world, all those who rightly see the cause of peace furthered by respect for the rights of Man, are waiting for this return to nonviolent means. All humanity's desire for peace argues for an end to the state of martial law in Poland.
>
> The Church speaks out for this desire. Soon it will be Christmas, when generation after generation of Poland's sons and daughters have been drawn together by Holy Communion. Every effort must be made so that our compatriots will not be

forced to spend this Christmas under the shadow of repression and death.

I appeal to your conscience, General, and to the conscience of all those who must decide this question.

The Vatican 18 December 1981
John Paul II

This letter, like all of the pope's responses to martial law, stemmed in part from a central premise. However repugnant, martial law, in the pope's phrase, was a "lesser evil" than civil war or Soviet intervention. The pope correctly assumed that Jaruzelski would eventually need the Church's cooperation to find a way out of the terrible situation in which he and the nation now found themselves. Since Jaruzelski had only two choices—to turn toward the Church or toward Moscow—the pope believed that Jaruzelski would ultimately seek the protection of the Church.

* * *

No moment of his young papacy was as delicate, no problem as vexing, as the situation that faced Wojtyla in 1983 on his second trip to Poland. That winter had been an especially depressing one for Poles. Martial law seemed unrelenting. Dismissals, secret accusations, and acts of repression had poisoned the air.

As he arrived on June 16, 1983, John Paul II did not hide his sadness at the condition of his country. It was evident in his first words at Warsaw's airport, after he had kissed the ground: "I ask those who suffer to be particularly close to me. I ask this in the words of Christ: I was sick, and you visited me, I was in prison and you came to me. I myself cannot visit all those in prison [the crowd gasped], all those who are suffering. But I ask them to be close to me in spirit to help me, just as they always do."

Later that same morning he held the first of two private meetings at Belweder Palace with Prime Minister Jaruzelski, sessions in which real negotiations finally began. The man who had crushed Solidarity looked stiff, correct, and expressionless as he greeted the pope. His pale face wasn't shielded by his usual dark glasses. His uniform gave him a certain patriotic elegance, but John Paul II noticed that when the general spoke, his right hand, which held his prepared remarks, trembled, and his left was clenched in a fist. Jaruzelski has since admitted that he felt extremely nervous and excited. When the time came for official speeches, the pope placed a microphone between himself and Jaruzelski, as if to distance himself as much as possible from the man in charge of martial law. Then the pope publicly addressed Jaruzelski and Jablonski in a televised speech, asserting Poland's right to independence, "her proper place among the nations of Europe, between East and West." The path to true sovereignty and reform, he said, must take into account "social agreements stipulated by representatives of state authorities with representatives of the workers," that is, the Gdansk accords.

His idea, which he now passed on to a whole nation, was a variation of his own experience as a youth during the war: Victory was within. Spiritual victory forged from the suffering of their nation, the path of martyrdom, was possible. "Man is called to victory over himself," he declared. "It is the saints and the beatified who show us the path to victory that God achieves in human history." To achieve that victory requires "living in truth. . . . It means love of neighbor; it means fundamental solidarity between human beings." In a theme he repeated over and over in the following days, to the chagrin of the regime, he said that victory means "making an effort to be a person with a conscience, calling good and evil by name and not blurring them . . . developing in myself what is good, and seeking to correct what is evil by overcoming it in myself.

"You come to the Mother of Czestochowa with a wound in the heart, with sorrow, perhaps also with rage," he preached. "Your presence shows the force of a testimony, a witnessing which has stupefied the whole world: when the Polish worker made his own person the object of a demand, with the Gospel in his hand and a prayer on his lips. The images transmitted to the world in 1980 have touched hearts and consciences,"

In his homily to another crowd of one million people in the steel town of Katowice (and to the Communist regime), he reiterated the basic rights of workers: "to a just salary," "to security," "to a day of rest." "Connected with the area of workers' rights is the question of trade unions," he said, "the right of free association," the right of all workers to form unions as "a mouthpiece for the struggle for social justice." Quoting the late Cardinal Wyszynski, he continued, "The state does not give us this right, it has only the obligation to protect and guard it. This right is given us by the Creator who made man as a social being." Each day his speeches alluded to these elements of the Gdansk agreements.

He met privately with Lech Walesa on the last day of his visit, as well as with intellectuals who were secretly in contact with the Solidarity underground. He received from them copies of underground newspapers.

After eighteen months of martial law, Solidarity was no longer a mass organization of labor, with membership cards and a list of workplace demands. The state had destroyed that body, and its resurrection seemed almost inconceivable. But with the pope's second visit, Solidarity became an idea, a consciousness, a set of values, even a way of life "in solidarity."

At the close of his visit, the pope and Jaruzelski met again, this time alone face to face for more than an hour and a half at the Wawel, "a place of great symbolic importance," as Jaruzelski noted. The meeting, unscheduled, had been requested the night before by the pope.

The pope stunned Jaruzelski with his directness: "I understand that socialism as a political system is a reality," he said, "but the point is that it ought to have a human face."

The pope always spoke "in terms of human rights or civil rights," the general noted. "And when we discussed rights we naturally mean[t] democracy, If there is democracy, then you have elections; if you have elections, then you have power. But he never put it that way. It showed his great culture and diplomacy, because in substance he used words and phrases that you couldn't argue with. Because if he had said, 'You have to share power with Solidarity,' we would have argued about it, naturally. But when one simply mentions human rights, it's such a general term, such a general notion, that you can have a constructive discussion, which eventually brought us [the regime] closer to that goal without losing face."

* * *

The pope's first real sign of "socialism with a human face"—three years and three months after the declaration of martial law in Poland —came in the unlikely form of a visit to the Vatican on February 27, 1985, by Soviet foreign minister Andrei Gromyko. In Moscow, unbeknownst to the pope, Konstantin Chernenko was near death. Twelve days later Gromyko, who had served every Soviet leader since Stalin, would play a crucial role in the selection of Mikhail Gorbachev to succeed Chernenko as general secretary of the Communist Party of the USSR.

Gromyko now let the pope know that the USSR might be interested in establishing diplomatic relations with the Holy See. When John Paul II voiced his concerns about world peace, particularly the need for progress at the stalled Geneva talks on arms control, and the plight of Catholics in the Soviet Union, Gromyko seemed unusually responsive. He suggested further explorations of such matters by representatives of the USSR and the Vatican. This overture took Wojtyla completely by surprise.

That spring, in May, he began receiving reports from Poland that Gorbachev might indeed be a different kind of Communist and that the Brezhnev era might finally be ending, two and a half years after his death. Gorbachev had traveled to Poland in late April to attend a meeting of the Consultative Political Committee of the Warsaw Pact. More consequentially, when the meeting adjourned, Gorbachev remained behind to speak with Jaruzelski. He had only an hour, the new general secretary said, but then the hour stretched into five as the two men conducted an exhaustive review of the situation in Poland and the USSR—and a long discussion about the pope and the Vatican.

From this discussion, Jaruzelski concluded that Gorbachev was a different kind of Communist and took steps, through the primate, to inform the pope of their meeting. "It was a critical moment," Jaruzelski disclosed almost a decade later (and Gorbachev too confirmed the portentous nature of their encounter): "Five hours of conversation face to face without an interpreter. Much of it centered on the Church and Wojtyla, but first "we spoke about the past, about the origins of the system, about the necessity for change." Gorbachev had been general secretary for only a few weeks and he wanted to learn firsthand as much as possible about the internal situation in Poland and about the Holy See. Jaruzelski got the impression that, "though he was broad-minded" and had been a member of the Politburo for several years, "his knowledge of the Church and religion was superficial."

Jaruzelski clung to Gorbachev like a drowning man to a life preserver: Finally someone in the Kremlin was giving him a sympathetic ear—and not just anyone, but the general secretary himself.

"First of all I tried to explain the difference, the uniqueness of the Church's role in Poland, compared with that of the Church in other countries," Jaruzelski recounted. As rigidly controlled as conditions were then in Poland, the country had engaged in a bold experiment with human rights before the imposition of martial law, and both men agreed that Communist societies had to evolve in the direction of that experiment.

Gorbachev had yet to use the term *perestroika*—meaning "restructuring"—but this talk with Jaruzelski turned on some of the concepts he was later to introduce, including a broad guarantee of religious rights for Communist citizens. He asked Jaruzelski many questions about the failures of Poland's planned economy and about the moribund state of the Polish Communist Party. But the conversation kept returning to the Church, and eventually to the pope himself.

"What kind of a man is he?" Gorbachev asked. "What is his intellectual training? Is he a fanatic? Or is he a man with his feet on the ground?"

Jaruzelski replied that the pope was "an outstanding personality, a great humanist, a great patriot," above all a man committed to peace.

Gorbachev now began talking enthusiastically about peaceful coexistence between East and West, arms reductions, even the radical elimination of armaments. Jaruzelski knew how important this was because he had heard the pope take a similar tack on such issues. When he did, Jaruzelski told Gorbachev, "it was not only as the leader of a great religion, a great Church, but also as the son of a nation whose lot had been particularly hard. When this particular pope spoke about peace, it sounded different than when, say, Pius XII talked about it."

It now occurred to Jaruzelski that he could become the intermediary between the pope and Gorbachev, that he could explain one to the other. Later, Gorbachev, like the pope, credited him with playing just such a role.

*   *   *

The advent of Gorbachev brought rapid changes to Church-state relations in Poland and created an atmosphere in which Jaruzelski felt safe to begin relaxing many of the restrictions that had accompanied martial law.

Then, on June 2, 1985, the pope issued one of his most important encyclicals, *Slavorum Apostoli* (Apostles to the Slavs), charged with both religious and secular significance. It was an invitation to ecumenical dialogue with the Eastern churches in the USSR.

With the coming of Gorbachev, the Kremlin would no longer automatically interpret such offers as insidious attempts to undermine the foundation of Communist legitimacy. Twice in the next year, at Jaruzelski's urging, Primate Glemp was permitted to visit Minsk and Moscow, where he met with Catholic and Russian Orthodox leaders and clergy, along with secular officials and scholars. Never before had a Polish cardinal visited the Soviet Union.

The "Slavic encyclical" commemorated the eleven hundredth anniversary of the evangelism of Sts. Cyril and Methodius, who brought Christianity to most of the Slavic peoples of Eastern Europe. In this document, the pope invoked the metaphor of Europe as one "body that breathes with two lungs." In 1980 he had made Sts. Cyril and Methodius co-patrons (with St. Benedict) of Europe.

Gorbachev, a Slav and a Communist, and Wojtyla, a Slav and a Christian, were moving toward each other, each increasingly aware of the other's power and potential for doing good. Later that June, the new general secretary propounded the economic changes that would come to be known as *perestroika*: He spoke of a humanism that united the aspirations of Europe for economic and political peace and security. Similarly, the pope's *Ostpolitik* was grounded in the belief that the Church must speak not just for Western Europe, but for a single undivided entity and culture, from the Urals to the Atlantic, "with a pan-European tradition of humanism that encompassed Erasmus, Copernicus, and Dostoevsky," in a historian's phrasing.

The pope was excited and hopeful about the changes Gorbachev was initiating. There was no doubt that Poland, the Communist nations of the East, and even the USSR were on the verge of a great transformation.

That spring of 1985, to the immense satisfaction of the pope, the USSR Council for Religious Affairs recommended Soviet participation in the interreligious convocation that John Paul had called for in Assisi. But Wojtyla was also a realist; he had long years of experience dealing with Communist ideologues. Early in Gorbachev's tenure, the pope had a lengthy discussion about the new general secretary with Rocco Buttiglione, an Italian intellectual who frequently visited the Vatican. "Well, he's a good man, but he'll fail," the pope declared, "because he wants to do something that's impossible. Communism can't be re-formed." The pope was never to change this judgment, though he hoped and prayed for Gorbachev's success. Gorbachev was already meeting resistance in the Soviet party and Politburo. *"Perestroika* is an avalanche that we have unleashed and it's going to roll on," the pope said to Father Mieczyslaw Maliliski, his fellow underground seminarian. *"Perestroika* is a continuation of Solidarity. Without Solidarity there would be no *Perestroika.*"

The avalanche was rumbling through Czechoslovakia. In the spring of 1985, in commemoration of the eleven hundredth anniversary of the death of St. Methodius, eleven hundred priests—one-third of the Catholic clergy in Czechoslovakia—concelebrated mass at the Moravian shrine of Velehrad. Cardinal Frantisek Tomasek, eighty–six years old, who had been imprisoned by the Communists, read a letter from the pope urging the priests "to continue intrepidly in the spirit of St. Methodius on the path of evangelization and witness, even if the present situation makes it arduous, difficult, and even bitter."

"We felt how strong we were," said Bishop Frantisek Lobkowicz, who was a thirty-six-year-old pastor at the time. Until then the Church had not figured conspicuously in the Czech opposition, though some prominent Catholic intellectuals were affiliated with Charter 77, the umbrella organization of Czech resistance groups. Three months later, in "normalized" Czechoslovakia, 150,000 to 200,000 Catholic pilgrims marched to Velehrad for another observance in honor of St. Methodius. For months the government had tried to transform the event into a "peace festival." But when the Communist leaders took to the microphones, the pilgrims shouted back, "This is a pilgrimage! We want the pope! We want mass!" It was the largest independent gathering in Czechoslovakia since the Prague Spring of 1968.

* * *

The definitive sign that the era of martial law in Poland was finally ending came on September 11, 1986, when the regime announced a general amnesty and released the 225 prisoners who had been considered most dangerous to the state. The release of political prisoners had been the number one demand made by the underground since 1981.

For the first time in almost five years, all of Solidarity's leaders could meet freely. Polish jails were once more reserved for criminals, not political prisoners.

* * *

On January 13, 1987, for the first time since their conversation in the Wawel in 1981, John Paul II and General Jaruzelski met, in the pope's study in the Vatican. Jaruzelski would later describe the visit as "historic," because of what he saw as a crucial meeting of minds. For different reasons the pope's closest aides have used the term "historic" for the session. The discussion lasted eighty minutes, during which Jaruzelski delivered a firsthand report on his conversations with Gorbachev and what the general secretary called his new thinking.

By now, the regime was easing more of the restrictions on civil rights imposed during martial law: Travel in and out of the country was relatively easy, censorship had become less pervasive, the police less conspicuous, and some independent organizations were reinstated.

"I found that [the pope] had a complete understanding of the processes through which we were living," Jaruzelski said of their meeting. "I concluded that the pope saw in the trends and changes occurring in Poland a significance well beyond the Polish framework . . . that they [were], to a great extent, an impulse for the changes occurring in the other countries, especially in the Soviet Union."

By this time, Jaruzelski was openly courting the pope—and the forces of history. As usual, he sought the approval of those he admired, whether in the Kremlin or in the Vatican. In his (dubious) version of events, he claimed that, after imposing the brutal restrictions of martial law, he suddenly reversed direction out of a long-standing democratic impulse.

The pope's view of Jaruzelski, according to the people closest to John Paul II, was somewhat cooler than the general's perception of it, though there is no doubt that Wojtyla regarded Jaruzelski as above all a patriot. But in his dealings with Jaruzelski, the pope always tried to offer the general a vision preferable to Moscow's. This was one of his great accomplishments.

"The pope was aware," says Cardinal Deskur, "that Jaruzelski had a very strong religious background . . . Catholic school, Marian Fathers, etcetera. 'I think he is a man deeply *credente*—believing,' the pope said. 'He hasn't lost his faith.'" And Wojtyla intended to make the most of it.

* * *

When Jaruzelski briefly visited Moscow in late April 1987 to sign a declaration of Soviet-Polish cooperation—in "ideology, science, and culture"—he was told by Gorbachev that *perestroika* was encountering fierce resistance.

John Paul II arrived triumphantly in Warsaw two months later, on June 8, 1987, for his third pontifical pilgrimage to his homeland, this time to reclaim Solidarity. Though his visit came against the backdrop of profoundly disturbing privation and suffering, the expectant spirit of his first pilgrimage—the hope, the excitement, the defiance—was in the air.

Solidarity was now operating in the open, though tentatively, and its adherents understandably held the authorities in great suspicion. During the week of his visit, the pope had met privately with Walesa near the Gdansk shipyard (after he finished his shift as an electrician) then served communion to him at a mass attended by hundreds of thousands. The pope made an unrelentingly emotional appeal to "the special heritage of Polish Solidarity," and each day his challenge to the regime became more overt.

At one of the most extraordinary masses of his pontificate, celebrated in Gdansk before a crowd of 750,000 workers and their families, the pope invoked the 1980 accords, tracing their roots to the bloody events at the shipyard in 1970. The Gdansk accords, he declared, "will go down in the history of Poland as an expression of the growing consciousness of the working people concerning the entire social-moral order on Polish soil." Looking out over a sea of Solidarity banners, the pope put aside his prepared text.

"I pray for you every day in Rome, I pray for my motherland and for you workers. I pray for the special heritage of Polish Solidarity." His audience was beside itself: weeping, applauding, praying, raising clenched fists.

John Paul II stood on a structure shaped like a gigantic ship, whose prow was in the form of St. Peter raising the keys to the kingdom and the Gospel in his hands. From his "ship," the pope told the crowd, "I'm glad to be here, because you have made me captain. . . . There is no struggle more effective than Solidarity!" He then asserted the workers' absolute right to "self-government." After the pope's speech in Gdansk, Walesa said, "I'm very happy. Now even a fool can understand that finding a passage in this labyrinth . . . requires Solidarity. This is the only road."

John Paul II used almost every stop of his journey to widen the perceived gulf between his vision and that of the regime—to the increasing chagrin of Jaruzelski. The pope called for a rethinking of the "very premises" of Poland's Communist order. "In the name of the future of mankind and of humanity the word 'solidarity' must be said out loud," he told hundreds of thousands of seamen at the port of Gdynia, near Gdansk, speaking from a towering altar set up near the harbor's gray waters. "This word was spoken right here, in a new way and in a new context. And the world cannot forget it. This word is your pride, Polish seamen."

The regime responded to the visit with television censorship, the deployment of tens of thousands of riot police, hundreds of detentions, and, finally, a bitter outburst by Jaruzelski at the farewell ceremonies for the pope at the Warsaw airport.

Following the pope's visit, events in Poland moved with methodical swiftness: At each important turn, the regime responded with half-measures to the pressures from Solidarity, the people, and the pope, and became overwhelmed. Recognizing that the economic reforms of the past five years had failed, it scheduled a referendum that asked Poles to vote for or against a program of radical economic change, dramatic austerity, and limited steps toward political pluralism. Solidarity urged a boycott of the referendum on the grounds that the government would use it as a vote of confidence. The boycott succeeded. When it failed to attract a majority of eligible voters to the polls, the government announced that it had lost the referendum, the first time in postwar history that a Communist government admitted that it had failed to win an election.

Trying to avoid direct negotiations with Walesa or other Solidarity leaders, Jaruzelski reached out to the Consultative Council, whose members included Jerzy Turowicz and other Catholic intellectuals close to the pope. More than anything, Jaruzelski did not want to be the first Communist leader in the Warsaw Pact to be replaced by a non-Communist. There would be scores to settle. But his gesture was too little too late.

A series of spontaneous strikes in 1988 proved the turning point. Walesa had always warned that the workers would take matters into their own hands. The strikes, in April and May, turned into a tidal wave. But they weren't called by Solidarity. The strikers were almost all young, impoverished factory workers for whom the events of 1980 were the stuff of myth. They struck in anger because they were disgusted with their constantly eroding standard of living. Their raw emotions threatened chaos. The government flinched and turned to Walesa himself to coax the strikers back to work. But they refused—hundreds of thousands of them—until Jaruzelski and the regime promised that the government would begin talks about the country's future with an opposition that included Walesa.

On January 18, 1989, Jaruzelski announced that Solidarity would once again be legally recognized as a trade union. He had resigned as prime minister to become the president of Poland, with full executive powers. His successor as prime minister, Mieczyslaw Rakowski, formerly his deputy, made an official visit to Primate Glemp, as protocol dictated. Their conversation turned on the political situation, and Glemp now told the Communist Rakowski how essential it was to support Gorbachev's policies in the Soviet Union; he added that the pope was committed to those policies both in the USSR and in Poland.

On February 6, even as demonstrators around the country were protesting price increases, representatives of the government and the opposition sat down at what became known as the Round Table negotiations on the future of Poland. The end of an epoch was at hand.

The talks, quietly conducted under the aegis of the Church, lasted eight weeks and covered subjects ranging from economic policy to health care, from political reforms to the inalienable rights of Polish citizens. Walesa, General Czeslaw Kiszczak (the interior minister who had placed him under arrest in 1980), Politburo member Stanislaw Ciosek, and a gaggle of party advisers carried out the most sensitive part of the negotiations themselves, with Cardinal Macharski of Kraków or his representatives in attendance. "If neither side gave in," said Ciosek, "we always knew we could go to the Vatican for help."

The crucial agreement reached by the Round Table mandated free and open elections in June for seats to a new body to be called the Senate. The full legalization of Solidarity was also agreed upon.

When elections were held on June 4, Solidarity won all but one of the 262 seats it was allowed to contest. Parish priests had called on the faithful at mass that Sunday to back Solidarity candidates against the Communists. "This is a terrible result," said Jaruzelski. "It's the Church's fault."

Jaruzelski, with unofficial support from the union, narrowly won the presidency. But such a shaky coalition of two old foes was bound to fail. On August 19, Jaruzelski asked Tadeusz Mazowiecki, a Catholic intellectual who had advised Walesa during the Gdansk strikes of 1980, to form a cabinet, and on August 24 Mazowiecki became prime minister and Solidarity officially came to power.

Meanwhile, Walesa's first act after the Round Table accords were signed was to fly to Rome with five associates to thank John Paul II on behalf of Solidarity and the Polish people.

* * *

The reverberations from the fall of Poland shook the Eastern bloc for the rest of the winter of 1989, until there was no bloc left.

And then there was the USSR.

* * *

On December 1, 1989, the sidewalks of the great avenue leading to the Vatican were thronged with tens of thousands of people in a state of anticipation and excitement. The general secretary of the Communist Party of the USSR and the supreme pontiff of the Roman Catholic Church were about to meet for the first time.

Virtually every monsignor and archbishop of the Curia had stopped work to witness, either from an office window or on television, the arrival of Mikhail Gorbachev in his limousine (bearing the red flag with its hammer and sickle). For more than sixty years the Catholic Church and the Kremlin had struggled fiercely, and these men in black attire, trained in their seminaries to despise and fight the "enemies of God" throughout the world, had been in the front lines.

Yet the day before, in a speech in the Italian Capitol, the general secretary had spoken of the need for spirituality in the world. He had called for a "revolution in men's souls" while exalting "the eternal laws of humanity and morality of which Marx spoke."

"Religion helps *perestroika*," he declared. "We have given up pretending to have a monopoly on truth. . . . We no longer think that those who don't agree with us are enemies." This was truly a "new world order."

The first meeting between a general secretary of the USSR and a pontiff of the Roman Catholic Church was rich in symbolism for a new era.

Wojtyla, wearing his white robes, greeted Gorbachev and his wife, Raisa, enthusiastically in the reception room of the papal apartments. Then the two men adjourned to the pope's study.

"Generally speaking," the pope declared, "there are quite a few spots on this earth where peace is having a hard time. Perhaps we could act together in concert here." He was thinking particularly of regions with large Christian populations and historic Soviet influence.

Then John Paul offered the general secretary a homily on the subject of human rights:

We have been waiting with great anxieties and hopes for the adoption, in your country, of a law on the freedom of conscience. We hope that the adoption of such a law will lead to a broadening of the possibilities of religious life for all Soviet citizens. A person becomes a believer by his own free will; it's impossible to force somebody to believe.

With such a law, the pope said, diplomatic relations between the Holy See and Moscow could move forward—something Gorbachev now desired more than the Vatican, owing to the need to strengthen his position at home and the pope's great international prestige. Gorbachev readily pledged that a law on freedom of conscience would soon be adopted by the Supreme Soviet.

* * *

In August 1991, the Red Empire went into its death throes. At dawn on the 19th, in a coup d'etat, conservative members of the Politburo seized power in Moscow and put Gorbachev under house arrest in his Crimean dacha, announcing that he had been taken ill. Boris Yeltsin, president of the Russian Federal Republic, rebelled against the coup and transformed the Russian parliament building (called the White House for its marble facing) into the headquarters of the resistance.

Thanks to a radio transmitter belonging to Father van Straaten, which was intended to broadcast Catholic-Orthodox religious programs and was smuggled into the parliament's kitchens in a vegetable truck, Yeltsin was able to maintain contact with the outside world. His resistance prompted the West to support him.

A sincere cry of joy can be heard in the telegram that John Paul II sent to Gorbachev on August 23, the day the coup leaders surrendered: "I thank God for the happy outcome of the dramatic trial which involved your person, your family, and your country. I express my wish that you may continue your tremendous work for the material and spiritual renewal of the peoples of Soviet Union, upon whom I implore the Lord's blessing."

John Paul II's hopes, like those of many other world leaders, were shortlived. Yeltsin's victorious resistance became a sign of the people's will to wipe out the Communist regime once and for all. On December 25, the man who invented *perestroika* left office, and in the afternoon the red flag was lowered over the green cupola of the Kremlin.

*   *   *

Years later, much of the world came to hail Wojtyla as the conqueror of a war he had begun in 1978. The pope himself took a sober view. He expressly avoided parading as a kind of superman who had floored the Soviet bear. He urged his audience not to oversimplify things, not even to ascribe the fall of the USSR to the finger of God. When the Italian writer Vittorio Messori asked him about this, John Paul II replied: "It would be simplistic to say that Divine Providence caused the fall of communism. It fell by itself as a consequence of its own mistakes and abuses. It fell by itself because of its own inherent weakness."

John Paul II had experienced the crisis of communism from within, and above all he had meditated as a philosopher on the essence of communism's contradictions. Better than many Western politicians he understood that the Soviet system had collapsed through implosion. The external pressures had revealed the cracks in the system, but in the end the collapse had come from deep internal flaws.

In this collapse, economic and moral factors were interwoven. The economic resources of the USSR simply couldn't guarantee every citizen a secure existence, at however poor a level, while maintaining all the military apparatus of a superpower fighting a cold war. This was even clearer in the case of Communist East Germany, which, though far better organized than the USSR, was still facing economic bankruptcy on the eve of its collapse.

But it was above all ethical contradictions that had undermined the system. With Khrushchev the need for truth had stimulated an attempt to reform the system. With Brezhnev the denial of truth had produced stagnation and massive cynicism. With Gorbachev the thirst for truth, for *glasnost*, had become so intense as to overturn the system itself.

This theme of the truth and of the unsustainability of lies has always fascinated John Paul II in his thinking on totalitarianism. He read the works of both Andrei Sakharov and Aleksandr Solzhenitsyn and was moved by their moral conviction. Above all, Solzhenitsyn's booklet *Don't Lie* made a great impression on him, because he was convinced that the refusal to lie was the most powerful means of provoking a crisis in any totalitarian state. John Paul II spoke at length about ethics when Solzhenitsyn came to visit him in the Vatican in 1994. Communism, the pope had said in his first visit to post-Communist Prague in 1990, had "revealed itself to be an unattainable utopia because some essential aspects of the human person were neglected and negated: man's irrepressible longing for freedom and truth and his incapacity to feel happy when the transcendent relationship with God is excluded."

CHAPTER NINE

John Paul II on Faith and Reason

Fides et Ratio and The Quest for Truth

Gregory R. Beabout

he first time I heard that John Paul II had completed his encyclical on faith and reason was while I was attending a banquet in France. I was there for the annual meeting of the International Association for Christian Social Teaching, a group dedicated to the study of social justice as articulated in the encyclical tradition of Catholic Social Thought. The Friday dinner of September 4, 1998 turned into a birthday party when the president of the association, Jacques DelCourt of Belgium, announced that it was his wife's birthday. She had come with him to the meeting in Angers, France. The representative from Brazil stood up and sang "Happy Birthday" in Portuguese to Mrs. DelCourt. Next, two Jesuits from India arose and sang a birthday song in Hindi. Then, a pair of scholars from Pamplona sang a Spanish birthday song. There were more than fifty scholars from seventeen nations at the meeting. Country by country, in more than a dozen languages, scholars took their turn singing. As the only North American at the meeting, I was called upon to give my American interpretation of "Happy Birthday" as well.

Amidst the singing and joy and laughter of embarrassed scholars who don't usually sing in public, someone at my table mentioned that the Holy Father had completed his encyclical on faith and reason. "They are only waiting for the official Latin version to be completed," I was told. "Then it will be issued." Ten days later, on September 14, 1998, *Fides et Ratio* was officially released. This association in my mind of John Paul II's thirteenth encyclical with a joyous party of scholars from around the world, is appropriate, for this encyclical is an occasion for joy. To scholars and intellectuals like those at this meeting (theologians, philosophers, economists, political scientists and social theorists), an encyclical that praises and defends the intellectual life and the scholarly pursuit of the truth is a welcome delight.

On October 15, 1998, the day that the English translation was made available, I heard a report about the new encyclical on the radio. Several of my students joined me in my office as we surfed the web to get to the Vatican internet site in order to print out our own early copy of the encyclical. As we took turns reading passages aloud from the just printed text, one of my colleagues stopped by my office to see why there was so much commotion. After I explained that these were philosophy students who were taken with the relationship between faith and philosophy that was articulated by the Holy Father in his latest encyclical, my colleague whispered to me, "It's a new day, isn't it? We have a whole different kind of student now. This isn't the 1960s."

The following day, October 16, 1998, was the twentieth anniversary of John Paul II's election to the papacy. The front page of the *New York Times* ran a story on the new encyclical that described *Fides et Ratio* as "one of his most personal pronouncements to date: a crystallization of his philosophical and theological thinking over a lifetime." Indeed, it is. In some ways, John Paul II's entire life has involved both theology and philosophy, both faith and reason. His vocations before the papacy included philosophy professor and then bishop. His books included a volume of moral theology on love, a philosophical examination of the meaning of human action, and an interpretation and application of the Second Vatican Council. While he was in his late 20s and early 30s, he wrote two doctoral dissertations. His first dissertation is theological; it is an interpretation of the meaning of faith in St. John of the Cross. His second dissertation is more philosophical in character; it is a critical assessment of the moral philosophy of the twentieth century German phenomenologist Max Scheler. His life has been a testament to the blend of faith and reason, of theology and philosophy, that he defends in the encyclical.

And yet, the voice of the pope in his praise of reason as the complement of faith is, in some ways, a voice crying in the intellectual wilderness. While there are still scholars and intellectuals devoted to the pursuit of truth, there are many others who proclaim, in various ways, that the only truth is that there is no absolute truth. To a significant extent, this individualism and relativism has become commonplace in contemporary culture. The result has been the widespread belief in "truth by consensus" and "morality by majority."

For example, in the same week that the English translation of *Fides et Ratio* was issued, the student newspaper on our campus made no mention of the event. (The encyclical was front page news in the *New York Times*, but entirely unreported in the student newspaper at our Catholic university). During the week in which one would have expected a story about the new encyclical, the student newspaper instead included a large advertisement by the letterhead group that is so-called "Catholics for a Free Choice." The ad, part of a fund raising campaign, declares "Most polls show that four out of five Catholics disagree with the official Church position . . ."[1] This is an uncanny instantiation of morality-by-majority thinking. Because this type of thinking has become so common in contemporary culture, the irrationality of it goes almost unnoticed. The advertisement then blames the pope and the bishops for thousands of "abortions and maternal deaths in our hemisphere alone."[2] No rational evidence is given in the ad to support this outrageous claim.

The cultural tendencies of twentieth century modernism and postmodernism provide the background for the encyclical. The desire to drive a wedge that separates faith and reason that marked so much of the modern project after the rise of modern science in the seventeenth century and into the Enlightenment has become part of the everyday world of the twentieth century. From the Enlightenment dream of a secularized society that celebrates science, morality and the arts—all separated from traditional religious faith—we have arrived at a culture that spends unprecedented time and money on soap operas and sit-coms that depict characters with no religious life and no sense of ultimate purpose. The split between faith and reason has brought about dual extremes. On the one hand, we have Carl Sagan exemplifying the hope for a scientific society devoid of religion. On the other hand, we have growing fundamentalisms, new age "spiritualities" and other quasi-religious movements where faith is separated from rationality. While political philosophers like Rawls and Habermas prescribe a public square based on reason alone and devoid of all religious and metaphysical questions, we have witnessed the rise of the Moral Majority and then the Christian Coalition speaking a political language devoid of philosophical nuance that almost seems to advocate a theocracy, with various voices calling for a literal application of biblical morality to governmental policy.

Within this cultural context, where the divorce between faith and reason has been so complete that it seems difficult for a conversation between the two to exist, the encyclical *Fides et Ratio* offers an alternative vision with a defense of both faith and reason, as well as an account of the complementary relation between faith and reason in the human quest for truth.

Summary of the Encyclical

The encyclical is written in an intellectual tone. It is written with the assumption that the reader is conversant with the history and terminology of theology and philosophy. Several parts are fairly technical. Though the details of the 35,000 word encyclical are dense and tightly argued, the central message is clearly accessible to a broad audience. The main conclusion is that both faith and reason are necessary complements in the quest for truth. The chief metaphor that is used to articulate this conclusion appears in poetic form in the first line of the encyclical. "Faith and reason are like two wings on which the human spirit rises to the contemplation of the truth."

The encyclical is divided into seven chapters that are framed by an introduction and a conclusion. After an introduction that urges intellectuals and those who shape the culture to pursue the truth by addressing the fundamental questions of human life, chapter one is a reflection on faith, where faith is understood as a free human response to entrust oneself personally and completely to the transcendent mystery of God. Chapter two is a meditation on the concept of wisdom in the Hebrew and Christian scriptures. Chapter three is a complex philosophical argument which shows that the honest use of reason in the quest for truth always entails a kind of faith and is compatible with Christian faith. Chapter four is a history of the encounter of the relationship between faith and reason from the time of St. Paul's preaching in Athens through the history of western philosophy to the contemporary setting. Chapter five, which focuses on the role of the magisterium in philosophical matters, is an extension of Leo XIII's 1879 encyclical *Aeterni Patris*. Chapter six shows several ways theology and philosophy need each other and why. Chapter seven identifies a number of current tasks for philosophy and theology. The encyclical ends with John Paul II offering encouragement to those he has addressed in their efforts to pursue the truth using faith and reason.

With this brief overview, I will spend the rest of this essay offering a more detailed examination of each of the parts of the encyclical.

Know Thyself

In every culture and society, there have been wise people who have taken up the quest for truth. The desire to understand the truth about the world also raises questions about oneself. In all of the ancient cultures (as examples, the pope mentions ancient India, China, Greece and the early mid-east) there have been wise people who have addressed the same fundamental questions that pervade human life: "Who am I? Where have I come from and where am I going? Why is there evil? What is there after this life?"[3] The Church is also concerned about these fundamental human questions. Over the course of the centuries, philosophy has developed as one of the central resources for taking up these questions that flow from the wonder awakened in us by the contemplation of creation. The Church considers philosophy an indispensable help in coming to a deeper understanding of the fundamental truths about human life (5).

In the contemporary situation, the search for ultimate truth about these basic human questions often seems to be neglected. Part of this neglect flows from tendencies in modern philosophy. Modern philosophical research has tended to focus on human knowing, especially accenting the ways in which human knowledge is limited and conditioned (5). There are important insights that are gained in this investigation, but it has tended to lead to a neglect or even abandonment of the quest for understanding of our being. With the abandonment of the contemplation of the mystery of our being and the turning away from our quest for transcendence and truth, there is a tendency for individuals to become reduced to objects of knowledge that are used for pragmatic purposes. Technology then becomes the trump card. This tendency to focus only on what is clearly knowable using empirical and logical categories is not merely a movement in modern academic philosophy. It has cultural effects in that it gives rise to widespread scepticism, agnosticism, and relativism. This leads to a sense of being adrift, stumbling through life with no clear sense of ultimate meaning or purpose, of standing at the edge of an abyss without knowing where one is going (6). In particular, the younger generation can be left with a sense that there are no valid points of reference.

Amidst this cultural climate, where there is a highly developed sense of scientific and technological understanding but a tendency to assume that reason can not gain any insights into the fundamental questions of human life, the pope makes a call to redouble our quest for truth. Echoing the admonition over the temple door at Delphi—"Know Thyself"—the pope urges us to pursue an understanding of what it means to be a human being. The encyclical primarily is addressed to bishops. John Paul II urges them to strengthen their contemporaries in the quest for truth. He also addresses himself to theologians, philosophers and "all those who are searching" (6). The pope issues a series of challenges. He urges his fellow bishops to witness to the truth that is entrusted to them. He then challenges theologians to explore and reaffirm the truth of faith. Next, he invites philosophers to recover and develop the full dignity of philosophy in its quest for understanding of the human condition. To all who seek, the pope calls us to a clearer sense of the great resources with which we have been endowed to pursue the truth, not only about the world, but about who we are and about our place in it.

The Revelation of God's Wisdom

Many of the intellectuals who discuss the role of dialogue in public life have begun with the presupposition that all public discourse should be based on claims that are reasonable and publicly defensible. Of course, this has generated tremendous debate about what constitutes "reasonableness." Still, the prevailing view has been that religious appeals or moral claims based on religious belief are ruled out of bounds. Further, any consideration of ultimate metaphysical issues of human purpose, the meaning of life or considerations of an afterlife are inappropriate for public discourse. In the apt phrase of Richard John Neuhaus, the cosmopolitan elite expect us to operate in a "naked public square." Public discourse about tax laws, building bridges, rights to expression and individual freedoms are all permitted. But it is viewed as gauche, as tacky, as out of place, to raise religious and metaphysical questions in public.

Having declared that this refusal of cultural leaders to discuss the fundamental questions of human life has led to a sense of a loss of meaning, the pope refuses to play by the cosmopolitan rules of the late twentieth century. Instead, he boldly proclaims that the Church is the "bearer of a message" from God (7). This message, God's revelation of Himself to the world, does not have its origin in human speculation or reasoning (7). It comes from an encounter initiated by God which is "utterly gratuitous, moving from God to men and women in order to bring them salvation" (7). This revelation from God of Himself to the world has occurred and continues to occur in history. While God continues to reveal Himself in the unceasing action of the Holy Spirit, God revealed Himself in a special way in the Incarnation. "In the Incarnation of the Son of God we see forged the enduring and definitive synthesis which the human mind of itself could not even have imagined: the Eternal enters time, the Whole lies hidden in the part, God takes on a human face" (12).

While truth is one, faith and reason provide different accesses to the truth. Philosophy and the sciences operate within the order of natural reason. Through ordinary sense perception and by the natural light of the intellect, the human person can gain some insight into the workings of the physical world and into a deeper understanding of one's being. Divine revelation is another access into the truth. Revelation is neither identical to nor mutually exclusive of natural reason (9). While Christ's revelation of Himself to the world occurs at a particular time and place, the truth communicated in Christ's revelation is offered to every man and woman, and is not confined to a particular place or culture (12).

Faith involves the free human response to entrust oneself personally and completely to the transcendent mystery of God (13). The human person is free to reject the gift of God, but human freedom only finds its completion in entrusting oneself to God who is the source of freedom and truth (13). The mystery of God is never exhausted by the human mind, but can only be received and embraced by faith. Human reason can, on its own and without reference to faith, discover signs that point beyond themselves (14). Philosophy, with its search for understanding, seeks to understand the truth of the meaning of life. Through the mystery of God's revelation, the eternal answer is disclosed in history by God in love. Yet the perception of the truth revealed in faith, our vision of the face of God, is fragmentary and can be deepened with the use of natural reason (13). With the revelation of faith, reason is compelled to extend the range of its power (14).

Faith Seeking Understanding

One of the marks of most of John Paul II's encyclicals has been his generous use of the sacred scriptures. For example, *Veritatis Splendor* begins with a detailed meditation on the gospel story of the rich young man. From that gospel story, the pope proceeds to reflect on the splendor of truth as revealed in the scriptural narrative. A similar biblical emphasis is present in many of John Paul II's other encyclicals and is employed in the second chapter of *Fides et Ratio*. In this chapter, the pope focuses on the concept of wisdom as it is developed in the scriptures. The first half of the chapter draws from the Hebrew scriptures, especially the Wisdom literature including the book of *Proverbs* and the deutero-canonical texts. In these texts, the sacred scriptures indicate that the truths of faith and the truths of reason are deeply related. For example, the encyclical quotes from *Sirach* 14:20: "Happy the man who meditates on wisdom and reasons intelligently" (16).

The second half of this chapter turns to the theme of wisdom in the New Testament. In *Romans* 1:20, St. Paul presents in popular form a philosophical argument affirming the human capacity for metaphysical insight (22). From observations of the created things of this world, we can reason to their transcendent source. While St. Paul affirms the power of reason to gain some insight into the divine, he denies that human argumentation can understand the central Christian mystery of Jesus' death and resurrection (23). The wisdom of this world can not comprehend this mystery, so that the wisdom of faith, which is open to all and is free of cultural limitations, is a wisdom that complements and exceeds human wisdom.

Understanding Seeking Faith

At the core of the third chapter are some important insights into the nature of the human person and the role of interpersonal relations in human knowledge that can be gained from phenomenological reflection. In that sense, this is a highly personal chapter that draws from the pope's reflection on his experience of interpersonal relationships. In another sense, the third chapter of the encyclical contains a rather detailed and technical argument that leads to the conclusion that faith and reason complement one another and together are both ordered toward the truth.

The argument has two parts. In the first part of the argument, the pope moves from the capacity of humans to use reason in a quest for truth to conclude that the use of reason entails faith in other persons. Then, having established that reason necessarily entails faith in other human persons, the pope moves to faith in Christ as a person who is the truth, and shows that this faith complements reason's quest for truth. In schematic form, the argument looks like this.

P1. Reason has the capacity to rise above the here and now to set out towards the infinite (24).

P2. All human beings desire to know the truth (25).

P3. The first absolutely certain truth (beyond the fact that we exist) is the inevitability of our death (26).

P4. Each of us has the desire to know the truth about our own death (26).

P5. Our desire is for a truth that is universal and absolute (27).

P6. The search for a truth that is universal and absolute reveals something about the kind of being a human being is, that is, a human being is the kind of being who seeks universal truth (28).

P7. The search for truth implies the rudiments of a response (29).

P8. The truth that we seek (about death and the meaning of life) will affect the way the seeker lives and regulates one's behavior (30).

P9. Some truths are verified by immediate evidence, confirmed by experimentation, or accepted after a process of critical inquiry (30).

P10. It is practically impossible and undesirable to personally verify all the information and scientific findings of modern life (30).

P11. Human beings develop in their quest for truth in a social context, that is, humans are born and raised in a family and immersed in a language and a tradition (31).

P12. Some truths are accepted based on believing the authority of qualified persons (31).

P13. In the life of a human being, many more truths are based on belief in the word of other persons than those verified by immediate evidence, confirmed by experimentation, or accepted after a process of critical inquiry (31).

P14. In believing another person, we entrust ourselves to the knowledge acquired by others.

P15. The capacity to entrust oneself to another reveals the ability of the person to enter into an interpersonal, intimate and enduring relationship with another person (32).

P16. The human quest for truth involves not only acquiring abstract knowledge but also entering into personal relationships of faithful self-giving (32).

C1.   In order for reason to be sustained, one must enter into interpersonal relationships of faithful self-giving.

Having arrived at this conclusion, the pope continues the argument to show that reason is compatible with Christian faith.

P17. The search for truth is also a search for a person to whom one might entrust oneself (33).

P18. In grace, Jesus Christ reveals himself as the truth and as a person to whom one may entrust oneself (34).

P19. Christian faith offers the concrete possibility of reaching the goal which men and women seek in their journey (34).

C2.   Faith and reason complement one another in the quest for truth "like two wings on which the human spirit rises to the contemplation of the truth."

Having established that faith and reason complement one another, John Paul turns in the subsequent chapters to explore more directly the relationship between revealed truth and philosophy.

The Relationship Between Faith and Reason

The fourth chapter of *Fides et Ratio* is a history of the encounter of the relationship between faith and reason. This history begins with Paul's preaching in Athens as recorded in the *Acts of the Apostles* (17:16–32). During his trip to Athens, St. Paul entered into discussion with Greek philosophers, and from there, the history of the dialogue between faith and philosophy unfolds. The early Church fathers were concerned with the relation between faith and reason and with various interpretations of the relation between Christian faith and philosophy, or between "Jerusalem and Athens." Iranaeus, Tertullian, Justin, Clement of Alexandria and Origen are all mentioned (37–39). The Greek notion of theology as the noblest part of philosophical discourse (especially in Aristotle's system) was transformed by the early Church fathers so that it came to signify "the reflection undertaken by the believer in order to express the true doctrine about God" (39). When the fathers adopted elements of Plato's philosophy into their reasoning about faith, theology underwent particularly profound changes. Augustine played an especially important role in Christianizing Platonic and Neo-Platonic thought (40). These early Church fathers are held up as models of thinkers who welcomed reason and who were willing to probe the questions of philosophy and "infuse it with the richness drawn from revelation" (41).

Next, the pope gives a special place to the synthesis between faith and reason forged in the thirteenth century by St. Thomas Aquinas. As Aquinas argued, there can be no contradiction between reason and faith, since both come from God. In the Catholic intellectual tradition, Thomas has been consistently held up as the Angelic Doctor who was willing to plumb the depths of reason, following it carefully toward the truth, recognizing where it is weak due to human fragility and limitations, and synthesizing the truth attained by the light of natural reason with faith that builds upon and perfects reason (43–44).

Though Aquinas insisted upon a legitimate distinction between faith and reason; later thinkers transformed this recognition of appropriate differences into a fateful separation. Ultimately this became the modern divorce between faith and reason. Though the pope does not name names in this part of the encyclical,[4] scholars of the history of philosophy are familiar with the array of modern philosophers who urged a radical breach between faith and reason. This began with rationalism and included thinkers who claimed that reason could prove (on its own) beliefs that had traditionally been understood as flowing from faith. This led ultimately to a rejection not only of faith but also of reason. Since reason claimed to be able to prove what had been previously believed by faith, the first step was that many thinkers came to view faith as unnecessary (at least for the cultured elite). Next, because reason (especially when transformed into a narrow, instrumental, utilitarian or positivistic tool wholly separated from faith) could not provide adequate answers to the ultimate questions of human life, thinkers began to despair of reason's ability to respond to the quest for ultimate meaning and truth. The dream of a society based on reason without need of faith has become instead the brooding anxiety of a society that despairs of reason's ability to ask ultimate questions. "As a result of the crisis of rationalism, what has appeared finally is nihilism" (46). As Walker Percy puts it, the Enlightenment dream of the freedom to pursue happiness "through work, participation in society, family, the market-place, the political process, cultural activities, sports, the sciences, and the arts" has become instead the insatiable pursuit of meaningless diversions: "TV, sports, travel, drugs, games, newspapers, magazines, Vegas."[5]

We find ourselves at a point where there is a widespread tendency, not only among many philosophers but also throughout various areas of cultural life, to believe that reason is inadequate to address the fundamental questions of human life. Among many contemporary philosophers, the effort to address the metaphysical questions of life's meaning and purpose have been disregarded, and religious belief is not even on the map for consideration. Increasingly, it is not just faith that has been written off, but also reason. The effect is that many philosophers have abandoned the search for truth. Likewise, in education and in the culture, the pursuit of wisdom about the human condition largely has been abandoned. While intellectual elites (from Rawls to Rorty) continue to despair of reason's ability to pursue the truth about ultimate questions about life's meaning and purpose, there is a growing ignorance in the broader culture that our heritage includes a host of thinkers over several millennia who have dedicated themselves to using reason in a quest for the truth.

The Hierarchy of the Roman Catholic Church and Philosophy

The pope begins this section by making it clear that the Church has no philosophy of her own (49). Philosophy has its own goals and methods. Still, since it is ordered to the truth, as is faith, and since philosophy often includes serious mistakes which can cause confusion to those who do not have philosophical training, it is an appropriate role for the magisterium to point out certain serious errors that have arisen in some philosophies (50). This is not primarily a negative task with the magisterium limiting certain philosophical approaches. Rather, it is a positive task with the magisterium encouraging more serious philosophical inquiry. Philosophers recognize and want criticism, especially when their inquiry is not oriented toward the truth. After reviewing the way the magisterium has challenged certain flawed philosophical approaches, the pope turns to the current situation. Many philosophers have abandoned the quest for metaphysical truth, settling for a view that "truth is born of consensus" rather than through the challenging work of reason (56). Amidst this postmodern tendency to despair of reason's ability to come closer to the truth, the pope encourages all philosophers "to trust in the power of human reason and not to set themselves goals that are too modest" (56). "It is necessary not to abandon the passion for ultimate truth, the eagerness to search for it or the audacity to forge new paths in the search" (56).

The second half of chapter five is an extension of the 1879 encyclical of Leo XIII, *Aeterni Patris*. In that encyclical, Leo emphasized the incomparable value of the philosophy of Thomas Aquinas. That encyclical led to a renewed interest in the thought of St. Thomas and a number of novel interpretations of Aquinas's thought as various thinkers brought St. Thomas into dialogue with the philosophical issues of their day. The Thomistic revival of the twentieth century included a powerful array of thinkers (58). Additionally, there have been important Catholic philosophers who have engaged the methods and approaches of other philosophical traditions and have produced fruitful and important results.

Next, the pope turns to the teaching of the Second Vatican Council with regard to philosophy. In *Gaudium et Spes* (the Vatican II document on the role of the Church in the modern world), especially in the chapter on the dignity of the human person, thinkers can find "a compendium of biblical anthropology from which philosophy too can draw inspiration" (60). The Council also stressed the importance of philosophy in the formation of candidates for the priesthood and by implication for all Christian education. Of course, it is well known that in the period after the Council, there has been a widening gap between theology and philosophy. In many Catholic seminaries, colleges and universities, philosophy was greatly reduced in the curriculum during the period immediately after the Council. The pope expresses concern that the teaching of the Council has been distorted. (Though the pope doesn't say so, it often seems that this distortion has occurred through the neglect of the study of the teaching of the Council by those who most claim to speak in the "spirit" of the council.) The pope concludes this section by emphasizing the "intimate bond which ties theological work to the philosophical search for truth" (63).

The Interaction Between Philosophy and Theology

The search for truth always entails the individual human person who is embedded in a particular culture entering a journey towards a truth which is universal and which transcends one's own particular culture. This universal character of truth is evident in both faith and reason. "The word of God is addressed to all people," (64) and hence has a universal character. Likewise, philosophy allows the person, through the power of reason, to transcend more concrete particularities and take up the quest for universal truth. Together, faith and reason deepen one another in this quest for universal truth.

There has been a tendency, especially after the Second Vatican Council, for some theologians to focus on issues of culture, history or the social sciences and to ignore philosophy. The pope acknowledges that there have been insights gained in emphasizing the particular. However, he emphasizes "the duty to go beyond the particular and concrete, lest the prime task of demonstrating the universality of faith's content be abandoned" (69). To provide an example of the way that theologians may engage a culture without getting stuck at the level of concrete particularities, the pope proposes that theologians might study more fully the philosophical tradition of India in a way analogous to the way St. Thomas synthesized the Christian tradition with Aristotle's philosophy. Just as Aristotle's philosophy was alien to Christianity and yet contained a rich reserve of universal truths, so too theologians might engage the philosophical traditions of the east in a dialogue with faith in a manner such that the dialogue might advance the quest for truth.

In the second part of chapter six, John Paul lays out three different stances of philosophy. First, there is a philosophy entirely independent of God's revelation. Historically, Greek philosophy preceded the Incarnation, so the Greek philosophers can be seen as models of thinkers on the quest for universal truth and using reason without the gift of faith. Nonetheless, we see in them an openness to the transcendent. In contrast, many philosophers in the modern period coupled the appropriate desire for autonomy in philosophy with an outright refusal of divine revelation, a refusal which is tantamount to turning away from an appropriate access to the truth (75).

A second stance is usually called Christian philosophy (76). This does not mean that there is an official philosophy of the Church or that these thinkers are working out a philosophy for the Church. Instead, it refers to Christians who philosophize and who pursue philosophical questions that flow from the direct or indirect contribution of Christian faith.

The pope notes a third stance: when theology calls upon philosophy. "Were theologians to refuse the help of philosophy, they would run the risk of doing philosophy unwittingly and locking themselves within thought structures poorly adapted to the understanding of faith. Were philosophers, for their part, to shun theology completely, they would be forced to master on their own the contents of Christian faith" (77). The pope is critical of either tendency—philosophy without theology and vice versa—because in both cases, the autonomy of the disciplines paradoxically would be violated. This is a subtle and nuanced position with a curious argument to support it. If theology ignores philosophy, it ends up tacitly doing philosophy, and it ends up doing poor philosophy. The inverse is true of philosophy. Therefore, philosophy and theology stand in need of each other and should be in dialogue with one another.

Current Requirements and Tasks

In the first half of chapter seven, the pope outlines four current tasks for philosophy and then five dangers to be avoided. Each of the tasks for philosophy flow from its responsibility to respond to the contemporary crisis of meaning. 1) The pope urges philosophers to recover philosophy's "sapiential dimension" of using reason in the search for ultimate meaning in life (81). 2) Philosophy is called to verify the human capacity to know the truth, including the truth about what it is to be a human being and about the other fundamental questions of human life (82). 3) The pope then challenges philosophers to transcend the merely empirical and to rise toward the genuinely metaphysical, specifically to reality and truth (83). 4) Philosophy needs to participate in helping people in the quest for a unified and organic vision, especially amidst the contemporary situation of the fragmentation of knowledge (85).

In addressing these four needs, there are five dangers to be avoided by philosophy. 1) *Eclecticism* is the tendency to treat ideas as a smorgasbord where various ideas are arbitrarily drawn from widely differing philosophies without concern for their internal coherence (86). 2) *Historicism* focuses on the way that a particular truth is related to the period or purpose in which the idea arose in a historical context while ignoring that there are truths and errors that can be evaluated as such despite the distance of space and time (87). 3) *Scientism* is the naive view that the only valid forms of knowledge are in the positive sciences, and hence all religious, theological, ethical, and aesthetic knowledge are matters of private taste or mere fancy (88). 4) *Pragmatism* is a mode of thinking that ignores principled moral considerations in making decisions and instead focuses solely on the practical consequences in determining a proposed line of action (89). 5) *Nihilism* is the view that nothing ultimately matters and that there is no ultimate foundation or objective truth (90). These five common tendencies in postmodern thought are cited as dangers to be avoided by those who philosophize.

In the second half of chapter seven, the pope outlines two current tasks for theology. First, he calls theology to renew its methods in order to serve evangelization more effectively. Second, theology should look to the ultimate truth which revelation entrusts to it (92). In trying to be sensitive to both the concrete particularities in which revelation is always addressed and the universal truth that is the content of every authentic divine revelation, theologians need an approach that looks at cultural context without neglecting truths that transcend a particular culture. "The use of a hermeneutic open to the appeal of metaphysics can show how it is possible to move from the historical and contingent circumstances in which the texts developed to the truth which they express, a truth transcending those circumstances" (95).

In order to accomplish its task of understanding revealed truth, theology needs philosophy, both to understand aspects of the mystery of being and to make sense of key ideas in moral theology (97). In addition, the philosophical implications of catechesis need to be explored more fully (99).

The Encyclical's Concluding Section

Throughout the encyclical, various approaches are used to articulate the complementary relationship appropriate to faith and reason. The conclusion is that faith and reason mutually support each other in the quest for truth. Their collaboration has contributed to humanity. The task of the Church is to defend human dignity and to proclaim the gospel. To do this, the Church needs to help people discover their capacity to know the truth and their yearning for the ultimate meaning of life. This means philosophers are called to do what they traditionally have done: pursue more comprehensively the true, the good and the beautiful (103). The encyclical then ends with a reflection on Mary, the seat of Wisdom, but not before the pope gives words of encouragement to five groups of people who are important members of the pilgrimage toward the truth. 1) Theologians are encouraged to pay special attention to the philosophical implications of the Word of God (105). 2) Those responsible for priestly formation are encouraged to pay special attention to the philosophical and theological preparation of seminarians (105). 3) Philosophers and teachers of philosophy are urged to have the courage to recover the authentic wisdom proper to philosophical enquiry (106). 4) Scientists are encouraged to continue their research, but to act within the horizon of wisdom about the ethical values appropriate to the human person (106). 5) Finally, everyone is encouraged to take up the search for truth in freedom, recognizing that freedom comes to its fulfillment in the truth (107).

NOTES

[1] The ad appeared in *The University News*, October 22, 1998, p. 4.

[2] *Ibid.*

[3] *Fides et Ratio,* section 1. Hereafter, all references to *Fides et Ratio* will appear as parenthetical references designating the section number from the encyclical.

[4] The pope treats this issue on pp. 50–53 of *Crossing the Threshold of Hope.* (New York: Alfred A Knopf, 1994). It is common in papal encyclicals not to speak ill of individuals, only of positions. But for those who would like a list of names of people John Paul II has in mind who have contributed to the divorce between faith and reason, in *Crossing the Threshold of Hope* he mentions DesCartes, Kant, Voltaire and Rousseau. The pope also mentions the Enlightenment in France and the French Revolution play an important part in reason's revolt against faith.

[5] Walker Percy, *Lost in the Cosmos.* (New York: Farrar, Straus & Giroux, 1983) 12.

CHAPTER TEN

John Paul II in
His Own Words

The following passages are from the writings of John Paul II on the themes covered in this book.

John Paul II and Theology

This passage is from John Paul II"s first encyclical, "Redemptor Hominis," *which was issued in 1979. This text is taken from sections 8–12 of the encyclical.*

The redeemer of the world! In him has been revealed in a new and more wonderful way the fundamental truth concerning creation to which the Book of Genesis gives witness when it repeats several times: 'God saw that it was good.' The good has its source in wisdom and love. In Jesus Christ the visible world which God created for man—the world that, when sin entered, 'was subjected to futility'—recovers again its original link with the divine source of wisdom and love. Indeed, 'God so loved the world that he gave his only son.' As this link was broken in the man Adam, so in the man Christ it was reforged. Are we of the twentieth century not convinced of the overpoweringly eloquent words of the apostle of the gentiles concerning the 'creation [that] has been groaning in travail together until now' and 'waits with eager longing for the revelation of the sons of God,' the creation that 'was subjected to futility'? Does not the previously unknown immense progress—which has taken place especially in the course of this century—in the field of man's dominion over the world itself reveal—to a previously unknown degree—that manifold subjection 'to futility'? It is enough to recall certain phenomena, such as the threat of pollution of the natural environment in areas of rapid industrialization, or the armed conflicts continually breaking out over and over again, or the prospectives of self-destruction through the use of atomic, hydrogen, neutron and similar weapons, or the lack of respect for the life of the unborn. The world of the new age, the world of space flights, the world of the previously unattained conquests of science and technology—is it not also the world 'groaning in travail' that 'waits with eager longing for the revealing of the sons of God'?

In its penetrating analysis of 'the modern world,' the Second Vatican Council reached that most important point of the visible world that is man, by penetrating like Christ the depth of human consciousness and by making contact with the inward mystery of man, which in biblical and non-biblical language is expressed by the word 'heart.' Christ, the redeemer of the world, is the one who penetrated in a unique unrepeatable way into the mystery of man and entered his 'heart.' Rightly therefore does the Second Vatican Council teach: 'The truth is that only in the mystery of the incarnate word does the mystery of man take on light. For Adam, the first man, was a type of him who was to come (*Romans* 5:14), Christ the Lord. Christ the new Adam, in the very revelation of the mystery of the Father and of his love, *fully reveals man to himself* and brings to light his most high calling.' And the council continues: 'He who is the "image of the invisible God" (*Colossians* 1:15), is himself the perfect man who has restored in the children of Adam that likeness to God which had been disfigured ever since the first sin. Human nature, by the very fact that it was assumed, not absorbed, in him, has been raised in us also to a dignity beyond compare. For, by his incarnation, he, the son of God, *in a certain way united himself with each man.* He worked with human hands, he thought with a human mind. He acted with a human will, and with a human heart he loved. Born of the Virgin Mary, he has truly been made one of us, like to us in all things except sin,' he, the redeemer of man.

As we reflect again on this stupendous text from the council's teaching, we do not forget even for a moment that Jesus Christ, the son of the living God, became our reconciliation with the Father. He it was, and he alone, who satisfied the Father's eternal love, that fatherhood that from the beginning found expression in creating the world, giving man all the riches of creation, and making him 'little less than God,' in that he was created 'in the image and after the likeness of God.' He and he alone also satisfied that fatherhood of God and that love which man in a way rejected by breaking the first covenant and the later covenants that God 'again and again offered to man.' The redemption of the world—this tremendous mystery of love in which creation is renewed—is, at its deepest root, the fullness of justice in a human heart—the heart of the first-born son—in order that it may become justice in the hearts of many human beings, predestined from eternity in the first-born son to be children of God and called to grace, called to love. The cross on Calvary, through which Jesus Christ—a man, the son of the Virgin Mary, thought to be the son of Joseph of Nazareth —'leaves' this world, is also a fresh manifestation of the eternal father-hood of God, who in him draws near again to humanity, to each human being, giving him the thrice holy 'Spirit of truth.'

This revelation of the Father and outpouring of the Holy Spirit, which stamp an indelible seal on the mystery of the redemption, explain the meaning of the cross and death of Christ. The God of creation is revealed as the God of redemption, as the God who is 'faithful to himself,' and faithful to his love for man and the world, which he revealed on the day of creation. He is a love that does not draw back before anything that justice requires in him. Therefore 'for our sake [God] made him [the son] to be sin who knew no sin.' If he 'made to be sin' him who was without any sin whatever, it was to reveal the love that is always greater than the whole of creation, the love that is he himself, since 'God is love.' Above all, love is greater than sin, than weakness, than the 'futility of creation;' it is stronger than death; it is a love always ready to raise up and forgive, always ready to go to meet the prodigal son, always looking for 'the revealing of the sons of God,' who are called to 'the glory that is to be revealed.' This revelation of love is also described as mercy; and in man's history this revelation of love and mercy has taken a form and a name: that of Jesus Christ.

Man cannot live without love. He remains a being that is incom-prehensible for himself, his life is senseless, if love is not revealed to him, if he does not encounter love, if he does not experience it and make it his own, if he does not participate intimately in it. This, as has already been said, is why Christ the redeemer 'fully reveals man to himself'. If we may use the expression, this is the human dimension of the mystery of the redemption. In this dimension man finds again the greatness, dignity and value that belong to his humanity. In the mystery of the redemption man becomes newly 'expressed' and, in a way, is newly created. He is newly created! 'There is neither Jew nor Greek, there is neither slave nor free, there is neither male nor female; for you are all one in Christ Jesus.' The man who wishes to understand himself thoroughly—and not just in accordance with immediate, partial, often superficial, and even illusory standards and measures of his being—he must with his unrest, uncertainty and even his weakness and sinfulness, with his life and death, draw near to Christ. He must, so to speak, enter into him with all his own self, he must 'appropriate' and assimilate the whole of the reality of the incarnation and redemption in order to find himself. If this profound process takes place within him, he then bears fruit not only of adoration of God but also of deep wonder at himself. How precious must man be in the eyes of the creator, if he 'gained so great a redeemer,' and if God 'gave his only son' in order that man 'should not perish but have eternal life.'

In reality, the name for that deep amazement at man's worth and dignity is the gospel, that is to say: the good news. It is also called Christianity. This amazement determines the Church's mission in the world and, perhaps even more so, 'in the modern world.' This amazement, which is also a conviction and a certitude—at its deepest root it is the certainty of faith, but in a hidden and mysterious way it vivifies every aspect of authentic humanism—is closely connected with Christ. It also fixes Christ's place—so to speak, his particular right of citizenship—in the history of man and mankind. Unceasingly contemplating the whole of Christ's mystery, the Church knows with all the certainty of faith that the redemption that took place through the cross has definitively restored his dignity to man and given back meaning to his life in the world, a meaning that was lost to a considerable extent because of sin. And for that reason, the redemption was accomplished in the paschal mystery, leading through the cross and death to resurrection.

The Church's fundamental function in every age and particularly in ours is to direct man's gaze, to point the awareness and experience of the whole of humanity towards the mystery of God, to help all men to be familiar with the profundity of the redemption taking place in Christ Jesus. At the same time man's deepest sphere is involved—we mean the sphere of human hearts, consciences and events.

The Second Vatican Council did immense work to form that full and universal awareness by the Church of which Pope Paul VI wrote in his first encyclical. This awareness—or rather self-awareness—by the Church is formed 'in dialogue'; and before this dialogue becomes a conversation, attention must be directed to 'the other', that is to say: the person with whom we wish to speak. The Ecumenical Council gave a fundamental impulse to forming the Church's self-awareness by so adequately and competently presenting to us a view of the terrestrial globe as a map of various religions. It showed furthermore that this map of the world's religions has superimposed on it, in previously unknown layers typical of our time, the phenomenon of atheism in its various forms, beginning with the atheism that is programmed, organized and structured as a political system.

With regard to religion, what is dealt with is in the first place religion as a universal phenomenon linked with man's history from the beginning, then the various non-Christian religions, and finally Christianity itself. The council document on non-Christian religions, in particular, is filled with deep esteem for the great spiritual values, indeed for the primacy of the spiritual, which in the life of mankind finds expression in religion and then in morality, with direct effects on the whole of culture. The Fathers of the Church rightly saw in the various religions as it were so many reflections of the one truth, 'seeds of the word,' attesting that, though the routes taken may be different, there is but a single goal to which is directed the deepest aspiration of the human spirit as expressed in its quest for God and also in its quest, through its tending towards God, for the full dimension of its humanity, or in other words for the full meaning of human life. The council gave particular attention to the Jewish religion, recalling the great spiritual heritage common to Christians and Jews. It also expressed its esteem for the believers of Islam, whose faith also looks to Abraham.

The opening made by the Second Vatican Council has enabled the Church and all. Christians to reach a more complete awareness of the mystery of Christ, 'the mystery hidden for ages' in God, to be revealed in time in the man Jesus Christ, and to be revealed continually in every time. In Christ and through Christ God has revealed himself fully to mankind and has definitively drawn close to it; at the same time, in Christ and through Christ man has acquired full awareness of his dignity, of the heights to which he is raised, of the surpassing worth of his own humanity, and of the meaning of his existence.

All of us who are Christ's followers must therefore meet and unite around him. This unity in the various fields of the life, tradition, structures and discipline of the individual Christian churches and ecclesial communities cannot be brought about without effective work aimed at getting to know each other and removing the obstacles blocking the way to perfect unity. However, we can and must immediately reach and display to the world our unity in proclaiming the mystery of Christ, in revealing the divine dimension and also the human dimension of the redemption, and in struggling with unwearying perseverance for the dignity that each human being has reached and can continually reach in Christ, namely the dignity of both the grace of divine adoption and the inner truth of humanity, a truth which—if in the common awareness of the modern world it has been given such fundamental importance—for us is still clearer in the light of the reality that is Jesus Christ.

Jesus Christ is the stable principle and fixed center of the mission that God himself has entrusted to man. We must all share in this mission and concentrate all our forces on it, since it is more necessary than ever for modern mankind. If this mission seems to encounter greater opposition nowadays than ever before, this shows that today it is more necessary than ever and, in spite of the opposition, more awaited than ever. Here we touch indirectly on the mystery of the divine 'economy' which linked salvation and grace with the cross. It was not without reason that Christ said that 'the kingdom of heaven has suffered violence, and men of violence take it by force' and moreover that 'the children of this world are more astute . . . than are the children of light.' We gladly accept this rebuke, that we may be like those 'violent people of God' that we have so often seen in the history of the Church and still see today, and that we may consciously join in the great mission of revealing Christ to the world, helping each person to find himself in Christ, and helping the contemporary generations of our brothers and sisters, the peoples, nations, states, mankind, developing countries and countries of opulence—in short, helping everyone to get to know 'the unsearchable riches of Christ,' since these riches are for every individual and are everybody's property.

In this unity in mission, which is decided principally by Christ himself, all Christians must find what already unites them, even before their full communion is achieved. This is apostolic and missionary unity, missionary and apostolic unity. Thanks to this unity we can together come close to the magnificent heritage of the human spirit that has been manifested in all religions, as the Second Vatican Council's declaration *Nostra Aetate* says. It also enables us to approach all cultures, all ideological concepts, all people of good will. We approach them with the esteem, respect and discernment that since the time of the apostles has marked the *missionary* attitude, the attitude *of the missionary*. Suffice it to mention St Paul and, for instance, his address in the Areopagus at Athens. The *missionary* attitude always begins with a feeling of deep esteem for 'what is in man,' for what man has himself worked out in the depths of his spirit concerning the most profound and important problems. It is a question of respecting everything that has been brought about in him by the Spirit, which 'blows where it wills.' The mission is never destruction, but instead is a taking up and fresh building, even if in practice there has not always been full correspondence with this high ideal. And we know well that the conversion that is begun by the mission is a work of grace, in which man must fully find himself again.

For this reason the Church in our time attaches great importance to all that is stated by the Second Vatican Council in its *Declaration on Religious Freedom*, both the first and the second parts of the document. We perceive intimately that the truth revealed to us by God imposes on us an obligation. We have, in particular, a great sense of responsibility for this truth. By Christ's institution the Church is its guardian and teacher having been endowed with a unique assistance of the Holy Spirit in order to guard and teach it in its most exact integrity. In fulfilling this mission, we look towards Christ himself, the first evangelizer, and also towards his apostles, martyrs and confessors. The *Declaration on Religious Freedom* shows us convincingly that, when Christ and, after him, his apostles proclaimed the truth that comes not from men but from God ('My teaching is not mine, but his who sent me,' that is the Father's), they preserved, while acting with their full force of spirit, a deep esteem for man, for his intellect, his will, his conscience and his freedom. Thus the human person's dignity itself becomes part of the content of that proclamation, being included not necessarily in words but by an attitude towards it. This attitude seems to fit the special needs of our times. Since man's true freedom is not found in everything that the various systems and individuals see and propagate as freedom, the Church, because of her divine mission, becomes all the more the guardian of this freedom, which is the condition and basis for the human person's true dignity.

Jesus Christ meets the man of every age, including our own, with the same words: 'You will know the truth, and the truth will make you free.' These words contain both a fundamental requirement and a warning: the requirement of an honest relationship with regard to truth as a condition for authentic freedom, and the warning to avoid every kind of illusory freedom, every superficial unilateral freedom, every freedom that fails to enter into the whole truth about man and the world. Today also, even after two thousand years, we see Christ as the one who brings man freedom based on truth, frees man from what curtails, diminishes and as it were breaks off this freedom at its root, in man's soul, his heart and his conscience. What a stupendous confirmation of this has been given and is still being given by those who, thanks to Christ and in Christ, have reached true freedom and have manifested it even in situations of external constraint!

When Jesus Christ himself appeared as a prisoner before Pilate's tribunal and was interrogated by him about the accusation made against him by the representatives of the Sanhedrin, did he not answer: 'For this I was born, and for this I have come into the world, to bear witness to the truth'? It was as if with these words spoken before the judge at the decisive moment he was once more confirming what he had said earlier: 'You will know the truth and the truth will make you free.' In the course of so many centuries, of so many generations, from the time of the apostles on, is it not often Jesus Christ himself that has made an appearance at the side of people judged for the sake of the truth? And has he not gone to death with people condemned for the sake of the truth? Does he ever cease to be the continuous spokesman and advocate for the person who lives 'in spirit and truth'? Just as he does not cease to be it before the Father, he is it also with regard to the history of man. And in her turn the Church, in spite of all the weaknesses that are part of her human history, does not cease to follow him who said: 'The hour is coming, and now is, when the true worshippers will worship the Father in spirit and truth, for such the Father seeks to worship him. God is spirit, and those who worship him must worship in spirit and truth.'

John Paul II and Philosophy

This passage is from the 1969 book "The Acting Person," which is a philosophical examination of the experience and meaning of human action. Originally published in Polish, the work was recognized as having international importance for the philosophical community and was thus translated into English just prior to Cardinal Wojtyla's ascendance to the Holy See. It was published in 1979 as Volume 10 in the Reidel book series "**Analecta Husserliana.**" *This section can be found in Chapter Three, "The Personal Structure of Self-Determination."*

Self-Determination Shows the Structure of Self-Governance and Self-Possession as Essential to the Person.

Owing to the will, self-possession finds its manifestation and its confirmation in action. The simple experience of "I will" can never be correctly interpreted in the dynamic, complex whole without reference to man's specific complexity, which is introduced by self-possession and is proper only to the person. Self-determination is possible only on the ground of self-possession. Every authentically human "I will" is an act of self-determination; it is so not in abstraction and isolation from the dynamic personal structure but, on the contrary, as the deep-rooted content of this structural whole. Because "I will" is an act of self-determination at a particular moment it presupposes structural self-possession. For only the things that are man's actual possessions can be determined by him; they can be determined only by the one who actually possesses them. Being in the possession of himself man can determine himself. At the same time the will, every genuine "I will," reveals, confirms, and realizes the self-possession that is appropriate solely to the person—the fact that the person is his own judge.

Self-possession has as its consequence still another relation that occurs in the very structure of man as a person and is most strictly connected with the will. It is the relation of self-governance, which is indispensable for the understanding and the interpretation of self-determination. Self-governance may also be expressed in terms of a specific complex whole: the person is, on the one hand, the one who governs himself and, on the other, the one who is governed. "Self-governance" is here used in a different sense than the "self-control" of colloquial speech; self-control is the power to control oneself and applies only to one of the functions of the dynamism appropriate to man, to one of his powers or virtues, or to a set of these. Self-governance, on the other hand, is something far more fundamental and far more strictly related to the inner personal structure of man who differs from all other structures and all other existents in that he is capable of governing himself. Thus self-governance is man's power to govern himself and not only to control himself.

John Paul II And Culture

This passage is from "Centesimus Annus," the 1991 encyclical that celebrates the 100th anniversary of Pope Leo XIII's encyclical on the condition of the working classes. This section can be found in Chapter Five, "State and Culture," 49.1; 50–51; and 52.2.

Apart from the family, other intermediate communities exercise primary functions and give life to specific networks of solidarity. These develop as real communities of persons and strengthen the social fabric, preventing society from becoming an anonymous and impersonal mass as unfortunately often happens today. It is in interrelationships on many levels that a person lives and that society becomes more 'personalized.' The individual today is often suffocated between two poles represented by the state and the marketplace. At times it seems as though he exists only as a producer and consumer of goods or as an object of state administration. People lose sight of the fact that life in society has neither the market nor the state as its final purpose, since life itself has a unique value which the state and the market must serve. Man remains above all a being who seeks the truth and strives to live in that truth, deepening his understanding of it through a dialogue which involves past and future generations.

From this open search for truth, which is renewed in every generation, the culture of a nation derives its character. Indeed, the heritage of values which has been received and handed down is always challenged by the young. To challenge does not necessarily mean to destroy or reject *a priori*, but above all to put these values to the test in one's own life and through this existential verification to make them more real, relevant and personal, distinguishing the valid elements in the tradition from false and erroneous ones or from obsolete forms which can be usefully replaced by others more suited to the times.

In this context, it is appropriate to recall that evangelization too plays a role in the culture of the various nations, sustaining culture in its progress toward the truth and assisting in the work of its purification and enrichment. However, when a culture becomes inward looking and tries to perpetuate obsolete ways of living by rejecting any exchange or debate with regard to the truth about man, then it becomes sterile and is heading for decadence.

All human activity takes place within a culture and interacts with culture. For an adequate formation of a culture, the involvement of the whole man is required, whereby he exercises his creativity, intelligence and knowledge of the world and of people. Furthermore, he displays his capacity for self-control, personal sacrifice, solidarity and readiness to promote the common good. Thus the first and most important task is accomplished within man's heart. The way in which he is involved in building his own future depends on the understanding he has of himself and of his own destiny. It is on this level that the church's specific and decisive contribution to true culture is to be found. The church promotes those aspects of human behavior which favor a true culture of peace, as opposed to models in which the individual is lost in the crowd, in which the role of his initiative and freedom is neglected and in which his greatness is posited in the arts of conflict and war. The church renders this service to human society by preaching the truth about the creation of the world, which God has placed in human hands so that people may make it fruitful and more perfect through their work; and by preaching the truth about the redemption whereby the Son of God has saved mankind and at the same time has united all people, making them responsible for one another. Sacred Scripture continually speaks to us of an active commitment to our neighbor and demands of us a shared responsibility for all of humanity.

This duty is not limited to one's own family, nation or state, but extends progressively to all mankind, since no one can consider himself extraneous or indifferent to the lot of another member of the human family. No one can say that he is not responsible for the well-being of his brother or sister (cf. *Genesis* 4:9; *Luke* 10:29–37; *Matthew* 25: 31–46). Attentive and pressing concern for one's neighbor in a moment of need—made easier today because of the new means of communication which have brought people closer together—is especially important with regard to the search for ways to resolve international conflicts other than by war. It is not hard to see that the terrifying power of the means of destruction—to which even medium- and small-sized countries have access—and the ever closer links between the peoples of the whole world make it very difficult or practically impossible to limit the consequences of a conflict.

This may mean making important changes in established lifestyles in order to limit the waste of environmental and human resources, thus enabling every individual and all the peoples of the earth to have a sufficient share of those resources. In addition, the new material and spiritual resources must be utilized which are the result of the work and culture of peoples who today are on the margins of the international community, so as to obtain an overall human enrichment of the family of nations.

John Paul II and the Gospel of Life

This passage is from John Paul II's 1995 encyclical "Evangelium Vitae." This text is taken from sections 83 and 87 of the encyclical.

Because we have been sent into the world as a "people for life," our proclamation must also become *a genuine celebration of the Gospel of life*. This celebration, with the evocative power of its gestures, symbols and rites, should become a precious and significant setting in which the beauty and grandeur of this Gospel is handed on.

For this to happen, we need first of all to *foster*, in ourselves and in others, *a contemplative outlook*. Such an outlook arises from faith in the God of life, who has created every individual as a "wonder" (cf. *Psalms* 19:14). It is the outlook of those who see life in its deeper meaning, who grasp its utter gratuitousness, its beauty and its invitation to freedom and responsibility. It is the outlook of those who do not presume to take possession of reality but instead accept it as a gift, discovering in all things the reflection of the Creator and seeing in every person his living image (cf. *Genesis* 1:27; *Psalms* 8:5). This outlook does not give in to discouragement when confronted by those who are sick, suffering, outcast or at death's door. Instead, in all these situations it feels challenged to find meaning, and precisely in these circumstances it is open to perceiving in the face of every person a call to encounter, dialogue and solidarity.

It is time for all of us to adopt this outlook, and with deep religious awe to rediscover the ability to *revere and honour every person*, as Paul VI invited us to do in one of his first Christmas messages. Inspired by this contemplative outlook, the new people of the redeemed cannot but respond with *songs of joy, praise and thanksgiving for the priceless gift of life*, for the mystery of every individual's call to share through Christ in the life of grace and in an existence of unending communion with God our Creator and Father.

By virtue of our sharing in Christ's royal mission, our support and promotion of human life must be accomplished through the *service of charity*, which finds expression in personal witness, various forms of volunteer work, social activity and political commitment. This is a *particularly pressing need at the present time*, when the "culture of death" so forcefully opposes the "culture of life" and often seems to have the upper hand. But even before that it is a need which springs from "faith working through love" (*Galatians* 5:6). As the Letter of James admonishes us: "What does it profit, my brethren, if a man says he has faith but has not works? Can his faith save him? If a brother or sister is ill-clad and in lack of daily food, and one of you says to them, 'Go in peace, be warmed and filled,' without giving them the things needed for the body, what does it profit? So faith by itself, if it has no works, is dead" (2:14–17).

In our service of charity, *we must be inspired and distinguished by a specific attitude:* we must care for the other as a person for whom God has made us responsible. As disciples of Jesus, we are called to become neighbours to everyone (cf. *Luke* 10:29–37), and to show special favour to those who are poorest, most alone and most in need. In helping the hungry, the thirsty, the foreigner, the naked, the sick, the imprisoned— as well as the child in the womb and the old person who is suffering or near death—we have the opportunity to serve Jesus. He himself said: "As you did it to one of the least of these my brethren, you did it to me" (*Matthew* 25:40). Hence we cannot but feel called to account and judged by the ever relevant words of Saint John Chrysostom: "Do you wish to honour the body of Christ? Do not neglect it when you find it naked. Do not do it homage here in the church with silk fabrics only to neglect it outside where it suffers cold and nakedness."

Where life is involved, the *service of charity must be profoundly consistent*. It cannot tolerate bias and discrimination, for human life is sacred and inviolable at every stage and in every situation; it is an indivisible good. We need then to "show care" for all life and for the life of everyone. Indeed, at an even deeper level, we need to go to the very roots of life and love.

It is this deep love for every man and woman which has given rise down the centuries to an *outstanding history of charity*, a history which has brought into being in the Church and society many forms of service to life which evoke admiration from all unbiased observers. Every Christian community, with a renewed sense of responsibility, must continue to write this history through various kinds of pastoral and social activity. To this end, appropriate and effective programs of *support for new life* must be implemented, with special closeness to mothers who, even without the help of the father, are not afraid to bring their child into the world and to raise it. Similar care must be shown for the life of the marginalized or suffering, especially in its final phases.

John Paul II and Non-Catholics

This passage is from John Paul II's 1995 encyclical "Ut Unum Sint," *(That They May Be One). While John Paul II has written and spoken on relations between non-Christians and Catholics (as covered in Jerram Barrs' essay in this volume),* "Ut Unum Sint" *focuses on the relation between Catholics and non-Catholic Christians. This text is taken from the opening of* "Ut Unum Sint."

The call for Christian unity made by the Second Vatican Ecumenical Council with such impassioned commitment is finding an ever greater echo in the hearts of believers, especially as the Year 2000 approaches, a year which Christians will celebrate as a sacred Jubilee, the commemoration of the Incarnation of the Son of God, who became man in order to save humanity.

The courageous witness of so many martyrs of our century, including members of Churches and Ecclesial Communities not in full communion with the Catholic Church, gives new vigour to the Council's call and reminds us of our duty to listen to and put into practice its exhortation. These brothers and sisters of ours, united in the selfless offering of their lives for the Kingdom of God, are the most powerful proof that every factor of division can be transcended and overcome in the total gift of self for the sake of the Gospel.

Christ calls all his disciples to unity. My earnest desire is to renew this call today, to propose it once more with determination, repeating what I said at the Roman Colosseum on Good Friday 1994, at the end of the meditation on the *Via Crucis* prepared by my Venerable Brother Bartholomew, the Ecumenical Patriarch of Constantinople. There I stated that believers in Christ, united in following in the footsteps of the martyrs, cannot remain divided. If they wish truly and effectively to oppose the world's tendency to reduce to powerlessness the Mystery of Redemption, they must *profess together the same truth about the Cross.* The Cross! An anti-Christian outlook seeks to minimize the Cross, to empty it of its meaning, and to deny that in it man has the source of his new life. It claims that the Cross is unable to provide either vision or hope. Man, it says, is nothing but an earthly being, who must live as if God did not exist.

No one is unaware of the challenge which all this poses to believers. They cannot fail to meet this challenge. Indeed, how could they refuse to do everything possible, with God's help, to break down the walls of division and distrust, to overcome obstacles and prejudices which thwart the proclamation of the Gospel of salvation in the Cross of Jesus, the one Redeemer of man, of every individual?

I thank the Lord that he has led us to make progress along the path of unity and communion between Christians, a path difficult but so full of joy. Interconfessional dialogues at the theological level have produced positive and tangible results: this encourages us to move forward.

Nevertheless, besides the doctrinal differences needing to be resolved, Christians cannot underestimate the burden of *long-standing misgivings* inherited from the past, and of mutual *misunderstandings* and *prejudices. Complacency, indifference* and *insufficient knowledge of one another* often make this situation worse. Consequently, the commitment to ecumenism must be based upon the conversion of hearts and upon prayer, which will also lead to the *necessary purification of past memories.* With the grace of the Holy Spirit, the Lord's disciples, inspired by love, by the power of the truth and by a sincere desire for mutual forgiveness and reconciliation, are called to *re-examine together their painful past* and the hurt which that past regrettably continues to provoke even today. All together, they are invited by the ever fresh power of the Gospel to acknowledge with sincere and total objectivity the mistakes made and the contingent factors at work at the origins of their deplorable divisions. *What is needed is a calm, clear-sighted and truthful vision of things,* a vision enlivened by divine mercy and capable of freeing people's minds and of inspiring in everyone a renewed willingness, precisely with a view to proclaiming the Gospel to the men and women of every people and nation.

At the Second Vatican Council, the Catholic Church committed herself *irrevocably* to following the path of the ecumenical venture, thus heeding the Spirit of the Lord, who teaches people to interpret carefully the "signs of the times." The experiences of these years have made the Church even more profoundly aware of her identity and her mission in history. The Catholic Church acknowledges and confesses *the weaknesses of her members,* conscious that their sins are so many betrayals of and obstacles to the accomplishment of the Saviour's plan. Because she feels herself constantly called to be renewed in the spirit of the Gospel, she does not cease to do penance. At the same time, she acknowledges and exalts still more *the power of the Lord,* who fills her with the gift of holiness, leads her forward, and conforms her to his Passion and Resurrection.

Taught by the events of her history, the Church is committed to freeing herself from every purely human support, in order to live in depth the Gospel law of the Beatitudes. Conscious that the truth does not impose itself except "by virtue of its own truth, as it makes its entrance into the mind at once quietly and with power," she seeks nothing for herself but the freedom to proclaim the Gospel. Indeed, her authority is exercised in the service of truth and charity.

I myself intend *to promote every suitable initiative* aimed at making the witness of the entire Catholic community understood in its full purity and consistency, especially considering the engagement which awaits the Church at the threshold of the new Millennium. That will be an exceptional occasion, in view of which she asks the Lord to increase the unity of all Christians until they reach full communion.

John Paul II and Economics

This passage is from "Centesimus Annus," the 1991 encyclical that celebrates the 100th anniversary of Pope Leo XIII's 1891 encyclical on the condition of the working classes. This section can be found in Chapter Four, "Private Property and the Universal Destination of Material Goods," from sections 32, 33, 35, and 48.

The modern business economy has positive aspects. Its basis is human freedom exercised in the economic field, just as it is exercised in many other fields. Economic activity is indeed but one sector in a great variety of human activities, and like every other sector, it includes the right to freedom as well as the duty of making responsible use of freedom. But it is important to note that there are specific differences between the trends of modern society and those of the past, even the recent past. Whereas at one time the decisive factor of production was the land and later capital—understood as a total complex of the instruments of production—today the decisive factor is increasingly man himself, that is, his knowledge, especially his scientific knowledge, his capacity for interrelated and compact organization as well as his ability to perceive the needs of others and to satisfy them.

However, the risks and problems connected with this kind of process should be pointed out. The fact is that many people, perhaps the majority today, do not have the means which would enable them to take their place in an effective and humanly dignified way within a productive system in which work is truly central. They have no possibility of acquiring the basic knowledge which would enable them to express their creativity and develop their potential. They have no way of entering the network of knowledge and intercommunication which would enable them to see their qualities appreciated and utilized. Thus, if not actually exploited, they are to a great extent marginalized; economic development takes place over their heads, so to speak, when it does not actually reduce the already narrow scope of their old subsistence economies. They are unable to compete against the goods which are produced in ways which are new and which properly respond to needs, needs which they had previously been accustomed to meeting through traditional forms of organization. Allured by the dazzle of an opulence which is beyond their reach and at the same time driven by necessity, these people crowd the cities of the Third World where they are often without cultural roots and where they are exposed to situations of violent uncertainty without the possibility of becoming integrated. Their dignity is not acknowledged in any real way, and sometimes there are even attempts to eliminate them from history through coercive forms of demographic control which are contrary to human dignity.

Many other people, while not completely marginalized, live in situations in which the struggle for a bare minimum is uppermost. These are situations in which the rules of the earliest period of capitalism still flourish in conditions of 'ruthlessness' in no way inferior to the darkest moments of the first phase of industrialization. In other cases the land is still the central element in the economic process, but those who cultivate it are excluded from ownership and are reduced to a state of quasi-servitude. In these cases it is still possible today, as in the days of *Rerum Novarum*, to speak of inhuman exploitation. In spite of the great changes which have taken place in the more advanced societies, the human inadequacies of capitalism and the resulting domination of things over people are far from disappearing. In fact, for the poor, to the lack of material goods has been added a lack of knowledge and training which prevents them from escaping their state of humiliating subjection.

Unfortunately, the great majority of people in the Third World still live in such conditions. It would be a mistake, however, to understand this 'world' in purely geographic terms. In some regions and in some social sectors of that world, development programs have been set up which are centered on the use not so much of the material resources available but of the 'human resources.'

Even in recent years it was thought that the poorest countries would develop by isolating themselves from the world market and by depending only on their own resources. Recent experience has shown that countries which did this have suffered stagnation and recession, while the countries which experienced development were those which succeeded in taking part in the general interrelated economic activities at the international level. It seems therefore that the chief problem is that of gaining fair access to the international market, based not on the unilateral principle of the exploitation of the natural resources of these countries but on the proper use of human resources.

However, aspects typical of the Third World also appear in developed countries, where the constant transformation of the methods of production and consumption devalues certain acquired skills and professional expertise, and thus requires a continual effort of retraining and updating. Those who fail to keep up with the times can easily be marginalized as can the elderly, the young people who are incapable of finding their place in the life of society and in general those who are weakest or part of the so-called Fourth World. The situation of women too is far from easy in these conditions.

The church acknowledges the legitimate role of profit as an indication that a business is functioning well. When a firm makes a profit, this means that productive factors have been properly employed and corresponding human needs have been duly satisfied. But profitability is not the only indicator of a firm's condition. It is possible for the financial accounts to be in order and yet for the people—who make up the firm's most valuable asset—to be humiliated and their dignity offended. Besides being morally inadmissible, this will eventually have negative repercussions on the firm's economic efficiency. In fact, the purpose of a business firm is not simply to make a profit, but is to be found in its very existence as a community of persons who in various ways are endeavoring to satisfy their basic needs and who form a particular group at the service of the whole of society. Profit is a regulator of the life of a business, but it is not the only one;

other human and moral factors must also be considered, which in the long term are at least equally important for the life of a business.

We have seen that it is unacceptable to say that the defeat of so-called 'real socialism' leaves capitalism as the only model of economic organization. It is necessary to break down the barriers and monopolies which leave so many countries on the margins of development and to provide all individuals and nations with the basic conditions which will enable them to share in development. This goal calls for programmed and responsible efforts on the part of the entire international community. Stronger nations must offer weaker ones opportunities for taking their place in international life, and the latter must learn how to use these opportunities by making the necessary efforts and sacrifices and by ensuring political and economic stability, the certainty of better prospects for the future, the improvement of workers' skills and the training of competent business leaders who are conscious of their responsibilities.

These general observations also apply to the role of the state in the economic sector. Economic activity, especially the activity of a market economy, cannot be conducted in an institutional, juridical or political vacuum. On the contrary, it presupposes sure guarantees of individual freedom and private property as well as a stable currency and efficient public services. Hence the principal task of the state is to guarantee this security so that those who work and produce can enjoy the fruits of their labors and thus feel encouraged to work efficiently and honestly. The absence of stability, together with the corruption of public officials and the spread of improper sources of growing rich and of easy profits deriving from illegal or purely speculative activities, constitutes one of the chief obstacles to development and to the economic order.

Another task of the state is that of overseeing and directing the exercise of human rights in the economic sector. However, primary responsibility in this area belongs not to the state, but to individuals and to the various groups and associations which make up society. The state could not directly ensure the right to work for all its citizens unless it controlled every aspect of economic life and restricted the free initiative of individuals. This does not mean, however, that the state has no competence in this domain, as was claimed by those who argued against any rules in the economic sphere. Rather, the state has a duty to sustain business activities by creating conditions which will ensure job opportunities, by stimulating those activities where they are lacking or by supporting them in moments of crisis.

The state has the further right to intervene when particular monopolies create delays or obstacles to development. In addition to the tasks of harmonizing and guiding development, in exceptional circumstances the state can also exercise a substitute function when social sectors or business systems are too weak or are just getting under way and are not equal to the task at hand. Such supplementary interventions, which are justified by urgent reasons touching the common good, must be as brief as possible so as to avoid removing permanently from society and business systems the functions which are properly theirs and so as to avoid enlarging excessively the sphere of state intervention to the detriment of both economic and civil freedom.

In recent years the range of such intervention has vastly expanded to the point of creating a new type of state, the so-called welfare state. This has happened in some countries in order to respond better to many needs and demands, by remedying forms of poverty and deprivation unworthy of the human person. However, excesses and abuses, especially in recent years, have provoked very harsh criticisms of the welfare state, dubbed the 'social assistance state.' Malfunctions and defects in the social assistance state are the result of an inadequate understanding of the tasks proper to the state. Here again the principle of subsidiarity must be respected: A community of a higher order should not interfere in the internal life of a community of a lower order, depriving the latter of its functions, but rather should support it in case of need and help to coordinate its activity with the activities of the rest of society, always with a view to the common good.

By intervening directly and depriving society of its responsibility, the social assistance state leads to a loss of human energies and an inordinate increase of public agencies which are dominated more by. bureaucratic ways of thinking than by concern for serving their clients and which are accompanied by an enormous increase in spending. In fact, it would appear that needs are best understood and satisfied by people who are closest to them and who act as neighbors to those in need. It should be added that certain kinds of demands often call for a response which is not simply material, but which is capable of perceiving the deeper human need. One thinks of the condition of refugees, immigrants, the elderly, the sick and all those in circumstances which call for assistance such as drug abusers: All these people can be helped effectively only by those who offer them genuine fraternal support, in addition to the necessary care.

John Paul II and the Family

This passage is from the 1981 Apostolic Exhortation of John Paul II, "Familiaris Consortio," "The Role of the Christian Family in the Modern World." This passage can be found in Part Three, "The Role of the Christian Family," sections 17–18.

The family finds in the plan of God the Creator and Redeemer not only its *identity*, what it *is*, but also its *mission*, what it can and should *do*. The role that God calls the family to perform in history derives from what the family is; its role represents the dynamic and existential development of what it is. Each family finds within itself a summons that cannot be ignored, and that specifies both its dignity and its responsibility: family, *become* what you *are*.

Accordingly, the family must go back to the "beginning" of God's creative act, if it is to attain self-knowledge and self-realization in accordance with the inner truth not only of what it is but also of what it does in history. And since in God's plan it has been established as an "intimate community of life and love," the family has the mission to become more and more what it is, that is to say, a community of life and love, in an effort that will find fulfillment, as will everything created and redeemed, in the Kingdom of God. Looking at it in such a way as to reach its very roots, we must say that the essence and role of the family are in the final analysis specified by love. Hence the family has *the mission to guard, reveal and communicate love*, and this is a living reflection of and a real sharing in God's love for humanity and the love of Christ the Lord for the Church His bride.

Every particular task of the family is an expression and concrete actuation of that fundamental mission. We must therefore go deeper into the unique riches of the family's mission and probe its contents, which are both manifold and unified.

Thus, with love as its point of departure and making constant reference to it, the recent Synod emphasized four general tasks for the family: 1) forming a community of persons; 2) serving life; 3) participating in the development of society; 4) sharing in the life and mission of the Church.

The family, which is founded and given life by love, is a community of persons: of husband and wife, of parents and children, of relatives. Its first task is to live with fidelity the reality of communion in a constant effort to develop an authentic community of persons.

The inner principle of that task, its permanent power and its final goal is love: without love the family is not a community of persons and, in the same way, *without love the family cannot live, grow and perfect itself as a community of persons.* What I wrote in the encyclical *Redemptor Hominis* applies primarily and especially within the family as such: "Man cannot live without love. He remains a being that is incomprehensible for himself, his life is senseless, if love is not revealed to him, if he does not encounter love, if he does not experience it and make it his own, if he does not participate intimately in it."

The love between husband and wife and, in a derivatory and broader way, the love between members of the same family—between parents and children, brothers and sisters and relatives and members of the household—is given life and sustenance by an unceasing inner dynamism leading the family to ever deeper and more intense *communion*, which is the foundation and soul of the *community* of marriage and the family.

John Paul II and the Fall of Communism

This passage is from "Crossing the Threshold of Hope," specifically from John Paul II's response to the question "Was God at work in the fall of communism?"

By your question you confirm that in *the fall of Communism* the action of God has become almost visible in the history of our century. We must be wary of oversimplification. What we refer to as Communism has its own history. It is the history of protest in the face of injustice, as I recalled in the encyclical *Laborem Exercens*—a protest on the part of the great world of workers, which then became an ideology. But *this protest has also become part of the teaching of the Church.* We need but recall the encyclical *Rerum Novarum*, from the end of the last century. We add: this *teaching is not limited to protest, but throws a farseeing glance toward the future.* In fact, it was Leo XIII who in a certain sense predicted the fall of Communism, a fall which would cost humanity and Europe dearly, *since the medicine*—he wrote in his encyclical of 1891—*could prove more dangerous than the disease itself!* The pope said this with all the seriousness and the authority of the Church's Magisterium.

And what are we to say of the *three children from Fatima* who suddenly, on the eve of the outbreak of the October Revolution, heard: "Russia will convert" and "In the end, my Heart will triumph. . . !" They could not have invented those predictions. They did not know enough about history or geography, much less the social movements and ideological developments. And nevertheless it happened just as they had said.

Perhaps this is also why the pope was called from "a faraway country," perhaps this is why it was necessary for the assassination attempt to be made in St. Peter's Square precisely on May 13, 1981, the anniversary of the first apparition at Fatima—so that all could become more transparent and comprehensible, so that the voice of God which speaks in human history through the "signs of the times" could be more easily heard and understood.

This, then, is the Father who is always at work, and this is the Son, who is also at work, and this is the invisible Holy Spirit who is Love, and as Love is ceaseless creative, saving, sanctifying, and life-giving action.

Therefore, it would be simplistic to say that Divine Providence caused the fall of Communism. In a certain sense Communism as a system fell by itself. It fell as a consequence of its own mistakes and abuses. *It proved to be a medicine more dangerous than the disease itself.* It did not bring about true social reform, yet it did become a powerful threat and challenge to the entire world. But *it fell by itself, because of its own inherent weakness.*

"My Father is at work until now, so I am at work" (*John* 5:17). The fall of Communism opens before us a *retrospective panorama of modern civilization's typical way of thinking and acting*, especially in Europe, where Communism originated. Modern civilization, despite undisputed successes in many fields, has also made many mistakes and given rise to many abuses with regard to man, exploiting him in various ways. It is a civilization that constantly equips itself with power structures and structures of oppression, both political and cultural (especially through the media), in order to impose similar mistakes and abuses on all humanity.

How else can we explain the increasing gap between the rich North and the ever poorer South! Who is responsible for this! Man is responsible—man, ideologies, and philosophical systems. I would say that *responsibility lies with the struggle against God, the systematic elimination of all that is Christian.* This struggle has to a large degree dominated thought and life in the West for three centuries. *Marxist collectivism is nothing more than a "cheap version" of this plan.* Today a similar plan is revealing itself in all its danger and, at the same time, in all its faultiness.

God, on the other hand, is faithful to His Covenant. He has made it with humanity in Jesus Christ. He cannot now withdraw from it, having decided once and for all that the destiny of man is eternal life and the Kingdom of Heaven. *Will man surrender to the love of God, will he recognize his tragic mistake?* Will the Prince of Darkness surrender, he who is "the father of lies" (*John* 8:44), who continually accuses the sons of men as once he accused Job (cf *Job* 1:9ff)? It is unlikely that he will surrender, but his arguments may weaken. Perhaps, little by little, humanity will become more sober, people will open their ears once more in order to hear that word by which God has said everything to humanity.

And there will be nothing humiliating about this. Every person can learn from his own mistakes. So can humanity, allowing God to lead the way along the winding paths of history. God does not cease to be at work. *His essential work will always remain the Cross and the Resurrection of Christ.* This is the ultimate word of truth and of love. This is also the unending source of God's action in the sacraments, as well as in other ways that are known to Him alone. His is an action which passes through the heart of man and through the history of humanity.

John Paul II on Faith and Reason

This passage is from "Fides et Ratio" (Faith and Reason), the Pope's most recent encyclical, issued on the 14th of September, 1998, and made available in English translation on October 15, 1998, the day before his twentieth anniversary as Pope. This passage begins with the opening line of the encyclical and then includes a summary passage from Chapter Three, section 33.

Faith and reason are like two wings on which the human spirit rises to the contemplation of truth; and God has placed in the human heart a desire to know the truth—in a word, to know Himself—so that, by knowing and loving God, men and women may also come to the fullness of truth about themselves.

It is the nature of the human being to seek the truth. This search looks not only to the attainment of truths which are partial, empirical or scientific; nor is it only in individual acts of decision-making that people seek the true good. Their search looks towards an ulterior truth which would explain the meaning of life. And it is therefore a search which can reach its end only in reaching the absolute. Thanks to the inherent capacities of thought, man is able to encounter and recognize a truth of this kind. Such a truth—vital and necessary as it is for life—is attained not only by way of reason but also through trusting acquiescence to other persons who can guarantee the authenticity and certainty of the truth itself. There is no doubt that the capacity to entrust oneself and one's life to another person and the decision to do so are among the most significant and expressive human acts.

It must not be forgotten that reason too needs to be sustained in all its searching by trusting dialogue and sincere friendship. A climate of suspicion and distrust, which can beset speculative research, ignores the teaching of the ancient philosophers who proposed friendship as one of the most appropriate contexts for sound philosophical enquiry.

From all that I have said to this point it emerges that men and women are on a journey of discovery which is humanly unstoppable—a search for truth and a search for a person to whom they might entrust themselves. Christian faith comes to meet them, offering the concrete possibility of reaching the goal which they seek. Moving beyond the stage of simple believing, Christian faith immerses human beings in the order of grace, which enables them to share in the mystery of Christ, which in turn offers them a true and coherent knowledge of the Triune God. In Jesus Christ, who is the Truth, faith recognizes the ultimate appeal to humanity, an appeal made in order that what we experience as desire and nostalgia may come to its fulfillment.

Afterword

Charles E. Ford

For our sake God made him to be sin him who knew no sin, so that in him we might become the righteousness of God. (2 Corinthians 5:21)

ne of the central and recurring themes, both in John Paul II's thought and in this volume, is the pope's insistence on the primacy of the spiritual. As John Paul II stated in his first encyclical, *Redemptor Hominis*, it is the Paschal Mystery that most reveals to us who we are. Every attempt to understand human life purely in material terms without acknowledging God's eternal love and our spiritual character ends in failure. But in the Paschal Mystery, where "God made him to be sin him who knew no sin," it was revealed that God's love "is always greater than the whole of creation,"[1] As the pope writes, "Man cannot live without love. He remains a being that is incomprehensible for himself, his life is senseless, if love is not revealed to him."[2]

From the beginning of his papacy, John Paul II has expressed concerns about the tendency in contemporary society to overemphasize the material and "production" to the neglect of the spiritual. He fears that in focusing only on what is produced, technology can turn against man. His central concern is whether in the context of material progress man—as man—"is becoming truly better, that is to say more mature spiritually, more aware of the dignity of his humanity, more responsible, more open to others, especially the neediest and the weakest, and readier to give and to aid all."[3]

We are called to a mature humanity. As John Paul II explains, this means "full use of the gift of freedom received from the Creator."[4] The freedom to which we are called is, however, not freedom as an end in itself, but rather freedom which takes concrete form in self giving and service. "The full truth about human freedom is indelibly inscribed on the mystery of the Redemption."[5]

A remarkable aspect of John Paul II's approach is his discussion of contemporary problems without an emphasis on the state. As George Weigel notes in chapter three, the heart of the pope's thought is "the primacy of the spiritual" which has "direct effects on the whole of culture."[6] The state is not irrelevant, but the pope's analysis focuses on the individual's vocation, on society, on the Church, on fraternal communities and the like.

The attempts in our century to uproot religion and reorganize society—so that the government is dominant and the spiritual character of human life is ignored or even annihilated—has led to incredible violence and the most massive destruction in history. This century has seen the attempted annihilation of religion, especially Christianity, by international socialism, and the attempted annihilation of the Jews of Europe by national socialism.[7]

In approaching the most profoundly destructive reality of this century, the assault on religion, John Paul II does not respond with a political program. Instead, he refers back to the center of the Christian faith, the Paschal Mystery. This is expressed in John Paul II's second encyclical, *Dives in Misericordia*, which appeared on November 13, 1980, not long after the formation of the Polish labor union Solidarity. *Dives in Misericordia* is perhaps the most theological of John Paul II's encyclicals and has the most sober tone. Despite his unequivocal support of justice for the workers of Poland, the emphasis in this encyclical is not on justice but on mercy. In fact the pope offered the following warning about the search for justice, a warning derived from the experience of revolutionary socialism in this century.

> It would be difficult not to notice that very often programs which start from the idea of justice . . . in practice suffer from distortions. Although they continue to appeal to the idea of justice, nevertheless, experience shows that other negative forces have gained the upper hand over justice, such as spite, hatred and even cruelty. In such cases, the desire to annihilate the enemy, limit his freedom, or even force him into total dependence, becomes the fundamental motive for action . . . It is obvious, in fact, that in the name of an alleged justice (for

example, historical justice or class justice) the neighbor is sometimes destroyed, killed, deprived of liberty or stripped of fundamental human rights. The experience of the past and of our own time demonstrates that justice alone is not enough, that it can even lead to the negation and destruction of itself, if that deeper power, which is love, is not allowed to shape human life in its various dimensions.[8]

What is the connection of love with the question of justice? First, love does not dismiss the question of justice. Rather it is viewed from the perspective of the perfect justice that is at the heart of the Paschal Mystery and which springs from love. In the Paschal Mystery, we find the ultimate relationship between justice and mercy. The Paschal Mystery offers full justice to God and radical mercy to man.

> Here, precisely in him, in Christ, justice is done to sin at the price of his sacrifice, of his obedience "even to death." He who was without sin, "God made him sin for our sake." Justice is also brought to bear upon death, which from the beginning of man's history had been allied to sin. Death has justice done to it at the price of the death of the one who was without sin and who alone was able—by means of his own death—to inflict death upon death. In this way the Cross of Christ, on which the Son, consubstantial with the Father, renders full justice to God, is also a radical revelation of mercy, or rather of the love that goes against what constitutes the very root of evil in the history of man: against sin and death.[9]

John Paul II's thought stands in marked contrast with many dominant contemporary approaches. Amidst the twentieth century tendency to focus only on what is observable, John Paul II places primary emphasis on the Paschal Mystery. Without an understanding of the spiritual character of life, we move from disquiet to fear and violence. The materialist view of life gives rise to a culture of death. In response, John Paul II proclaims the "gospel of life."[10] The neglect of the spiritual character of human life gives rise to the false dream of a perfect state over everything. In response, John Paul II recognizes that, as spiritual creatures, we are nourished in the family, the basic cell of society "established in God's plan" as "a community of life and love."[11] By ignoring the spiritual freedom to which men and women are called by

God, there arises the rationalist's hope for a planned economy. In response, John Paul II states that economic activity "includes the right to freedom as well as the duty of making responsible use of freedom."[12]

In *Fides et Ratio*, John Paul II's latest encyclical, the pope mentioned two series of important contemporary religious thinkers. The first lists Roman Catholics; the second Russian Orthodox.[13] It is perhaps significant that each list includes a twentieth century martyr, one to each of the two branches of revolutionary socialism. The Roman Catholic martyr is the Carmelite nun Edith Stein, a martyr to national socialism, gassed at Auschwitz on August 9, 1942. The Russian Orthodox martyr is the priest Pavel A. Florensky, a martyr to international socialism, executed after four years in slave labor camps, on December 8, 1937.

The central principle of revolutionary socialism was put forward by Karl Marx in 1843: "it is man who makes religion, and not religion which makes man." Marx considered his socialism to be scientific precisely because it rejected religious explanations for human behavior. This, indeed, is the fundamental principle of scientific socialism. Revolutionary socialists began a search for the "real" explanation of Christianity and Judaism. They eventually settled on class and race respectively as the fundamental explanations. The international socialists talked about class and the struggle between classes while the national socialists talked about race and the struggle between races. The fundamental category, however, has been religion, and this century's struggles of revolutionary socialism have been attempts to annihilate religion, especially Christianity and Judaism.

The writings of John Paul II represent precisely the opposite view from Marx, that Christianity comes from God, not from the human imagination. In *Fides et Ratio*, John Paul II expressed it this way.

> Underlying all the Church's thinking is the awareness that she is the bearer of a message which has its origin in God himself. The knowledge which the Church offers to man has its origin not in any speculation of her own, however sublime, but in the word of God which she has received in faith. At the origin of our life of faith there is an encounter, unique in kind, which discloses a mystery hidden for long ages but which is now revealed: In his goodness and wisdom, God chose to reveal himself and to make known to us the hidden purpose of his will, by which, through Christ, the Word made flesh, man has

access to the Father in the Holy Spirit and comes to share in the divine nature. This initiative is utterly gratuitous, moving from God to men and women in order to bring them to salvation.[14]

Here again is expressed the primacy of the spiritual over the material, the economic, and the political. In the thought of John Paul II, the centrality of the spiritual is understood above all by reference to the Paschal Mystery. Thus, the unprecedented martyrdom of this century is voiced by reference to the most unprecedented martyrdom in all history. That mystery is expressed in St. Paul's words, "God made him to be sin him who knew no sin." Through this mystery, justice is transformed to mercy, sin to righteousness, sorrow to joy, death to life.

NOTES

[1] *Redemptor Hominis*, 9.2.

[2] *Redemptor Hominis*, 10.1.

[3] *Redemptor Hominis*, 15.4.

[4] *Redemptor Hominis*, 21.4.

[5] *Redemptor Hominis*, 21.5.

[6] *Redemptor Hominis*, 11.2.

[7] Many millions of people were tortured and killed under national socialism. Many millions more have been imprisoned, tortured and killed at the hands of international socialists. For an account of the effort to destroy the Church under international socialism, see Dimitry Pospielovsky, *The Russian Church Under the Soviet Regime 1917–1982*. (Crestwood NY: St. Vladimir's Seminary Press, 1984). Also see Robert Conquest, *The Harvest of Sorrows*. (New York: Oxford, 1986). Accounts of more recent efforts to destroy religion can be found in the journal *Religion in Communist Lands*. For example, a survey of the journal beginning with volume seven will provide accounts of communist governments in the effort to annihilate religion during the years of John Paul II's papacy. Documented accounts of such events in the Soviet Union, Ethiopia, Mozambique, Angola, Nicaragua, Grenada and elsewhere are provided.

[8] *Dives in Misericordia*, 12.3.

[9] *Dives in Misericordia*, 8.1.

[10] See *Evangelim Vitae*, especially 78–101.

[11] *Familiaris Consortio*, 17.

[12] *Centesimus Annus*, 32.3.

[13] "We see the same fruitful relationship between philosophy and the word of God in the courageous research pursued by more recent thinkers, among whom I gladly mention, in a Western context, figures such as John Henry Newman, Antonio Rosmini, Jacques Maritain, Etienne Gilson and Edith Stein and, in an Eastern context, eminent scholars such as Vladimir S. Soloviev, Pavel A. Florensky, Petr Chaadaev and Vladimir N. Lossky." *Fides et Ratio*, 74.

[14] *Fides et Ratio*, 7.

Bibliography

Before his election to the Holy See, Karol Wojtyla wrote and published a wide range of books, articles, poems and plays. Much of this has been translated into English and is available. The first part of this list covers key works by Karol Wojtyla written before his election to the papacy that are available in English translation.

The Acting Person. Holland: D. Reidel, 1979. This philosophical magnum opus was published in 1969 in Polish. It was soon recognized by the philosophical community as an important work deserving of translation. The English translation includes some revisions to the original Polish text. It was published as volume 10 in Reidel's series *Analecta Husserliana.*

The Collected Plays and Writings on Theater. Berkeley: University of California Press, 1987. Wojtyla's first vocation was as an actor and playwright. During the Nazi occupation of Poland he was part of an underground "rhapsodic" theater. This collection includes his scripted plays and reflections on theater.

Collected Poems. New York: Random House, 1982. This collection of Wojtyla's poetry includes works from his youth as well as poetry composed after becoming bishop.

Faith According to Saint John of the Cross. San Francisco: Ignatius, 1981. This is an English translation of Wojtyla's first doctoral dissertation.

Love and Responsibility. San Francisco: Ignatius Press, 1981. First published in Polish in 1960, this is a book of moral theology that treats issues of love and responsible sexuality.

Person and Community: Selected Essays. New York: Peter Lang, 1993. This helpful collection includes English translations of Wojtyla's scholarly essays, many of which were published while he was a philosophy professor and then as a bishop.

Sources of Renewal: The Implementation of Vatican II. San Francisco: Harper & Row, 1980. First published in Polish in 1972, this volume contains Wojtyla's interpretation of Vatican II as well as his outline of how dioceses, parishes and the laity might apply the teachings of the Council.

Even after his election in 1978, John Paul II has continued to write and publish books. Listed below are books published during his papacy that go beyond his official writings as pope.

Celebrate 2000! Ann Arbor: Servant Publications, 1996. The coming millennium has been a favorite topic of the pope. As a way of preparing, the pope reflects on the significance of living in this time in history.

Crossing the Threshold of Hope. New York: Knopf, 1994. This book arose out of an exclusive interview the pope gave to an Italian journalist. It provides an insightful look into the pope's thought on many varying issues from prayer to non-Christian religions to issues of life and "eternal salvation."

Gift and Mystery: On the Fiftieth Anniversary of My Priestly Ordination. New York: Doubleday, 1996. This is a reflection by the pope on what it has meant for him to be a priest, bishop, and the pope. It is one of the pope's most personal works.

Lift Up Your Hearts: Daily Meditations. Ann Arbor: Servant Publications, 1995. This is a collection of daily meditations inspired by the pope's spiritual understanding of the liturgical year.

Spiritual Pilgrimage. New York: Crossroad Publishing Company, 1995.

As the bishop of Rome, the pope has a special charism as teacher of the faith. Since the 18th century, one of the principle ways that popes have exercised this responsibility is by publishing encyclical letters. It is one of the most authoritative forms of teaching in the Church. By the time of his twentieth anniversary as pope, John Paul II had issued thirteen encyclicals listed below. All of them are available and have been published individually by various presses in English translation. The St. Paul editions are widely available. The encyclicals are also easily accessed at the Vatican site on the internet (*www.vatican.va/*). All of them, except for *Fides et Ratio*, are available in a very helpful collection, listed below.

The Encyclicals of John Paul II. Miller, I. Michael, ed. Huntington, Ind.: Our Sunday Visitor, 1996.

Redemptor Hominis	1979	*The Redeemer of Man*
Dives in Misericordia	1981	*Rich in Mercy*
Laborem Exercens	1981	*On Human Work*
Slavorum Apostoli	1985	*The Apostles to the Slavs*
Dominum et Vivificantem	1986	*Lord and Giver of Life*
Redemptoris Mater	1987	*The Mother of the Redeemer*
Sollicitudo Rei Socialis	1988	*On Social Concern*
Redemptoris Missio	1990	*The Mission of the Redeemer*
Centesimus Annus	1991	*On the Hundredth Anniversary of Rerum Novarum*
Veritatis Splendor	1993	*The Splendor of the Truth*
Evangelium Vitae	1995	*The Gospel of Life*
Ut Unum Sint	1995	*That They May Be One*
Fides et Ratio	1998	*Faith and Reason*

While encyclicals are one type of papal teaching (exceeded only by Apostolic Constitutions in their formal authority), other forms of teaching include Apostolic Exhortations. They follow closely after encyclicals in formal authority, and they are often more pastoral in tone. Like his encyclicals, the Apostolic Exhortations of John Paul II are available individually, both in print and on the internet. They have been collected in a helpful volume.

The Post-Synodal Apostolic Exhortations of John Paul II. Miller, I. Michael, ed. Indiana: Our Sunday Visitor, 1998.

Catechesi Tradendae	1979	*On Catechesis in Our Time*
Familiaris Consortio	1982	*The Role of the Christian Family in the Modern World*
Reconciliatio et Paenitentia	1984	*Reconciliation and Penance*
Redemptionis Donum	1984	*The Gift of the Redemption*
Christifideles Laici	1989	*On the Vocation and Mission of the Lay Faithful in the Church and in The World*
Redemptoris Custos	1989	*The Custodian of the Redeemer*
Pastores Dabo Vobis	1992	*I Will Give You Shepherds*
Ecclesia in Africa	1995	*On the Church in Africa*
Vita Consecrata	1996	*On the Consecrated Life*

The number of books about Pope John Paul II is growing. While the authors in this volume have referred to various sources that are mentioned in the notes at the end of each chapter, this list of books about John Paul II surveys some of the major works about John Paul II. Buttiglione's book includes a helpful annotated bibliography that is more extensive than this short list. It might also be noted that the 1986 volume of the *Proceedings of the American Catholic Philosophical Association* is devoted to the philosophy of Karol Wojtyla.

Bernstein, Carl and Politi, Marco. *His Holiness: John Paul II and the Hidden History of Our Time.* New York: Doubleday, 1996.

Buttiglione, Rocco. *Karol Wojtyla: The Thought of the Man Who Became John Paul II.* Translated by Paolo Guietti and Francesca Murphy. Grand Rapids: Eerdmans, 1997.

Kwitny, Jonathan. *Man of the Century: The Life and Times of Pope John Paul II.* New York: Henry Holt, 1997.

Lawler, Ronald. *The Christian Personalism of John Paul II.* Chicago: Franciscan Herald Press, 1982.

The Pope speaks to the American church: John Paul II's homilies, speeches, and letters to Catholics in the United States. San Francisco: Harper, 1992.

McDermott, J.M. *The Thought of John Paul II: A Collection of Essays and Studies.* Editrice Pontificia Universita Gregoriana, 1993

Schmitz, Kenneth L. *At the Center of the Human Drama.* Washington, D.C.: The Catholic University of America Press, 1993.

Szulc, Tad. *Pope John Paul II: The Biography.* New York: Scribner, 1995.

Weigel, George. *The Final Revolution: The Resistance Church and the Collapse of Communism.* New York: Oxford University Press, 1992.

Weigel, George, ed. *A New Worldly Order: John Paul II and Human Freedom.* D.C.: Ethics and Public Policy Center, 1992.

Weigel, George. *Soul of the World: Notes on the Future of Public Catholicism.* D.C.: Ethics and Public Policy Center, 1996.

Weigel, George. *Witness to Hope.* San Francisco: Harper Collins, 1999 (forthcoming).

Williams, George Hunston. *The Mind of John Paul II.* New York: Seabury, 1981.

Woznicki, Andrew N. *A Christian Humanism: Karol Wojtyla's Existential Personalism.* Connecticut: Mariel Publications, 1980.

Woznicki, Andrew N. *The Dignity of Man as a Person.* San Francisco: Society of Christ Publications, 1987.

About the Authors

Helen Alvare is the Director of Planning and Information for Pro-Life Activities at the National Conference of Catholic Bishops. Prior to holding this position, she served as an attorney in the Office of General Counsel for the United States Catholic Conference, the public policy arm of the NCCB. In this role, Ms. Alvare co-authored briefs for major abortion, euthanasia, and First Amendment cases.

Jerram Barrs is the Director of the Francis Schaeffer Institute, which is affiliated with Covenant Seminary, in St. Louis. He joined the Seminary faculty in 1989 after 16 years with L'Abri Fellowship in England, where he also pastored the International Presbyterian Church. He has frequently written and spoken about Christian dialogue with non-Christians. He is the author of *Being Human, Shepherds and Sheep, Who Are the Peacemakers?* And *The Great Rescue.*

Gregory R. Beabout is an Associate Professor in the Department of Philosophy at Saint Louis University. He has published on Catholic Social Thought, Kierkegaard and ethics. His books include *Freedom and its Misuses* and *Applied Professional Ethics* (with Daryl Wennemann).

Carl Bernstein gained fame in the early 1970s after breaking the Watergate scandal. With Bob Woodward, he co-authored two best selling books about Watergate, *All the President's Men*, and *The Final Days*. After leaving the *Washington Post*, Mr. Bernstein served as a foreign correspondent for *Time*, and as a senior correspondent for ABC-TV and CBS-TV. In 1996, he published *His Holiness: John Paul II and the Hidden History of Our Time.*

Avery Dulles is the Laurence J. McGinley Professor of Religion and Society at Fordham University. He has held numerous academic appointments and has authored over 600 articles and books, including *Models of the Church* in 1974. Fr. Dulles has also served as the president of both the Catholic Theological Society of America and the American Theological Society.

Charles E. Ford is a Professor in the Department of Mathematics and Computer Science at Saint Louis University. He has a longstanding interest in the history of mathematics and in the relation between science and religion. His current research focuses on Russian Orthodox mathematicians during the Soviet period. Dr. Ford's publications on these topics have appeared in both English and Russian.

John Kavanaugh is a Professor in the Department of Philosophy and Director of the Center for Ethics Across the Curriculum at Saint Louis University. He has frequently published on issues of consumerism, intrinsic value, and the ethics of life (euthanasia, abortion, and war). He is the author of *Following Christ in a Consumer Society, On Christian Faith vs Capitalism*, and *Faces of Poverty*. Fr. Kavanaugh's columns appear regularly in *America* magazine.

Rev. Robert Sirico is the co-founder and president of the Action Institute for the Study of Religion and Liberty, a non-profit, free-market educational organization. Fr. Sirico's columns appear frequently in newspapers including The *New York Times* and *The Wall Street Journal*. CNN, ABC, the BBC, NPR and other news media have called upon him for his expertise on religion and economics. Fr. Sirico is a parochial vicar at St. Joseph's parish in St. Johns, Michigan.

Janet E. Smith is a frequent lecturer and has published extensively on natural law as well as Catholic social and moral thought, including *Why Humanae Vitae was Right: A Reader* and *Pope John Paul II, Feminists, Women, and the Church*. She is a professor in the philosophy department at the University of Dallas and a columnist for *Catholic Dossier.*

George Weigel is a Senior Fellow at the Ethics and Public Policy Center. Mr. Weigel's articles have appeared in magazines such as *First Things*, *Crisis*, and *Commentary*. His books include *Soul of the World* and *Idealism Without Illusions*. His biography of John Paul II, *Witness to Hope*, which will appear worldwide in 1999, will be published in English by Harper Collins in October 1999.

Index